Unity & Strategy
Ideas for Revolution

Unity & Strategy
Ideas for Revolution

the transitional program for socialist revolution and other writings

By Leon Trotsky, John Riddell, Duncan Hallas, James Burnham, Steve Bloom, Daniel Bensaïd and Michel Pablo

Introduction by Piers Mostyn

International Institute for Research & Education
Amsterdam, Islamabad, Manila

Resistance Books
London

The International Institute for Research and Education and Resistance Books would be glad to have readers' opinions of this book, its design and translations, and any suggestions you may have for future publications or wider distribution.

Our books are available at special quantity discounts to educational and non-profit organizations, and to bookstores.

To contact us, please write to: IIRE, Lombokstraat 40 1094 AL Amsterdam, Netherlands, email iire@iire.org or visit: iire.org

Published by IIRE and Resistance Books, March 2015

Printed in Britain by Lightning Source

Cover Design: Maral Jefroudi

Cover photograph: Getty Images International

Published as issue 51 of the Notebooks for Study and Research.

ISSN 0298-7902

ISBN 978-0-902869-66-0

Contents

Introduction.
Piers Mostyn

Two problems have confronted the socialist movement since its earliest days: How to unite the working class? How to build a bridge between the existing consciousness of the working class and the socialist program?

Without a relationship with the mass forces at the heart of successful struggle, the struggle for socialism will be irrelevant. Unity is a precondition for struggles to succeed, but unity with whom? And to what end?

Nearly two centuries of tackling these questions have thrown up a rich seam of experiences. The answers point to a process of working class radicalisation through the experience of struggle. But the mere fact of struggle is no guarantee that political consciousness, combativity and organisation will be strengthened – particularly in the wake of setbacks and defeats.

So the question then becomes: how best to facilitate, encourage and assist this process. That possibility only arises through being a part of it and not simply preaching from the sidelines.

Two methods of tackling these issues, called "The United Front" and "The Transitional Program", have evolved over the decades.

The transitional method is the idea of a program of demands that will meet the immediate needs of workers and the oppressed, but simultaneously have a dynamic that breaks with the logic of capitalism. These demands will be "reasonable" - connecting to the existing consciousness of the class and therefore readily accessible. But their full implementation would radically undermine the basic principles on which capitalism rests. A classic example of the latter would be the unfettered "right" of capitalists to manage business enterprises. A demand such as "open the books", if implemented, would immediately threaten that principle and even make it unworkable.

The first transitional program was a ten point list of demands drafted by Marx and Engels in the Communist Manifesto of 1848. In their 1872 preface to the Manifesto they made it clear that "no special stress" should be placed on this list, as its application depended on the historic conditions of the time. The Paris Commune of 1871 and other developments in the 24 years since it was first drafted meant, they concluded, that it would, "in many respects be very differently worded today".

The idea was revived by the Bolsheviks with a five-point program drafted by Lenin. The need for a new Transitional Program was part of the debates of the Left Opposition in the 1930s and Leon Trotsky drafted one in 1938 for the founding conference of the Fourth International that year.

Since then a number of efforts have been made to further update the concept – for instance incorporating the struggles of black communities, women and LGBT people and the challenge of eco-socialism. It is a continuous work in progress.

The United Front, put at its simplest, means joint action for a common goal in the interests of the working class. This involves diverse political forces within the working class movement working together, irrespective of their broader perspectives, in support of particular action goals. The trade union is a basic example. Others include movements, campaigns and action committees. Its highest expression is the Soviet for which the goal is the struggle for workers power.

Putting aside other differences to focus on the action goal enables the class to maximise its strength and effectiveness in the fight. It also allows lessons to be learnt. Having tried and tested the tactics, demands, methods of organisation and leaders on offer – which proved their worth? It is through this process of learning through experience that consciousness can be raised and radicalisation occurs.

But for a United Front to achieve this, it must facilitate the experience of large masses in struggle, with a free exchange of information and ideas. Democracy, accountability, freedom of criticism and expression, pluralism and transparency are therefore of the essence. And bureaucratic control from above, frontism or the exclusion or marginalisation of sections of the movement or their leaders are counter-productive.

United Front formations have, since the earliest days of the movement, been thrown up organically by the working class in struggle, dictated by the urgent need for unity. Theoretical debate on the subject also dates back to the Communist Manifesto, but is particularly associated with the 1920s and 1930s.

The setbacks imposed on the international communist movement after the initial revolutionary upsurge following 1917 forced a rethink.

A new reality, in which the mass of workers were not going to readily break from reformism, had to be faced.

How should revolutionaries, who had fought for and hoped for an international extension of revolutionary struggle, act when does this not occur? What tactics are required when they find themselves not only in the minority, but in some cases significantly marginalised? An ultra-left refusal to acknowledge this threatened isolation from the class and worse, the danger of serious defeats.

Faced with this challenge the fourth world congress of the Communist International adopted a policy on the United Front in 1922. How this method should be applied was a matter of heated debate over the next 15 years.

Ultra-left adventures in some sections led to serious setbacks. And the leadership of the Communist International, increasingly dominated by Stalinism, lurched from opportunism to ultra-left sectarianism and back again over the following decade. The so-called "Third Period" in which the German Social Democratic Party was denounced as "social fascist" was sectarianism at its most dangerous, as subsequent events showed.

The mid-1930s policy of the Popular Front followed, in which an alliance with the liberal bourgeoisie was privileged over the pursuit of class struggle, with dire consequences particularly in France and Spain.

The debates on the subject helped give rise to and shape the emerging Left Opposition within the Communist International and have left a rich legacy. The relevance of this topic remains undiminished – as the anti-austerity, anti-war or anti-fascist campaigns of more recent times will demonstrate.

The starting point for a consideration of either method has to be an analysis of the actual situation. This involves an honest and accurate assessment of the consciousness, formation and organisation of the working class, the balance of class forces, the politics of the bourgeoisie and its state and the international context.

Retreating to the comfort-zone of timeless nostrums or what socialists might like to be the case is of no value whatsoever. The same goes for any crude reduction of the class struggle to the purely economic. And the frank assessment has to include the weaknesses as well as the strengths of the revolutionary left itself, not just numerically but in terms of political and social weight.

Consequently, by definition these methods are not transferable "off the peg" solutions, applicable without reference to time and place, but rather always require specific adaptation.

Theoretical work on both United Front and Transitional Program has tended to focus on the same core problems. How to organise class struggle in the context of mass adherence to reformist organisations that have, whatever the intentions of individual members, always capitulated to bourgeois politics? How to simultaneously create the most favourable conditions for a break with reformism?

At heart there is a binary tension pulling in two opposite directions - the paramount requirement for unity against the need for full political freedom of the competing currents; the necessity to unite in action with reformists against the historic necessity to encourage the masses to break from reformism etc.

Getting the balance right, requires a very precise assessment in a given context, its history and its dynamics. Get it wrong one way and the revolutionary left finds itself in a sectarian wilderness of irrelevance. Get it wrong the other and that same left is reduced to opportunism, providing left cover for precisely the political forces it seeks to replace.

Revolutionary Marxists have unfortunately sometimes tried to avoid the risks involved in approaching these contradictions by lapsing into dogma, ahistorical tropes, propagandism and frontism. Maintaining an organisation, recruiting individual members and avoiding an accusation of "sell out" in the short term becomes a substitute for the uncertainty of engagement with the class and its struggles.

History has shown that such engagement necessitates an approach stripped of schemas and ultimatums – regarding political goal or organisational form. It involves seizing all openings and opportunities that facilitate dialogue with the most advanced sections of the class. The analysis and judgement at its centre measures success according to the extent to which the consciousness, confidence, combativity and independence of the class is strengthened. It is largely through their own experience of struggle that the different sections of the working class will unite and radicalise and there is no substitute for this.

From this it also follows that recognition of the heterogeneous nature of working class movements is essential, as against a reductionist or economist approach. The very real divisions (fomented by capitalism and its advocates) based on nation, gender, race, sexuality, occupation, age, disability etc have to be recognised.

Formations that don't reflect the range of political currents within the movement will fail to unify. On the contrary the right of political currents to organise and the right of self-organisation for oppressed sections is part of the process by which a broader unity can be maximised.

The united front and the transitional method are always rooted in actual experiences of struggle. What is right and what is wrong, what works and what doesn't is historically relative and therefore can only be analysed in context. So there is little substitute for immersion in the debates of the past and the struggles that gave rise to them. This is precisely what this book hopes to encourage.

John Riddell's exposition on Clara Zetkin is an ideal starting point. Zetkin's role in Germany in the early decades of the 20th century placed her at the heart of some of the most important discussions on the United Front. In the process she became the Communist International's best known non-Russian leader and led significant work on women's liberation and international solidarity.

Duncan Hallas, looking at the retreats imposed on the revolutionary movement in 1921 and after, asks, "What should a revolutionary party do in a non-revolutionary situation?" He focuses on Italy and Germany where ultra-leftism led to crisis and defeat and shows how lessons were learnt by the CI.

Leon Trotsky's theses on the subject were central to this discussion. He demonstrated how the United Front is acutely posed where, as in France, the Communist Party is a large minority component of the proletariat. He rejected the idea of "the United Front from below" as sectarian and counter-productive because there will be no mass radicalisation unless the reformist leaders are held to account. He also addressed the internal tasks for the party: in particular the need for discipline, for independence and for freedom of political agitation and criticism within the Front.

Trotsky's "What Next" written ten years later as a polemic against the Third International's ultra-left turn is an overview of the lessons to be learnt in the period since the Russian revolution – including a discussion on the character of Soviets as the highest form of United Front. And his "United Front for defence, letter to a social democratic worker" from 1933 is a rallying call for working class unity against fascism in Germany.

The continuing relevance of these debates is reflected in Tom Kerry's 1967 piece on the urgent task of the day, Vietnam solidarity. It is a critique of those who abstained from this activity on the false grounds that only propaganda was possible until a mass party could be built – a result of mechanically transposing the methods of one time and place to another.

Daniel Bensaid draws together the question of the United Front and the Transitional program in considering the fight against fascism. He argues that the appropriateness of demands depends on their mobilising value in the concrete situation and their educational value for those who enter struggle. The difference between revolutionaries and reformists is not that revolutionaries oppose demands for reform, but rather locate them in the closest possible relationship to their goals and aims.

The Transitional Program, a founding document of the Fourth International in 1938 shows how this method was implemented in the very testing circumstances of the period. The need for it to be constantly re-assessed and amended does not detract from the fact that it has stood the test of time.

The book closes with three documents from the mid-1930s: a defence of the United Front method against the Popular Front; James Burnham's critique of the CI's turn to popular frontism and Trotsky on how Stalinism sold out the Spanish revolution in the civil war.

But there are limitations to any reliance on the analysis of 70 to 90 years ago. Much has changed since then. The "high point" for the United Front as a policy of the Communist International was a time when the Russian revolution was a living recent event, its leadership winning tremendous authority among the working class and oppressed globally. The formation of mass Communist Parties was in progress.

The advanced sections of the workers movement were fully conversant with this history: from the splits in the 2nd international around the First World War, through 1917 and into the early 1920s. At both rank and file and leadership level the reformists and revolutionaries often faced each other as old comrades. The same was true, though to a lesser extent, for the developing left opposition within the communist movement internationally in the decade that followed.

It was possible for Trotsky to write in 1922 that "The Communist Party is the organisation of the proletarian vanguard for the ideological fructification of the labour movement and the assumption of leadership in all spheres – first and foremost in the unions" ("On the United Front etc" p.50). Four years on from 1917 that may not have been unreasonable. But such a formulation would today come across as sectarian.

Much water has since flowed under the bridge. The Second World War, the post-war boom, the more recent defeats imposed by neo-liberalism and the deepening globalisation of capitalism has had an impact on the consciousness and organisation of the class as a whole and its vanguard. It goes without saying that the revolutionary left has had to continuously re-earn its ability to influence and lead in way that may not have been so obvious in the aftermath of 1917.

Of course the struggles of the class haven't ceased: from defending living standards, workers rights, democratic rights and the environment; to opposition to imperialist war, racism and fascism. This has generated new political formations and demands.

Important new experiences have been thrown up of how to link up with those in the vanguard of struggle; how the most advanced sections of the class can be drawn towards the project of building new leaderships and organisations for change; how the experience of struggle can be harnessed to educate and raise consciousness on a mass level.

The inter-war debate was largely in the context of a working class dominated by two giant highly organised currents – social democracy and communism – facing each other in an era of wars and revolutions against the backcloth of the conquest of workers power in Russia. Other currents – syndicalism, anarchism, the left opposition etc - played a role, but very much within this framework. The United Front was classically conceived as an almost formal agreement between the two mass parties. In the current period it will only occasionally be posed in this way.

Since the fall of the Berlin Wall in particular this has become very much the exception. In some cases social democracy is hegemonic. In many others there is a complex pattern of reformism, green parties, communist and ex-communist parties and a variety of new left parties and small revolutionary formations.

The earlier emphasis on the internal "discipline" of the party will often be inappropriate today. The intervention of revolutionary organisations as highly disciplined formations into United Fronts can be counter-productive as it cuts across the building of trust, the sharing of ideas and information, the accountability, the pluralism and democracy that is required.

The last decade has seen a new range of experiences, all producing new challenges in the application of these methods: the global justice movement and the social forums; the campaign against imperialist wars in Iraq and Afghanistan; the campaign for climate justice; the experience of building new broad parties of the left, recent struggles against austerity and the Arab revolts. Many lessons are yet to be learnt.

PART 1
WHAT IS THE UNITED FRONT?

Class Unity, the Working-Class United Front and the Allies of the Proletariat.
Fourth International

Unity of the proletariat, forged in action, must be at the heart of any strategy for a socialist revolution in the imperialist countries of Europe.[*]

The unification of the key sectors of the proletariat—essentially, those in industry, transport, and communications—is the cornerstone of building such unity and of rallying the oppressed and exploited layers, those who have no objective interest in preserving private ownership of the major means of production, behind the cause of the working class.

An orientation calling for an alliance with the so-called middle classes on the basis of respecting private ownership of the means of production and the market economy, as is involved in a class collaborationist policy, creates division in the ranks of the wage earners. A section of these are impelled, even to defend their elementary demands, such as halting layoffs, to want to do away with capitalist ownership here and now.

Such workers tend immediately to refuse to subordinate their interests to the needs of an alliance with "antimonopoly sectors" of the bourgeoisie, or even with the; monopolist bourgeoisie itself, as is the case in the Italian "historic compromise." The orientation of the reformists thus dampens their spirits, may discourage them, and keep them from winning more backward layers to their cause.

Other sections of the working class, which are not confronted with the same difficulties, do not have the same experience in struggle, and have not yet been won over to independent working-class action, may wait and see what the results of such a class-collaborationist policy are. But their expectations will be disappointed, with the resulting risks of an erosion of their forces.

Thus, any strategy of alliances on a conservative basis with "middle layers," any class-collaborationist policy, introduces a dividing line

---

[*] This is an extract from the resolution on Europe of the 1979 world congress of the Fourth International.

into the working class itself. The unity of the workers is thus inextricably tied up with class independence.

Such strategies make the unity of the workers organizations and their leaderships a prior condition for any mobilization of the exploited and oppressed layers themselves for their demands. To the contrary, any real mass movement may serve as a catalyst in unifying the proletariat.

For example, if the unemployed are organized and led in struggle, this can inspire sections of the proletariat that are tending to be reduced to a precarious existence by the crisis with a confidence in their power. Along with this, such action can raise in the mass workers organizations the question of uniting the proletariat.

Moreover, if immigrant workers go into action in defense of their specific demands, this also provides a basis for raising the need for uniting the class, that is, for bringing the immigrants into a united battle line of the working class as a whole. In such mobilizations, we support demands and forms of action that facilitate a linkup with the workers movement.

Achieving an alliance with sections of the petty bourgeoisie-small shop keepers, small farmers, and artisans—remains an important problem for the workers. An alliance with the small peasants is a strategic, question first of all because of the social weight they wield in a series of countries (Ireland, Portugal, Greece, Spain, southern Italy, and certain regions of France). But it is a vital question also as a result of the role they play in supplying food to the urban complexes in most European countries.

It is necessary to convince the small peasants, artisans, and shopkeepers, many of whom are being expropriated by big capital, that the expropriation of the expropriators is not aimed at confiscating small property. What needs to be done is to show that a working-class plan for solutions to the crisis offers the means for meeting their own special needs.

In Portugal, among sections of the peasantry in the north, of the small shopkeepers, and artisans, the hope of getting long-term credit at very low interest rates as a result of the nationalization of the banks created a favorable attitude toward the nascent revolution for a period. The same reaction could be seen when the Portuguese petrochemical trust (SACOR) was nationalized under workers control, and the possibility appeared of its supplying fertilizer on unprecedentedly favorable credit terms.

Every means possible has to be used to demonstrate to these petty-bourgeois layers that there is no antagonism between workers control over the banks and industry, a monopoly of foreign trade, and setting up a unified banking system, on the one hand, and what is favorable to their interests. They look for distribution of the land, getting what is necessary to cultivate it (fertilizer, machinery), and easy credit terms. It is necessary also to demonstrate to the peasants, artisans, and small merchants that there is no contradiction between these first steps in setting up a planned economy and their enjoying favorable conditions for buying raw materials and distributing their products. This can encourage them to organize in cooperatives on a voluntary basis.

A series of working-class demands may also answer the most pressing needs of such petty-bourgeois layers—improving or establishing a genuine social welfare system, developing social and collective infrastructures (hospitals, housing, nurseries, etc.), education and vocational training in all fields (crafts, industry, agriculture).

Decisiveness on the part of the workers movement in providing positive answers to crucial socio-economic problems, such as the destruction of the environment, capitalist squandering of energy potential, the anarchy in scientific research and its subordination to the narrow needs of monopolies such as the military-industrial complex, and the threadbare system of public health can attract to the side of the workers sections of the "new middle layers of wage earners" (engineers, scientists, university teachers, and house physicians in hospitals, etc.)

In order to forge the unity of the working class in action and advance the proletariat along the road of class independence, the united front tactic assumes an important role.

The strategy of uniting the proletariat for the conquest of power must not be reduced to this tactic alone. This strategy requires a complex combination of actions and methods and slogans to go along with them. Nonetheless, the tactic of the workers united front assumes a special place today among the tasks to be pursued by the sections for the following reasons:

- The economic offensive of the bourgeoisie.
- The objective division that this offensive is creating in the working class, helped along by the bureaucratic apparatuses.
- Growing violations of democratic rights.
- The divisiveness engendered directly by the reformist leaderships on the trade-union and political levels.

- The need for large-scale mobilizations to block the austerity policies of the governments and the bosses during which large sectors of the masses can test the validity of the alternative policy we put forward.
- The urgent need to offer a rallying point for the struggles of the various social movements.

The united front tactic cannot be focused exclusively on agreements between the major organizations in the working class, Nonetheless, such accords are often decisive in mobilizing the class, since the new layers of the working class that are going into action insist on unity, an attitude they take in response to the attacks of the capitalists. This aspect of the united front takes on its greatest importance in those countries where the workers movement is split from top to bottom along party lines (SP, CP).

The united front at the top must not be counterposed to unity in action in various forms at the rank-and-file level or in specific sectors. What is important is to start from the objective needs of the working masses and to combine this activity with an orientation to the workers organizations, both at the top and at the bottom.

The Trotskyists do not take a wait-and-see attitude, making their initiatives de pendent on a prior agreement or under standing among the big workers organizations. By themselves, or together with other organizations, they can and must promote mobilizations. But in formulating slogans and selecting forms of action, they have to combine two objectives. One is to broaden the mobilization as much as possible by including, if feasible, activists and sections of the traditional organizations. The other is to maintain a united-front approach to these organizations, even when the chances of achieving any unity with them are slight.

Differentiations within the reformist parties, as well as changes in the relationship of forces between the apparatuses and the working-class vanguard may offer greater opportunities for the sections to formulate their proposals for unity in concrete terms on all the levels on which they raise them.

Depending on the relationship of forces and the concrete political situation, propaganda as well as agitation for a working class united front may be focused primarily on a united front between the big organizations of the working class on the national level—for example, united actions of the SP and the CP and the trade-union organizations led by them against an austerity plan.

We campaign constantly to explain our entire program to as broad an audience as possible, posing it as an alternative to the program of the reformist leaderships.

But this is not enough to win broad layers of workers away from the influence of the reformists or even of the centrists. Only experience in action can raise the consciousness of major sections of the working class. This enables them to see in practice what an obstacle the reformist policy represents to the advancement of the movement in which they are involved.

Of course, we do not make acceptance of our program a condition for establishing a united front. We base our united-front initiatives on the tasks flowing from the needs of the masses, which are dictated by the objective situation. To this end, we put forward immediate, democratic, or transitional demands that offer a basis for the unity in action of the masses and the organizations of the workers movement both in the plants and outside. At the same time, we campaign to get the workers organizations to break with the bourgeoisie. This can take different forms, depending on the country and the situation. We may focus on the need to break with a bourgeois party, oppose restrictions on the right to strike, oppose participation (by the unions or workers parties) in labor management boards, etc. Although such a break from the bourgeoisie cannot be complete except on the basis of the revolutionary program and although the Trotskyists explain this publicly, they do not make adopting the revolutionary program a precondition for movements going in this direction.

In the framework of this battle for unifying the working class and achieving its political independence, we maintain the need for building a revolutionary party to facilitate united action by the masses and to make it easier for them to take the initiative on the political level. The united-front tactic is not an end in itself, but a means for mobilizing the masses, for winning influence over them, and wresting them away from the domination of the reformist leaderships. Our objective remains the advancement of united, broad, and militant mass mobilizations, democratically organized and led.

The highest form of such class unity is embodied in the setting up, extension, and coordination of councils and committees. When this is achieved, the power of the ruling class on the governmental and state level will in fact be put in question.

Clara Zetkin's struggle for the united front.
John Riddell

Genossinnen und Genossen! -- That is how Clara Zetkin began her speeches. It is German for "women comrades and men comrades". Few socialists used that salutation in her time, and there were few women at their meetings. But that was beginning to change, and Zetkin was part of those changes.[*]

Clara Zetkin was a revolutionary leader, who over her long life took part in many struggles, on many issues. This article will consider only a small slice of her activity, one that was central to the tragedy of German communism in the 1920s.

Our topic today is the united front policy – a crucial part of our political inheritance from the era of the Russian Revolution. This policy, adopted by the world communist movement in December 1921, proposed that revolutionary socialists should press for unity with other political forces in action for demands benefiting working people. The character of such a united front was a topic of dispute among socialists then, and remains so today.

Let us examine this policy through Zetkin's eyes.

Clara Zetkin was the outstanding woman communist leader of the 1920s, and she is best known today as an apostle of women's emancipation. However, she also helped shape the communist movement's policy on unity in action. She favoured a broad and non-partisan approach, aiming for unity with non-revolutionary currents; action in the interests of the working class as a whole; and efforts to win social layers outside the industrial working class. She stressed the need for communist policy to reach out to the less radical layers of working people and producers. She opposed a focus on the concerns of the revolutionary vanguard.

---

[*] A version of this article was first published in the November-December 2009, issue of *International Socialist Review* (www.isreview.org) and is reprinted here with permission. John Riddell is editor of seven annotated volumes of Communist International documents, including two announced for publication in 2011, and was co-editor of *Socialist Voice* (www.socialistvoice.ca) where this version first appeared.

Zetkin - a pioneer Marxist

When the Communist (or Third) International (Comintern) adopted the united front policy in 1921, Zetkin, at 64, was more than a dozen years older than any other of its main leaders.[1] She had joined the German Social Democratic party in its early, heroic days. A friend of Friedrich Engels, she later formed a close partnership with Rosa Luxemburg to defend this party's revolutionary heritage and oppose its right-wing current, which sought to make peace with Germany's capitalist state.

In this period, women were almost completely excluded from political life. Zetkin and Luxemburg were the first women to fight their way into the central leadership of socialist parties. To this day, few women have been able to follow them down this path.

Zetkin led the Socialist (or Second) International's work among women, and in this capacity she called the first international socialist conference in opposition to the World War I.[2] This war was ended by revolutions in Russia and Germany in 1917 and 1918. In 1919, Zetkin joined the newly formed German Communist Party, the KPD. That same year, most of the party's central leaders, including Rosa Luxemburg, fell victim to a wave of government terror.

Zetkin was an influential figure in the party's new leadership and, from 1921, in the Communist International – the world union of revolutionary organisations formed two years earlier in Moscow.

Origin of the united front policy

After the German revolution of 1918, Social Democratic Party leaders had led and organised the restoration of capitalist power in the country, and had been notoriously complicit in the terror against revolutionary workers. Nonetheless, they had retained the support of most workers, while the Communist Party led a small minority.

In March 1920, when extreme rightists staged a military takeover, the Social Democrats played a major role in the massive general strike that defeated the coup. How could the momentum of this victory be maintained?

A fruitful initiative to break the stalemate came later that year from revolutionary metalworkers in Clara Zetkin's home base, Stuttgart. It was here that worker activists, six years earlier, had convinced Karl Liebknecht to launch open socialist opposition in Germany to the imperialist world war.[3]

In December, an assembly of Stuttgart's metalworkers, acting on the initiative of Communist Party activists, adopted a resolution calling on the leadership of their trade union, and of all unions, to launch a joint struggle for tangible improvements in workers' conditions. This campaign, the resolution stated, should call for the following five demands "shared by all workers":

- Reduced prices for food and essentials of life.
- Opening of the capitalists' financial records and higher jobless benefits.
- Lower taxes on workers and higher taxes on the rich.
- Workers' control of raw material and food production and distribution.
- Disarming of reactionary gangs and arming of the workers.[4]

Strikingly, the Stuttgart demands embraced not only issues of bread and pay but to initial steps toward workers' power. This was an early example of the communist concept of transitional demands, which are rooted in immediate needs but point toward workers' rule.

The Social Democrats, then organised in two parties, first ignored, then rejected this appeal, some saying the demands were too aggressive, others that they did not go far enough. But the Communists campaigned to rally support for the Stuttgart appeal, and a great many union councils voted their support.[5]

The 'Open Letter'

A month later, in January 1921, the German Communist Party central bureau made a more comprehensive appeal to all workers' organisations, including the Social Democrats, for united action. Zetkin was a leading member of this body, but the appeal's main author was party co-chairperson Paul Levi.

Known as the "Open Letter", this call included the Stuttgart five points, in more detailed form, plus demands for the release of political prisoners and resumption of Germany's trade and diplomatic relations with the Russian Soviet republic.

The Open Letter, too, was rejected by Social Democratic Party and union national leaderships. Union officials began expelling the appeal's supporters. But this time, the campaign to rally rank-and-file support was broader and more successful – to the point where the national union confederation felt compelled to issue counterproposals. Subsequent exchanges, while they did not achieve

agreement, showed that fruitful negotiations between Social
Democrats and Communists were possible.[6]

Reparations crisis

The month of January 1921 also saw Britain, France and other victors
of the world war levy their demands for reparations. They demanded
that Germany pay a sum equivalent to a dozen times the entire yearly
revenue of the near-bankrupt German state, and threatened military
occupation in case of non-payment. All shades of German opinion
held the reparations to be unpayable, and a wave of indignation swept
the country.[7]

The Communists responded by elaborating the final point of their
Open Letter and calling for Germany to conclude an alliance with
Soviet Russia. Clara Zetkin had already raised this call in her first
speech in the Germany's parliament, the Reichstag, on July 2, 1920.[8]
As the reparations crisis came to a head, she raised this demand again
in the Reichstag on January 24, 1921, as "the only way to achieve a
revision of the Versailles Treaty and ultimately to tear it up".

By promoting united action on this demand, Zetkin sought to point
the indignation of the German masses against the Versailles Treaty in
a socialist direction. The establishment of workers' power, she said,
will be "the hour when the German nation will be born, the birth of a
unified German people, no longer divided into lords and servants".[9]

A storm of controversy

The Stuttgart and Open Letter initiative marked a sharp change in
direction for the Communist Party. Instead of merely denouncing the
Social Democrats' pro-capitalist course, Communists were now
proposing a test in action of Social Democrats' capacity to struggle for
demands consistent with the Social Democrats' formal program.

This shift alarmed many German Communists, who felt their party
was playing down the goal of overthrowing the government and
concentrating on moderate demands more acceptable to Social
Democrats. They feared that Zetkin's invocation of a workers'
Germany as a new nation gave ground to reactionary nationalism.

The initiatives of Levi, Zetkin and their allies also encountered
objections abroad. A current led by Hungarian communists such as
Béla Kun called on communists to sharpen their slogans and initiate
minority actions that could sweep the hesitant workers into action –
the so-called "theory of the offensive". Although criticised by Lenin,

this concept found some support in the Moscow-based Executive Committee of the Communist International (ECCI), including from Nikolai Bukharin and Gregory Zinoviev.[10]

The ECCI initially criticised the Open Letter. Lenin supported it, however, and the matter was referred to the next world congress.[11]

Divided working class

The dispute on the united front policy was rooted in a dilemma facing the German working class. It had been defeated, with heavy casualties, in the civil war organised against it by the Social Democratic leaders in 1919. In the following years, hunger and destitution spread: average grain consumption was now little more than half pre-war levels; meat consumption was reduced by two-thirds. Capitalist attacks rained down, and the workers' movement was in retreat.

By the end of 1920, the Communist Party had grown into a mass party, with more than 400,000 members, but it held the support of fewer than 20 per cent of workers voting socialist.[12]

This produced a division among German workers. A Communist vanguard was frustrated and impatient to act, while the majority of workers were pessimistic and passive. In Zetkin's words, the workers were "almost desperate" yet "unwilling to struggle".[13]

Zetkin and her colleagues urged efforts to unite workers in a defensive struggle, in which they could regain the confidence needed for a renewed and concerted offensive for workers' power. However, her left-wing opponents within the party urged minority action to provoke a crisis. As one of them later commented, "A stagnant swamp was everywhere. A wall of passivity was rising. We had to break through it at any cost."[14]

Leadership was needed to rein in impatience and pursue consistent work for unity in action – but this was lacking, both in Berlin and in Moscow.

The 'March Action'

The tensions in the KPD exploded over an issue not directly related to the united front issue. At the January 1921 congress of the Italian Socialist Party, until then affiliated to the Communist International, a wing of the Comintern supporters walked out to form a Communist Party – with strong backing from the ECCI representatives, the Hungarian Mátyás Rákosi and the Bulgarian Kristo Kabakchiev. A larger and less radical grouping, who claimed to support of the Comintern but opposed an immediate break with the party's right-wing, reformist minority, stayed in the Socialist Party.

In a subsequent discussion among KPD leaders, Levi and Zetkin argued that the split, while inevitable, had been driven through by representatives of the Comintern ECCI in an aggressively inflexible manner that unnecessarily divided the pro-Comintern forces. Karl Radek, then representing the ECCI in Germany, defended its actions in Italy, winning the support of the KPD leadership's radical wing. The dispute became heated, touching off tensions in the KPD regarding united front policy, the theory of the offensive and the ECCI's role.

The party's central bureau adopted a motion by Zetkin that smoothed over the difference, but it soon flared up again.

At a KPD central committee meeting on February 22, Rákosi, representing the ECCI, reopened the debate, going so far as to suggest that a split of the type that had occurred in Italy might be needed in Germany as well. By 28 votes to 23, the central committee backed Rákosi and rejected Levi's position. In protest, Levi, Zetkin and three others resigned from the central bureau, the day-to-day leadership body. They were replaced by new, more radical leaders, who had been critical of the party's united front initiatives. Zinoviev, addressing a Russian party congress, greeted the overturn.[15]

There were precedents in communist history for Zetkin's demonstrative resignation. Zinoviev himself had quit the Bolshevik central committee in this manner only a few days before the October 1917 insurrection that established Soviet power. However, the resignation of Zetkin and her allies from the German leadership had disastrous results. The new leadership viewed it as disloyal – an act of desertion. Moreover, it placed Zetkin outside the day-to-day leadership discussions during the decisive events that soon followed.

In March, the KPD, with strong encouragement from ECCI envoys, put the "offensive" concept into action, attempting to launch an insurrectional general strike based on the party's forces alone. The so-called "March Action" was a costly failure, but party leaders held to their course. Paul Levi publicly denounced the party's conduct as a "putsch", an action for which he was expelled.

Correction at world congress

This left Zetkin as the most prominent advocate of a united front course in the KPD and the Communist International. At the April 7-8 meeting of the KPD's central committee, she condemned the party's central bureau for having abandoned the Open Letter and the alliance with Soviet Russia and for launching the party on a confrontation course that excluded the masses. "Party campaigns can prepare the road for mass action, can provide goals and leadership for them, but cannot replace them", her proposed resolution stated.[16]

Yet Zetkin stood almost alone, surrounded by "a frigid wall of rejection, mistrust, and hostility" and branded as an "opportunist" and "renegade", writes biographer Louise Dornemann. Zetkin "felt herself dreadfully alone, as never before in her life".[17]

When the Comintern met in congress in Moscow, in June, Zetkin found support. Lenin and Leon Trotsky launched a campaign to overturn the ultraleft "theory of the offensive" and won the Communist International to a course similar to what Zetkin had advocated.

Meanwhile, the dispute among German Communists raged at the congress, with Zetkin leading the critics of the March Action. In her view, the party leaders had shown no sense of reality. "They treated ... trends as already-existing facts", she said. "Concentrating on what was conceivably possible, they overlooked what was real. They believed that a resolution concocted in a test tube ... could master the situation and instantly reorient the party rank and file", who were entirely unprepared.[18]

In a compromise decision, the congress adopted the essence of the political course that Zetkin had advocated. This outcome opened the door to the Comintern's adoption of the united front policy in December 1921. It enabled Zetkin to carry out two years of fruitful work as the Communist International's best-known non-Russian leader.

United front in practice

As the head of the Communist International's work among women, Zetkin sought to imbue it with united front concepts. This work was never a high priority for party leaders, and women made up at best 10 per cent of the total membership. Still, the Communist Women's International had its own publications and conferences both internationally and nationally, which reached far beyond the party membership. Zetkin "wanted to win not only women [industrial] workers, but women who were office employees, peasants, civil servants, intellectuals", writes biographer Gilbert Badia. "She favoured appealing to Social Democratic women, setting aside invective in order to win a hearing."[19]

In the mid-1920s, as the Comintern was bureaucratised under Joseph Stalin, the Communist Women's International was among the first victims. In 1925, Zetkin's international women's magazine was shut down as "too costly"; the next year, over strenuous objections by Zetkin and her colleagues, the women's secretariat was dissolved and formation of further women's organisations prohibited, amid warnings regarding "feminism" and "Social Democratic methods".[20]

Zetkin also was among the central leaders of two organisations established to coordinate solidarity across borders: International Workers Aid, which provided humanitarian relief, and International Red Aid, which defended victims of political persecution. Established to help counter the famine in Russia in 1921, Workers' Aid soon had 200,000 people fully under its care; it then provided funds for industrial development equal to half what the Soviet government summoned up from its own resources. This vast effort rested on workers' donations and also contributions from more affluent friends of Soviet Russia; even some banks were induced to provide loans.[21]

These efforts were organised on a non-partisan basis; sponsors included Anatole France and Albert Einstein.[22] But later, in the Stalin era, the non-partisan principle could not survive. Despite Zetkin's vehement protests, these organisations were purged in the late 1920s, eliminating all critics of Stalin, including her closest collaborators.[23]

Zetkin was an exponent of the concept of a workers' government, that is, a government based on the mass movement of working people and acting in their interests. This was an application of the united front that originated in Germany and became part of the political tool-chest of communists in Lenin's time. I leave this topic for separate discussion.[24]

Unity with the peasants

The Bolsheviks' agrarian policies, aimed at forging an alliance with small-scale, exploited farmers, had aroused objections from many Marxists elsewhere in Europe, including Rosa Luxemburg. Zetkin, however, in a November 1922 speech on the fifth anniversary of Soviet power, emphasised the Bolsheviks' achievements in reaching out to the peasantry. In the following passage, she expresses a thought that I have not found elsewhere in world communist literature of the time.

Among the Russian poor peasants there are old and deeply felt traditions of indigenous village communism that have not entirely died away. They have been sustained and reinforced by primitive religious feelings that view all property as ultimately from God, as God's property.... And these beginning of communist understanding are systematically encouraged and promoted by the measures of the proletarian state.[25]

This conception reaches back to ideas of Marx that were unknown in Zetkin's time, and reaches forward to the positions of José Carlos Mariátegui of Peru and Marxists today regarding survivals of original communism among Indigenous peoples.

Uniting creative producers

The dominant event in European politics in the 1920s was the rise of fascism, which triumphed in Italy in 1922, and was then gaining strength in Germany. Zetkin made an important contribution to Marxism's understanding of this unprecedented phenomenon.

Zetkin believed that in these conditions of generalised social crisis, the workers' united front must be extended far beyond the industrial proletariat. Her distinctive approach is indicated by a word used by her, and only by her, with reference to the forces that must be united: *die Schaffenden*, a German word combining the meaning of "producers" and "creators". The *Schaffenden*, Zetkin says, are "all those whose labour, be it with hand or brain, increases the material and cultural heritage of humankind, without exploiting the labour of others".[26] They include many who are not exploited wage labourers – whether fisherfolk, artists or physicians – but are nonetheless victims of capitalism whom the proletariat must strive to win.

Commenting on a strike by German civil servants working on the railways, she viewed it as symptomatic of disintegration in the German state. Communists should "develop their ties among all public employees – not just railwaymen and postal workers but teachers, judicial clerks, etc.".

Addressing a united front, anti-fascist conference in 1923, Zetkin explained that "broad layers of petty bourgeois and intellectuals have lost the conditions of life of the pre-war period. They are not proletarianised but pauperised". Their hopes in capitalist democracy have been betrayed; it no longer produces reforms. But the proletariat offers them a road forward, because "only revolutionary class struggle wins reforms".[27]

The struggle against fascism

Zetkin's concept of creative producers gives depth to her analysis of fascism. Unlike other forms of right-wing dictatorship, fascism is sustained "not by a narrow caste but by broad social layers, large masses that reach even into the proletariat", she told a Comintern conference in 1923. "We cannot defeat them through military means alone."[28]

She regarded fascism as "an expression of the decay and disintegration of the capitalist economy and a symptom of collapse of the bourgeois state". In these social conditions, Zetkin continued, not only is the proletariat driven into poverty, but petty-bourgeois layers, peasants and intellectuals are proletarianised.[29]

These layers "have lost faith not only in reformist [Social Democratic] leaders but in socialism itself."

Fascism offers a "refuge for the politically homeless and socially uprooted, who are disillusioned and deprived of the basis for living". Yet "the vital interests of these layers is in growing contradiction to the capitalist order", as is also their "longing to rise to a higher cultural level". Such "despairing layers need hope, a new world outlook", which the proletariat can provide.[30]

These ideas were taken up by the International Provisional Committee Against Fascism, formed in 1923 with Zetkin and the French author Henri Barbusse as co-chairs.[31]

Zetkin in Stalin's Comintern

This promising beginning was undone the following year when the Communist International and its KPD reverted to a more extreme version of the ultraleftism of the "theory of the offensive" period. Social Democracy was now seen as a "wing of German fascism", or, in Stalin's word, its "twin". The term "united front" was still used, but it was now to be a "united front from below", that is, no appeals to leaders of other political currents; instead, attempts to win rank-and-file workers to Communist-led movements.

This reversal was dictated by the tactical needs of a bureaucratic faction that ruled in Moscow, in the first stage of a process that quickly led to the Communist International's degeneration.

Except for a partial respite in 1926-27, Zetkin now became an oppositionist, expressing her most deeply held views only in private letters, closed meetings and confidential memos.

The then-dominant left faction of the KPD was aligned with Comintern president Gregory Zinoviev, and in 1926 they followed him into the United Opposition, led by Zinoviev and Trotsky. Zetkin allowed her animosity to the German ultralefts to colour her assessment of this new opposition. She lined up with Nikolai Bukharin, then allied with Stalin, in a combination that was promoting bureaucratisation of the Communist International. Tragically, in 1927 she vocally supported measures to expel the United Opposition's supporters.

Only two years later, Zetkin supported the current led by Bukharin, the so-called "Right Opposition", in its rebellion against an ultraleft turn in Stalin's policies. Bukharin's tendency was defeated, and its supporters expelled or forced to recant. Zetkin alone remained at her post, never recanting her views, and proclaiming them when she could in letters, memos and personal discussions. She made no secret of her scorn for Stalin, once writing of him, in the chauvinist idiom of the era, as "a schizophrenic woman wearing men's pants".[32]

During these tormented years, her health, never good, gave way. Circulatory problems increasingly impeded her walking. She suffered the after effects of malaria, and in her last years she was almost blind.

She held to the hope that the Communist International could be reformed – as did Bukharin, Trotsky and almost all Communist oppositionists at that time. She did not quit the official Communist movement. But she could not prevent Stalin from utilising her enormous prestige for his own purposes.

On one occasion she managed to assert in print that she disagreed with the Comintern's line. Two of her closely argued critiques of Stalinist policy somehow reached independent socialist periodicals, which published them.

Zetkin's greatest concern was the rise of German fascism. Faced with this threat, the Communist International retreated into sectarianism, branding the Social Democrats as fascist, rejecting a broad alliance against Hitlerism, and making no attempt to prepare concerted resistance. Zetkin favoured a united front response, a position similar to that championed by Trotsky and the Left Opposition.

When the German parliament reconvened in 1932, it was Zetkin's right, as its oldest member, to officially open the session. When she heard this, she exclaimed, "I'll do it, dead or alive." The Nazis vowed to kill her if she appeared. Now near death, she was carried in a chair to the speaker's platform, to face an arrogant throng of uniformed Nazi deputies. Her voice, weak at first, grew in volume and passion,[33] expressing both her defiance and her insight into how the fascist menace could be defeated:

The most important immediate task is the formation of a United Front of all workers in order to turn back fascism... Before this compelling historical necessity, all inhibiting and dividing political, trade union, religious and ideological opinions must take a back seat.[34]

Nonetheless, the German workers' movement went down without making a stand. In the early months of 1933, the Nazis took power and crushed the Communist Party and the workers' movement.

Clara Zetkin died in July that year. It was a time of defeat and demoralisation. Had she lived five years longer, she would have witnessed the Communist International turn sharply to the right, embracing alliances with bourgeois forces in defence of capitalism, while Stalin organised the murder of almost all her friends and colleagues then living in the Soviet Union.

What does Clara Zetkin say to us today? Let me suggest three points:

1. Political conditions and class relations have changed enormously since Zetkin's time. But her insistence on the need for unity in action on the road toward workers' power remains valid.

2. As a communist leader, Zetkin was distinguished by her attention and sensitivity to the moods of more backward and more privileged working people. A revolutionary party leadership should not consist solely of such leaders. On the other hand, such a leadership needs to encompass this outlook. Zetkin's example illustrates the need for inclusivity and breadth in the leadership of a revolutionary party.

3. Clara Zetkin was often wrong, sometimes tragically so. Yet she succeeded in contributing enormously to the struggle for human liberation in her time. She provides an example of

what we, working together, can achieve in the coming decades.

Zetkin: A life of struggle for socialism

Clara Zetkin was one of the most prominent leaders of the world movement for socialism from 1890 until her death in 1933.

Zetkin was born in 1859 in Saxony, when it was still one of several dozen German feudal principalities then in the earliest stages of industrialisation. Trained as a teacher, in 1878 she joined the German socialist movement, later known as the Social Democratic Party of Germany (SPD). The repressive policies of the newly established German empire forced her into exile in 1882. She returned in 1890 and joined her party's publishing apparatus as editor of a women's rights magazine, *Die Gleichheit* (Equality).

Ten years later, Zetkin joined her close friend Rosa Luxemburg in opposing the "revisionist" policies of Eduard Bernstein, who had abandoned the goal of socialist revolution. She also led the struggle to win the Socialist International to a campaign for women's personal freedom, political rights, and to equality on the job.

During the first years of the new century, Zetkin resisted the SPD leadership's drift to the right and took part in the initial steps towards creation of a revolutionary opposition current. When war broke out in 1914, the SPD leaders betrayed socialist principles by committing the party to support of German government's war effort. Zetkin was among the first party leaders to protest. In 1915, she convened a socialist women's conference that was the first international gathering to reassert the principle of unity of working people across the battle lines.

Zetkin joined Luxemburg during the war in launching the Spartacus League, the revolutionary current that founded the German Communist Party (KPD) in January 1919. *Die Gleichheit* was reborn under her editorship as *Kommunistin* (Communist Woman). She served as an elected deputy in Germany's parliament from 1920 until her death. From 1921, she supported the wing of the German party most committed to the united front policy. She was a prominent leader of resistance to international fascism.

Zetkin headed the Communist Women's International from 1921 until its dissolution in 1926. During this period, and until her death, she worked primarily in Moscow as part of the Communist

International's apparatus. She carried out major responsibilities in international efforts to defend workers from political repression.

In 1928, Joseph Stalin imposed an ultraleft policy on the Communist International, rejecting the united front approach. Zetkin strongly opposed this turn. Defeated but unrepentant, she continued her work in the International until her death near Moscow in 1933.

Notes

1. Lenin, whom Russian communists often called "the old man", was born 13 years after Zetkin.
2. See John Riddell, ed., *Lenin's Struggle for a Revolutionary International* (New York: Monad Press, 1984), pp. 276-79.
3. Riddell, *Lenin's Struggle*, p. 172.
4. Pierre Broué, *The German Revolution 1917-1923* (London: Merlin Press, 2006), pp. 468-69; Arnold Reisberg, *An den Quellen der Einheitsfrontpolitik* (Berlin: Dietz Verlag, 1971), pp. 50-51.
5. Reisberg, pp. 51-53.
6. Reisberg, pp. 53-62, 65-67.
7. Sigrid Koch-Baumgarten, *Aufstand der Avantgarde: Die Märzaktion der KPD 1921* (Frankfurt: Campus Verlag, 1986), pp. 99-101.
8. The winning of women's suffrage had been one of the gains of the German revolution of 1918; only then was Zetkin eligible to stand for election.
9. Reisberg, p. 71. Zetkin's statement recalls a passage in the *Communist Manifesto*: "The working men have no country. We cannot take from them what they have not got. Since the proletariat must first of all acquire political supremacy, must rise to be the leading class of the nation, must constitute itself *the* nation, it is so far, itself national, though not in the bourgeois sense of the word." Karl Marx and Frederick Engels, *Collected Works* (Moscow: Progress Publishers, 1984), pp. 502-03.
10. Koch-Baumgarten 81. Lenin, "'Kommunismus'", in *Collected Works*, vol. 31 (Moscow: Progress Publishers, 1960-71), pp.165-67.
11. Broué, p. 473.
12. Reisberg, p. 97; Koch-Baumgarten, p. 87.
13. Zetkin, "Die Lehren des deutschen Eisenbahnerstriks", in *Kommunistische Internationale* 20 (1922), p. 1.

14. Quoted by Trotsky in *Protokoll des III Weltkongresses der Kommuinistischen Internationale* (Hamburg: Verlag der Kommunistischen Internationale, 1921), p. 274.
15. The complex story of the Italian split and its impact on German Communists is well told by Broué, pp. 474-90.
16. Reisberg, p. 125.
17. Luise Dornemann, *Clara Zetkin: Leben und Wirken* (Berlin: Dietz Verlag, 1973), p. 423.
18. *Protokoll des III Weltkongresses*, p. 601.
19. Gilbert Badia, *Clara Zetkin, féministe sans frontières* (Paris: Les Éditions Ouvrières, 1993), p. 256.
20. Badia, p. 257; Bernhard Beyerlein, "Zwischen Internationale und Gulag. Präliminarien zur Geschichte der internationalen kommunistischen Frauenbewegung (1919-1945). Teil 1.", in *The International Newsletter of Communist Studies Online*, vol. 12 (2006), no. 19, pp. 38-42.
21. *Protokoll des Vierten Kongresses der Kommuinistischen Internationale* (Hamburg: Verlag der Kommunistischen Internationale, 1923), p. 550, p. 555
22. Badia, p. 265
23. Badia, p. 267.
24. See Zetkin, "Die Arbeiterregierung", *Die Kommunistische Fraueninternationale* 9-10 (1922), pp. 651-57.
25. *Protokoll des Vierten Kongresses*, p. 250.
26. From a speech to the German Reichstag (parliament), March 7, 1923, published that year by the KPD and quoted in Tânia Puschnerat, *Clara Zetkin: Bürgerlichkeit und Marxismus* (Essen: Klartext Verlag, 2003), p. 346.
27. Zetkin, "Kampf gegen den internationalen Faschismus", in *Internationale Presse-Korrespondenz* 52 (1923), p. 418.
28. *Protokoll der Konferenz der erweiterten Executive der Kommunistischen Internationale Moscau 12-23. Juni 1923* (Hamburg: Verlag Carl Hoym, 1923), p. 205.
29. *Protokoll der Konferenz*, pp. 205-09.
30. *Protokoll der Konferenz*, p. 222.
31. Puschnerat, p. 283
32. Puschnerat 374.
33. Badia, pp. 302-303.
34. Philip S. Foner, ed., *Clara Zetkin: Selected Writings* (New York: International Publishers, 1984), p. 174.

The Communist International & the united front.
Duncan Hallas

In the most critical year for the bourgeoisie, the year 1919, the proletariat of Europe could have undoubtedly have conquered state power with minimum sacrifices, had there been at its head a genuine revolutionary organisation, setting forth clear aims and capably pursuing them, i.e. a strong Communist Party. But there was none ... During the last three years the workers have fought a great deal and have suffered many sacrifices. But they have not won power. As a result the working masses have become more cautious than they were in 1919-20.
(Trotsky, The Main Lesson of the Third Congress, 1921)

WHAT SHOULD a revolutionary party do in a non-revolutionary situation? [*] In 1919 this was not an issue. By 1921 it was central. As the Theses on the World Situation', adopted by the Third World Congress in 1921, put it:

> During the year that has passed between the second and third congresses of the Communist International, a series of working-class risings and struggles have ended in partial defeat (the advance of the Red Army on Warsaw in August 1920, the movement of the Italian proletariat in September 1920, the rising of the German workers in March 1921).

> The first period of the post-war revolutionary movement, distinguished by the spontaneous character of its assaults, by the marked imprecision of its aims and methods, and by the extreme panic which it aroused amongst the ruling classes, seems in essentials to be over. The self-confidence of the bourgeoisie as a class, and the outward stability of their state organs, have undeniably been strengthened... The leaders of the bourgeoisie are even boasting of the power of their state machines and have gone over to an offensive against the workers in all countries both on the economic and or, the political front. [1]

The recovery of capitalism was shaky and uneven. 1921 saw the onset of a serious, if shortlived, economic crisis. Nevertheless the receding of the revolutionary wave of 19 19-20 meant that the immediate perspective of which Zinoviev had spoken in 1920, "the World

---

[*] From *International Socialism* (1st series), No.74, January 1975.

Congress of Soviet Republics", was now unreal. Revolutionary opportunities could, and indeed did, arise in the next few years. But the international movement as a whole had to come to terms with a new situation.

In Russia the year 1921 saw the abandonment of "War Communism" and the adoption of the "New Economic Policy", a policy which Lenin described as "a strategical retreat". "We said, in effect," he wrote, "'Before we are completely routed, let us retreat and reorganise everything, but on a firmer basis.' If Communists deliberately examine the question of the New Economic Policy there cannot be the slightest doubt that we have sustained a very severe defeat on the economic front." [2]

On the international field a corresponding turn was essential. This was not at all a question of an automatic reflection of events in Russia. The changed situation in the world, above all in Europe, was one of the two main factors forcing the retreat to the NEP.

That changed situation put the choice squarely before European communists (and communism was still, in 1921, essentially a European movement); find ways and means of making revolutionary politics meaningful and important to workers in a (for the time being) non-revolutionary situation, or face relegation to the position of revolutionary sects without serious influence on the course of events.

From the day of its foundation – declared the Third World Congress's *Theses on Tactics* – the Communist International has clearly and unambiguously made its goal the formation not of small communist sects, trying by propaganda and agitation only to establish their influence over the working masses, but participation in the struggle of the working masses, the direction of this struggle in a Communist spirit, and the creation in the course of this struggle of experienced, large, revolutionary, mass communist parties. [3]

How was this to be done in the new situation? On the basis of what the *Theses on Tactics* called "partial struggles and partial demands", that is, demands about wages, conditions, unemployment and so on.

After stating that there was no *permanent* solution to any of the problems facing the working class on a reformist basis, after re-affirming that the destruction of capitalism remained the "guiding aim and immediate mission", the *Theses* argued:

But to carry out this mission the communist parties must put forward demands whose fulfilment is an immediate and urgent working class need, and they must fight for these demands in mass struggle, regardless of whether they are compatible with the profit economy of the capitalist class or not [i.e. even if they are compatible, are "reformist" demands – DH] ... The task of the communist parties is to extend, to deepen, and to unify this struggle for concrete demands:.. Every objection to the putting forward of such partial demands, every charge of reformism on this account, is on emanation of the same inability to grasp the essential conditions of revolutionary action as was expressed in the hostility of some revolutionary groups to participation in the trade unions or to making use of parliament. It is not a question of proclaiming the final goal to the proletariat, but of intensifying the practical struggle which is the only way of leading the proletariat to the struggle for the final goal ... [4]

Powerful tendencies in a number of important communist parties rejected this approach. For them, the struggle for "partial and immediate demands" smacked of reformism. A set of ultra-leftist amendments to the *Thesis on Tactics* were submitted by the German, Austrian and Italian parties.

Lenin wrote later: "At that Third Congress I was on the extreme right flank. I am convinced that it was the only correct stand to take." [5]

Ultra-leftist ideas had gained sustenance in the course of the struggle against centrism, a struggle that was far from ended in 1921-although the centrists were now a lesser danger than the ultra-lefts. Indeed the two trends reinforced each other to some extent as can be seen from the contrasting examples of Italy and Germany. The debacle into which the centrist leadership of the Italian party had led the working class in the autumn of 1920 encouraged the ultra-leftist adventurism of the theory of the offensive in Germany.

The Italian Debacle

The present phase of the class struggle in Italy is the phase that precedes either the conquest of political power by the revolutionary proletariat ... or a tremendous reaction by the capitalists and the governing caste. Every kind of violence will be used to subjugate the agricultural and industrial working class.
(Gramsci writing in L'Ordine Nuovo, May 1920)

ITALY EMERGED from the war as the weakest of the "victors". Its rulers had very little to show for the half a million dead and the huge war debt. The cost of living had risen sixfold since before the war and was still climbing. "The Italian liberal state was rapidly disintegrating, there was widespread sedition in the army and inflation was rampant." [6]

At the Second World Congress (1920), Serrati, leader of the centrist majority of the Italian Socialist Party (PSI), had declared: "Thus the political and economic conditions in Italy are such that they inevitably drive towards revolution. The party is so powerful that it may be said that the Italian proletariat is almost ready to seize power." [7]

The PSI had, however, no plan of action for any such thing. As has been noted, Serrati and his associates had earlier refused to support the considerable land-seizure movements of peasants and agricultural labourers on the grounds that it was "demagogic and petty-bourgeois".

At the end of August 1920 a wage dispute in the Milan engineering industry led to a national lock-out and a massive wave of factory occupations involving 600,000 workers. This was no ordinary dispute. Social tensions were extreme. There had already been a general strike in Turin in April. "Several workers were killed during the May Day celebrations, and later conflicts between the workers and the police or army were frequent and bloody." [8]

Factory councils controlled the occupied plants. "Red Guards" were set up in them. A new land seizure movement got underway in the south, notably in backward Sicily.

The PSI leadership encouraged all these movements, using the most extreme language. "Everything written in *Avanti* [the party's daily – DH] and everything uttered by the spokesmen of the Socialist Party was taken by the masses as a summons to the proletarian revolution. And this propaganda struck a responsive chord in the hearts of the working class, awakened their will and called forth the September events," said Trotsky. "... the PSI verbally conducted a revolutionary policy, without ever taking into account any of its consequences. Everybody knows that during the September events no other organisation so lost its head and became so paralysed by fear as the PSI which had itself paved the way for these events." [9]

For the PSI majority had, literally, no consistent policy. Its revolutionary rhetoric notwithstanding, it had agreed early in September with the trade union federation (CGL), whose leaders were party members, to confine the struggle to the original economic demands. Yet it still spoke the language of insurrection. It provoked, indeed terrified, the ruling class and at the same time remained politically passive, giving no concrete lead at all to the hundreds of thousands of workers under its influence and the millions they in turn influenced.

Late in August the executive of the International sent a letter to the PSI signed by Bukharin, Lenin and Zinoviev. "In Italy there are at hand all the most important conditions for a genuinely popular, great proletarian revolution ... Every day brings news of disturbances. All eye-witnesses – including the Italian delegates – assert and reiterate that the situation in Italy is profoundly revolutionary. Nevertheless in many cases the party stands aside, without attempting to generalise the movement, to give it slogans ... to turn it into a decisive offensive against the bourgeois state. [10]

On 22 September the ECCI sent another urgent call to the party leaders. "You cannot win by the seizure of factories and workshops alone ... the scope of this movement must be extended, generalised, the question raised to a general political level, in other words the movement broadened into a general uprising with the object of overthrowing the bourgeoisie by the seizure of power by the working class ... This is the only way to salvation; otherwise the disintegration and collapse of the mighty and magnificent movement that has begun is inevitable ..." [11]

None of this had any effect. The PSI failed to give the mass movement an overall political direction, failed to direct it towards the seizure of power, failed to make technical preparations for an insurrection. It drifted. The crisis passed. Inevitably, the predicted "disintegration and collapse" set in.

The outcome was disastrous. The thoroughly frightened ruling class began to turn to fascism. "Mussolini's movement, weak and negligible before September 1920, grew with extraordinary rapidity in the last three months of the year." [12]

The September crisis proved that the PSI, affiliated to Communist International since 1919, was in fact not a communist party at all. It was symptomatic that the Serrati leadership had persistently refused to expel its right wing led by the unreconstructed reformist Turati in spite of the Second World Congress decision and repeated demands by the ECCI.

At the PSI's Congress held at Livorno in January 1921, the International forced a split. But unlike the splits at Halle and Tours the previous year, the left did not succeed in winning the bulk of the membership away from the centrists. The card vote showed 14,695 votes for Turatti's right wing, 58,785 for the left and 98,028 for Serrati's centre group. The left seceded.

This relationship of forces would not have been so bad if the left, now the Italian Communist Party (PCI), had had an aggressive but flexible strategy for winning the workers who followed Serrati. It had no such strategy. It was dominated by the sterile ultra-leftism of Amadeo Bordiga and his group. Not until the middle-twenties was the hold of the ultra-lefts in the PCI finally broken. By then it was too late. Fascism had triumphed.

The March Action

> *The crux of the matter is that Levi in many respects is right politically. Unfortunately he is guilty of a number of breaches of discipline for which the party expelled him. Thalheimer's and Bela Kun's theses are politically utterly fallacious. Mere phases and playing at Leftism.* (Lenin, Letter to Zinoviev, 6 June 1921)

IN ITALY in the second half of 1920 a genuine mass revolutionary movement, a movement that could have led to the destruction of the Italian bourgeois state, to a soviet Italy, and so to a fundamental shift in the balance of power in Europe, was mined by the spinelessness of a centrist party leadership.

In Germany in March 1921, in the absence of a nationwide mass revolutionary movement, a party leadership tried to force the pace, to *substitute* the party militants for the mass movement. The result was a severe defeat. Not, indeed, a disaster on the Italian scale, but a serious defeat nonetheless, a defeat that was to have a profound and unfavourable influence on the German workers' movement.

There was a connection between the two events. On the surface it concerned the leadership of the German Party (KPD). Paul Levi, the outstanding KPD leader, had attended the Congress of Livorno. After the Congress he had criticised the tactical clumsiness of the International's representatives. They were Kristo Kabakchiev, a Bulgarian who Trotsky described as "a lifeless doctrinaire" and Matyas Rakosi, a Hungarian "organisation man", an "apparatchnik" without a serious political idea in his head who much later (1944-56) became the Stalinist boss of Hungary.

Levi's criticisms, which may have been broadly speaking correct, led Rakosi to demand an endorsement of his actions and a condemnation of Levi from the German party leadership. He gained his point (by 28 votes to 23). Levi, Clara Zetkin (the outstanding women's leader of the KPD, and previously of the SPD), Ernst Däumig (a prominent leader of the Berlin shop stewards' movement during the war and now head of the KPD's "military apparatus") and two other members of the right wing of the party leadership resigned in protest. The left gained a majority.

This shift in the political balance in the "general staff" had important consequences. It gave temporary dominance to a groups of lefts – Maslow, Fischer, Thalheimer, Frölich and others – who believed in the "theory of the offensive", the view that "the working class could be moved only when set in motion by a series of offensive acts" as Ruth Fischer put it. [13]

According to Fischer, "In the months preceding the Kronstadt revolt, March 1921, an action in Germany to divert the Russian workers from their own troubles bad been concocted by a caucus of the Russian party centring around Zinoviev and Bela Kun". [14]

This is an excuse, a justification after the event. The fact is that amongst the ex-members of the USPD who had been won to the Communist International after the Congress of Halle (300,000 to 350,000 of them), there was a strong sentiment for immediate revolutionary action. The lefts gave expression to this impatience, developed a theoretical justification for it and used it to overthrow their factional opponents in the leadership. These, the Levi group, were already attempting to direct the party along the lines that Lenin and Trotsky were to direct the whole International after the Third World Congress. But Levi lacked the authority, the patience and the tactical skill for this task.

It is true enough that Zinoviev (and Bukharin) were toying with the half-Blanquist notion that the German workers might be "galvanised" by an "offensive" by party militants and that they were guilty of the gross irresponsibility of sending Bela Kun to Germany as Comintern representative with undefined powers.

Kun, "my dear Bela", as Lenin said of him, "who also belongs to a poetically gifted nation and considers himself obliged to be constantly more left than the left" [15], was an ardent advocate of the "offensive at all costs". But the ECCI had not ordered the "offensive". Kun acted on his own responsibility and the truth is that his adventurist tendencies met a ready response from the new German leadership. Even without Kun, even without Zinoviev's equivocal encouragement, they would probably have acted no differently; Fischer's subsequent excuses notwithstanding. It was a case of "success has a thousand fathers; failure is always an orphan".

On 16 March 1921 the Social-Democratic Oberpräsident of Saxony, Otto Horsing, ordered his police to occupy the Mansfeld copper mines, a communist stronghold, and a number of factories on the pretext that "robbery and looting" were rife. This was almost certainly a calculated provocation. The police and the Social-Democratic leaden were well aware that the "offensive" was coming and Horsing preferred to deal with it at a time of his own choosing. [16]

The immediate outcome was indeed a rising of sorts, a series of armed clashes between workers and police and soldiers in the Mansfeld region and at the Leuna chemical plants near Halle. Aside from the resources of the party's military apparatus, the workers had quantities of arms left over from 1919. For a brief period red guards, led by the anarchist guerrilla leader Max Holz, dominated the Mansfeld area. But the action was extremely localised.

This type of situation would have been a difficult one for the most sober party leadership. As in the July Days in Petrograd in 1917, the workers in one centre were moving to armed insurrection whilst the mass of the working class was far from any such thought. The problem was to check the most advanced sections, to organise a retreat whilst minimising losses – an extremely hard and tricky operation.

The left leaders of the KPD, intoxicated with romantic notions, pursued the opposite course. They called for a general strike and armed actions against the state. The party's military units were ordered to "provoke" the authorities and so "galvanise" the workers. "Several bombs were exploded in Breslau and Halle; several other bombings planned for Berlin did not materialise." [17] When the strike call fell on deaf ears – as, in general, it did – the party militants were ordered to force the workers out.

"The Friederich-Albert-Hütte in Rheinhausen, owned by Krupp, was the scene of heavy fighting on Thursday," said one party report quoted by Levi, "between communists who occupied the plant and workers who wanted to go to work. Finally the workers attacked the communists with clubs and forced their way into the plant. Eight men were wounded." [18] There were big clashes in the Hamburg shipyards between social-democratic and communist workers. In Berlin the party attempted to organise the unemployed to seize the plants and keep the workers out! Everywhere, outside a limited area in central Germany where there was real support, a minority of communist influenced workers acted without, and often against, the mass of the working class.

The inevitable collapse of the adventure was followed by a savage repression. The party suffered a massive haemorrhage, membership fell catastrophically (to 150,000 or less) and thousands of militants were in prison.

Towards the United Front

The most important question before the Communist International today is to win predominating influence over the majority of the working class, and to bring its decisive strata into the struggle. For despite the objectively revolutionary situation ... the majority of workers are still not under communist influence.
(Resolution of the Third World Congress 1921)

THE MOVEMENT originated out of the split in the working class movement in 1914 and grew in the course of the struggle against the centrist leaders in 1919-20, a struggle leading to further splits.

Perhaps inevitably, hostility and contempt for the reformist and centrist leaders tended to spill over into a dangerous lack of regard for the workers who still followed these leaders. The lunacy of the March Action was the danger signal. A sharp turn "to the right" was essential if the International was to avoid increased isolation from the class it was trying to lead.

Trotsky later claimed: "At the Third World Congress the overwhelming majority called to order those elements in the International whose views involved the danger that the vanguard might, by precipitate action, be tattered against the passivity and immaturity of the working masses, and against the strength of the capitalist state. That was the greatest danger." [19]

In fact the majority was anything but overwhelming. Certainly the *Theses on Tactics* are an implicit condemnation of putschism and adventurism as well as of the passive, propagandist variant of ultra-leftism. But it was a hard fight to get them adopted.

And on the March Action itself, Lenin's "extreme right flank" had to be content with an equivocal resolution which declared:

The action of last March was forced on the KPD by the government attack on the workers of central Germany ... The KPD committed a number of errors of which the chief one was that it did not clearly understand the defensive nature of the struggle ... The Congress considers the March Action of the KPD as a step forward ... the KPD must in future better adapt its battle cry to the actual situation. [20]

This unsatisfactory compromise was, in part, the result of Paul Levi's public attack on the KPD, an attack which led to his expulsion. Levy published a pamphlet, *Our Course Against Putschism*, which contained an essentially correct, if exaggerated, criticism of the party leaders, written in extremely violent terms ("the greatest Bakunist Putsch in history") and which gave the authorities valuable evidence against the party. But the main factor was the continuing strength of the lefts. Not until after the Congress did the ECCI feel strong enough to draw the logical conclusions of the new line and address itself to formally spelling out its consequences.

In December it declared: "the ECCI is of the opinion that the slogan of the Third World Congress of the Communist International 'To the Masses', and the interests of the communist movement generally, require the communist panics and the Communist International as a whole to *support the slogan of the united front of the workers* and to take the initiative in this matter." [21] (The emphasis is in the original.) This, it was made clear, meant a determined attempt to force the *Ieaderships* of the reformist and centrist organisations into limited co-operation on concrete issues by winning their followers for unity in action, not merely an attempt to draw those followers into action behind the communist parties.

In January 1922 the ECCI called publicly for "the establishment of a united front of all parties supported by the proletariat, regardless of the differences separating them, so long as they are anxious to wage a common fight for the immediate and urgent needs of the proletariat ... No worker, whether communist or social-democrat or syndicalist or even a member of the Christian or liberal trade unions, wants his wages further reduced. None wants to work longer hours ... And therefore all must unite in a common front against the employers' offensive ..." [22]

This was an enormous retreat from the positions of 1919-20. Yet it was essential in the new conditions. The new line itself was fraught with difficulties and dangers, above all the danger of the communist parties losing their revolutionary elan and ability to shift rapidly to the left when the tide turned again. It was to be tested in revolutionary crises in Bulgaria and Germany in 1923.

Notes

1. Degras, *The Communist International 1919-43*, Vol.1, p.230.
2. Lenin, *Collected Works*, Vol.33, p.63.
3. Degras, Vol.1, p.243.
4. Degras, Vol.1, p.249-50.
5. Lenin, *CW*, Vol.33, p.208.
6. Cammett, *Antonio Gramsci and the Origins of Italian Communism*, p.69.
7. Degras, Vol.1, p.188
8. Cammett, p.111.
9. Trotsky, *The First Five Years of the Communist International*, Vol.1, p.262.
10. Degras, Vol.1, p.190.
11. Degras, Vol.1, p.193.
12. Cammett, p.133
13. Fischer, *Stalin and German Communism*, p.176.
14. Fischer, p.174-5.
15. Zetkin, *Reminiscences of Lenin*, quoted from Gruber, *International Communism in the Era of Lenin*, p.306.
16. Borkenau, *World Communism*, p.214.
17. Fischer, p.175.
18. Borkenau, p.216.
19. Degras, p.225.
20. *Decisions of the Third Congress of the Communist International*, p.18.
21. Degras, Vol.1, p.311.
22. Degras, Vol.1, p.317-9.

On the United Front: Material for a Report on the Question of French Communism.
Leon Trotsky

General Considerations on the United Front[1]

1) The task of the Communist Party is to lead the proletarian revolution. In order to summon the proletariat for the direct conquest of power and to achieve it the Communist Party must base itself on the overwhelming majority of the working class.[*]

So long as it does not hold this majority, the party must fight to win it.

The party can achieve this only by remaining an absolutely independent organization with a clear program and strict internal discipline. That is the reason why the party was bound to break ideologically and organizationally with the reformists and the centrists who do not strive for the proletarian revolution, who possess neither the capacity nor the desire to prepare the masses for revolution, and who by their entire conduct thwart this work.

Any members of the Communist Party who bemoan the split with the centrists in the name of "unity of forces" or "unity of front" thereby demonstrate that they do not understand the ABC of Communism and that they themselves happen to be in the Communist Party only by accident.

2) After assuring itself of the complete independence and ideological homogeneity of its ranks, the Communist Party fights for influence over the majority of the working class. This struggle can be accelerated or retarded depending upon objective circumstances and the expediency of the tactics employed.

But it is perfectly self-evident that the class life of the proletariat is not suspended during this period preparatory to the revolution. Clashes with industrialists, with the bourgeoisie, with the state power, on the initiative of one side or the other, run their due course.

In these clashes – insofar as they involve the vital interests of the entire working class, or its majority, or this or that section – the working masses sense the need of unity in action, of unity in resisting the onslaught of capitalism or unity in taking the offensive against it.

---

[*] From *The First Five Years of the Communist International*, Vol. 2, 1924.

Any party which mechanically counterposes itself to this need of the working class for unity in action will unfailingly be condemned in the minds of the workers.

Consequently the question of the united front is not at all, either in point of origin or substance, a question of the reciprocal relations between the Communist parliamentary fraction and that of the Socialists, or between the Central Committee of the two parties, or between *l'Humanité* and *Le Populaire*. [2] The problem of the united front – despite the fact *that a split is inevitable in this epoch between the various political organizations basing themselves on the working class* – grows out of the urgent need to secure for the working class the possibility of a united front in the struggle against capitalism.

For those who do not understand this task, the party is only a propaganda society and not an organization for mass action.

3) In cases where the Communist Party still remains an organization of a numerically insignificant minority, the question of its conduct on the mass-struggle front does not assume a decisive practical and organizational significance. In such conditions, mass actions remain under the leadership of the old organizations which by reason of their still powerful traditions continue to play the decisive role.

Similarly the problem of the united front does not arise in countries where – as in Bulgaria, for example – the Communist Party is the sole leading organization of the toiling masses.

But wherever the Communist Party already constitutes a big, organized, political force, but not the decisive magnitude: wherever the party embraces organizationally, let us say, one-fourth, one-third, or even a larger proportion of the organized proletarian vanguard, it is confronted with the question of the united front in all its acuteness.

If the party embraces one-third or one-half of the proletarian vanguard, then the remaining half or two-thirds are organized by the reformists or centrists. It is perfectly obvious, however, that even those workers who still support the reformists and the centrists are vitally interested in maintaining the highest material standards of living and the greatest possible freedom for struggle. We must consequently so devise our tactic as to prevent the Communist Party, which will on the morrow embrace the entire three-thirds of the working class, from turning into – and all the more so, from actually being – an organizational obstacle in the way of the current struggle of the proletariat.

Still more, the party must assume the initiative in securing unity in these current struggles. Only in this way will the party draw closer to those two-thirds who do not as yet follow its leadership, who do not as yet trust the party because they do not understand it. Only in this way can the party win them over.

4) If the Communist Party had not broken drastically and irrevocably with the Social Democrats, it would not have become the party of the proletarian revolution. It could not have taken the first serious steps on the road to revolution. It would have for ever remained a parliamentary safety-valve attached to the bourgeois state.

Whoever does not understand this, does not know the first letter of the ABC of Communism.

If the Communist Party did not seek for organizational avenues to the end that at every given moment joint, co-ordinated action between the Communist and the non-Communist (including the Social-Democratic) working masses were made possible, it would have thereby laid bare its own incapacity to win over – on the basis of mass action – the majority of the working class. It would degenerate into a Communist propaganda society but never develop into a party for the conquest of power.

It is not enough to possess the sword, one must give it an edge it is not enough to give the sword an edge, one must know how to wield it.

After separating the Communists from the reformists it is not enough to fuse the Communists together by means of organizational discipline, it is necessary that this organization should learn how to guide all the collective activities of the proletariat in all spheres of its living struggle.

This is the second letter of the alphabet of Communism.

5) Does the united front extend only to the working masses or does it also include the opportunist leaders?

The very posing of this question is a product of misunderstanding.

If we were able simply to unite the working masses around our own banner or around our practical immediate slogans, and skip over reformist organizations, whether party or trade union, that would of course be the best thing in the world. But then the very question of the united front would not exist in its present form.

The question arises from this, that certain very important sections of the working class belong to reformist organizations or support them. Their present experience is still insufficient to enable them to break with the reformist organizations and join us. It may be precisely after engaging in those mass activities, which are on the order of the day, that a major change will take place in this connection. That is just what we are striving for. But that is not how matters stand at present. Today the organized portion of the working class is broken up into three formations.

One of them, the Communist, strives toward the social revolution and precisely *because of this* supports concurrently every movement, however partial, of the toilers against the exploiters and against the bourgeois state.

Another grouping, the reformist, strives toward conciliation with the bourgeoisie. But in order not to lose their influence over the workers reformists are compelled, against the innermost desires of their own leaders, to support the partial movements of the exploited against the exploiters.

Finally, there is a third grouping, the centrist, which constantly vacillates between the other two, and which has no independent significance.

The circumstances thus make wholly possible joint action on a whole number of vital issues between the workers united in these three respective organizations and the unorganized masses adhering to them.

The Communists, as has been said, must not oppose such actions but on the contrary must also assume the initiative for them, precisely for the reason that the greater is the mass drawn into the movement, the higher its self-confidence rises, all the more self-confident will that mass movement be and all the more resolutely will it be capable of marching forward, however modest may be the initial slogans of struggle. And this means that the growth of the mass aspects of the movement tends to radicalize it, and creates much more favourable conditions for the slogans, methods of struggle, and, in general, the leading role of the Communist Party.

The reformists dread the revolutionary potential of the mass movement; their beloved arena is the parliamentary tribune, the trade-union bureaux, the arbitration boards, the ministerial antechambers.

On the contrary, we are, apart from all other considerations, interested in dragging the reformists from their asylums and placing them alongside ourselves before the eyes of the struggling masses. With a correct tactic we stand only to gain from this. A Communist who doubts or fears this resembles a swimmer who has approved the theses on the best method of swimming but dares not plunge into the water.

6) Unity of front consequently presupposes our readiness, within certain limits and on specific issues, to correlate in practice our actions with those of reformist organizations, to the extent to which the latter still express today the will of important sections of the embattled proletariat.

But, after all, didn't we split with them? Yes, because we disagree with them on fundamental questions of the working-class movement.

And yet we seek agreement with them? Yes, in all those cases where the masses that follow them are ready to engage in joint struggle together with the masses that follow us and when they, the reformists, are to a lesser or greater degree compelled to become an instrument of this struggle.

But won't they say that after splitting with them we still need them? Yes, their blabbermouths may say this. Here and there somebody in our own ranks may take fright at it. But as regards the broad working masses − even those who do not follow us and who do not as yet understand our goals but who do see two or three labour organizations leading a parallel existence − these masses will draw from our conduct this conclusion, that despite the split we are doing everything in our power to facilitate unity in action for the masses.

7) A policy aimed to secure the united front does not of course contain automatic guarantees that unity in action will actually be attained in all instances. On the contrary, in many cases and perhaps even the majority of cases, organizational agreements will be only half-attained or perhaps not at all. But it is necessary that the struggling masses should always be given the opportunity of convincing themselves that the non-achievement of unity in action was not due to our formalistic irreconcilability but to the lack of real will to struggle on the part of the reformists.

In entering into agreements with other organizations, we naturally obligate ourselves to a certain discipline in action. But this discipline cannot be absolute in character. In the event that the reformists begin putting brakes on the struggle to the obvious detriment of the movement and act counter to the situation and the moods of the masses, we as an independent organization always reserve the right to lead the struggle to the end, and this without our temporary semi-allies.

This may give rise to a new sharpening of the struggle between us and the reformists. But it will no longer involve a simple repetition of one and the same set of ideas within a shut-in circle but will signify – provided our tactic is correct – the extension of our influence over new, fresh groups of the proletariat.

8) It is possible to see in this policy a rapprochement with the reformists only from the standpoint of a journalist who believes that he rids himself of reformism by ritualistically criticizing it without ever leaving his editorial office but who is fearful of clashing with the reformists before the eyes of the working masses and giving the latter an opportunity to appraise the Communist and the reformist on the equal plane of the mass struggle. Behind this seeming revolutionary fear of "rapprochement" there really lurks a political passivity which seeks to perpetuate an order of things wherein the Communists and reformists each retain their own rigidly demarcated spheres of influence, their own audiences at meetings, their own press, and all this together creates an illusion of serious political struggle.

9) We broke with the reformists and centrists in order to obtain complete freedom in criticizing perfidy, betrayal, indecision and the half-way spirit in the labour movement. For this reason any sort of organizational agreement which restricts our freedom of criticism and agitation is absolutely unacceptable to us. We participate in a united front but do not for a single moment become dissolved in it. We function in the united front as an independent detachment. It is precisely in the course of struggle that broad masses must learn from experience that we fight better than the others, that we see more clearly than the others, that we are more audacious and resolute. In this way, we shall bring closer the hour of the united revolutionary front under the undisputed Communist leadership.

Groupings in the French Labour Movement

10) If we propose to analyse the question of the united front as it applies to France, without leaving the ground of the foregoing theses which flow from the entire policy of the Communist International, then we must ask ourselves: Do we have in France a situation in which the Communists represent, from the standpoint of practical actions, an insignificant magnitude (*quantité négligeable*)? Or do they, on the contrary, encompass the overwhelming majority of organized workers? Or do they perhaps occupy an in-between position? Are they sufficiently strong to make their participation in the mass movement of major importance, but not strong enough to concentrate the undisputed leadership in their own hands?

It is quite incontestable that we have before us precisely the latter case in France.

11) In the party sphere the predominance of the Communists over the reformists is overwhelming. The Communist organization and the Communist press surpass by far in numbers, richness and vitality the organization and press of the so-called Socialists.

This overwhelming preponderance, however, far from secures to the French Communist Party the complete and unchallenged leadership of the French proletariat, inasmuch as the latter is still strongly under the influence of anti-political and anti-party tendencies and prejudices, the arena for whose operation is primarily provided by the trade unions.

12) The outstanding peculiarity of the French labour movement consists in this: that the trade unions have long served as an integument or cover for a peculiar anti-parliamentary political party which bears the name of syndicalism. Because, however the revolutionary syndicalists may try to demarcate themselves from politics or from the party, they can never refute the fact that they themselves constitute a political party which seeks to base itself on trade-union organizations of the working class. This party has its own positive, revolutionary. proletarian tendencies, but it also has its own extremely negative features, namely, the lack of a genuinely definitive program and a rounded organization. The organization of the trade unions by no means corresponds with the organization of syndicalism. In the organizational sense, the syndicalists represent amorphous political nuclei, grafted upon the trade unions.

The question is further complicated by the fact that the syndicalists, like all other political groupings in the working class, have split, after the war, into two sections: the reformists who support bourgeois society and are thereby compelled to work hand in hand with parliamentary reformists; and the revolutionary section which is seeking ways to overthrow bourgeois society and is thereby, in the person of its best elements, moving toward Communism.

It was just this urge to preserve the unity of the class front which inspired not only the Communists but also the revolutionary syndicalists with the absolutely correct tactic of fighting for the unity of the trade-union organization of the French proletariat. On the other hand, with the instinct of bankrupts who sense that before the eyes of the working masses they cannot, in action, in struggle, meet the competition of the revolutionary wing, Jouhaux, Merrheim and Co. have taken the path of split. The colossally important struggle now unfolding throughout the entire trade-union movement of France, the struggle between the reformists and the revolutionists, is for us at the same time a struggle for the unity of the trade-union organization and the trade-union front.

The Trade-Union Movement and the United Front

13) French Communism finds itself in an extremely favourable position precisely with regard to the idea of the united front. In the framework of political organization, French Communism has succeeded in conquering the majority of the old Socialist Party, whereupon the opportunists added to all their other political credentials the quality of "Dissidents", that is, splitters. Our French party has made use of this in the sense that it has branded the social-reformist organization with the label of Dissidents (splitters), thus singling out the fact that the reformists are disrupters of unity in action and unity of organization alike.

14) In the field of the trade-union movement, the revolutionary wing and above all the Communists cannot hide either from themselves or their adversaries how profound are the differences between Moscow and Amsterdam – differences which are by no means simple shadings within the ranks of the labour movement but a reflection of the profoundest contradiction which is tearing modern society apart, namely, the contradiction between the bourgeoisie and the proletariat. But at the same time the revolutionary wing, i.e., first and foremost the conscious Communist elements, never sponsored, as has been said, the tactic of leaving the trade unions or of splitting the trade-union organization. Such slogans are characteristic only of sectarian groupings of "localists", of the KAPD, of certain "libertarian" anarchist grouplets in France, which never wielded any influence among broad working masses, which neither aspire nor strive to gain this influence but are content with small churches of their own, each with its rigidly demarcated congregation. The truly revolutionary elements among the French syndicalists have felt instinctively that the French working class can be won on the arena of the trade-union movement only by counterposing the revolutionary viewpoint and the revolutionary methods to those of the reformists on the arena of mass action, while preserving at the same time the highest possible degree of unity in action.

15) The system of cells in the trade-union organizations adopted by the revolutionary wing signifies nothing else but the most natural form of struggle for ideological influence and for unity of front without disrupting the unity of organization.

16) Like the reformists of the Socialist Party, the reformists of the trade-union movement took the initiative for the split. But it was

precisely the experience of the Socialist Party that largely inspired them with the conclusion that time worked in favour of Communism, and that it was possible to counteract the influence of experience and time only by forcing a split. On the part of the ruling CGT (the French Confederation of Labour) clique we see a whole system of measures designed to disorganize the left wing, to deprive it of those rights which the trade-union statutes afford it, and, finally, through open expulsion – counter to all statutes and regulations – to formally place it outside the trade-union organization.

On the other hand, we see the revolutionary wing fighting to preserve its rights on the grounds of the democratic norms of workers' organizations and resisting with all its might the split implanted from above by appealing to the rank and file for unity of the trade-union organization.

17) Every thinking French worker must be aware that when the Communists comprised one-sixth or one-third of the Socialist Party they did not attempt to split, being absolutely certain that the majority of the party would follow them in the near future. When the reformists found themselves reduced to one-third, they split away, nursing no hopes to again win the majority of the proletarian vanguard.

Every thinking French worker must be aware that when the revolutionary elements were confronted with the problem of the trade-union movement, they, still an insignificant minority at the time, decided it in the sense of working in common organizations, being certain that the experience of the struggle in the conditions of the revolutionary epoch would quickly impel the majority of the unionized workers to the side of the revolutionary program. When the reformists, however, perceived the growth of the revolutionary wing in the trade unions, they – nursing no hopes of coping with it on a competitive basis – resorted immediately to the methods of expulsion and split.

Hence flow conclusions of greatest importance:

- First, the full depth of the differences which reflect, as has been said, the contradiction between the bourgeoisie and the proletariat, becomes clarified.

- Secondly, the hypocritical "democratism" of the opponents of proletarian dictatorship is being exposed to the very roots, inasmuch as these gentlemen are averse to tolerating methods of democracy, not only in the framework of the state, but also in the framework of workers' organizations.

Whenever the latter turn against them, they either split away themselves, like the Dissidents in the party, or expel others, like the clique of Jouhaux-Dumoulin. It is truly monstrous to suppose that the bourgeoisie would ever agree to permit the struggle against the proletariat to come to a decision within the framework of democracy, when even the agents of the bourgeoisie inside the trade-union and political organizations are opposed to solving the questions of the labour movement on the basis of norms of workers' democracy which they themselves voluntarily adopted.

18) The struggle for the unity of the trade-union organization and trade-union action will remain in the future as well one of the most important tasks of the Communist Party – a struggle not only in the sense of constantly striving to unite ever larger numbers of workers around the program and tactics of Communism, but also in the sense that the Communist Party – on the road to the realization of this goal – both directly and through Communists in the trade unions, strives in action to reduce to a minimum those obstacles which are placed before the workers' movement by an organizational split.

If in spite of all our efforts to restore unity, the split in the CGT becomes sealed in the immediate future, this would not at all signify that the CGT *Unitaire* [3] regardless of whether half or more than half of the unionized workers join it in the next period, will conduct its work by simply ignoring the existence of the reformist CGT. Such a policy would render difficult in the extreme – if not exclude altogether – the possibility of co-ordinated militant actions of the proletariat, and at the same time would make it extremely easy for the reformist CGT to play, in the interests of the bourgeoisie, the role of *La Ligue Civique* [4] as regards strikes, demonstrations, etc.; and it would simultaneously provide the reformist CGT with a semblance of justification in arguing that the revolutionary CGTU provokes inexpedient public actions and must bear full responsibility for them. It is perfectly self-evident that in all cases where circumstances permit, the revolutionary CGTU will, whenever it deems it necessary to undertake some campaign, openly address itself to the reformist CGT with specific proposals and demands for a concrete plan of co-ordinated actions, and bring to bear the pressure of labour's public opinion and expose before this public opinion each hesitating and evasive step of the reformists.

In this way, even in the event that the split of the trade-union organization becomes permanent, the methods of struggle for the united front will preserve all their meaning.

19) We can, therefore, state that in relation to the most important field of the labour movement – the trade unions – the tactic of the united front demands that those methods, by which the struggle against Jouhaux and Co. has already been conducted on our side, be applied more consistently, more persistently and resolutely than ever before.

The Political Struggle and the United Front

20) On the party plane there is, to begin with, a very important difference from the trade unions in this, that the preponderance of the Communist Party over the Socialist, both in point of organization and the press, is overwhelming. We may consequently assume that the Communist Party, as such, is capable of securing the unity of the political front and that therefore it has no impelling reasons for addressing itself to the organization of the Dissidents with any sort of proposals for concrete actions. This strictly businesslike and legitimate method of posing the question, on the basis of evaluating the relationship of forces and not on the basis of verbal radicalism, must be appraised on its substantive merits.

21) If we take into account that the Communist Party numbers 130,000 members, while the Socialists number 30,000, then the enormous successes of Communist ideas in France become apparent. However, if we take into account the relation between these figures and the numerical strength of the working class as a whole, together with the existence of reformist trade unions and of anti-Communist tendencies within the revolutionary trade unions, then the question of the hegemony of the Communist Party inside the labour movement will confront us as a very difficult task, still far from solved by our numerical superiority over the Dissidents. The latter may under certain conditions prove to be a much more important counter-revolutionary factor within the working class than might appear, if one were to judge solely from the weakness of their organization and the insignificant circulation and ideological content of their paper, *Le Populaire*.

22) In order to evaluate a situation, it is necessary to take clear cognizance of how this situation took shape. The transformation of the majority of the old Socialist Party into the Communist Party came as a result of a wave of dissatisfaction and mutiny engendered in all countries in Europe by the war. The example of the Russian Revolution and the slogans of the Third International seemed to point a way out. The bourgeoisie, however, was able to maintain itself throughout 1919-20 and was able, by means of combined measures, to establish on post-war foundations a certain equilibrium, which is

being undermined by the most terrible contradictions and which is heading toward vast catastrophes, which meanwhile provides relative stability for the current day and for the period immediately ahead. The Russian Revolution, in surmounting the greatest difficulties and obstacles created by world capitalism, has been able to achieve its socialist tasks only gradually, only at the cost of an extraordinary strain upon all its forces. As a result, the initial flood-tide of vague, uncritical, revolutionary moods has been unavoidably superseded by an ebb. Only the most resolute, audacious and youthful section of the world working class has remained under the banner of Communism.

This does not mean naturally that those broad circles of the proletariat who have been disillusioned in their hopes for immediate revolution, for swift radical transformations, etc., have wholly returned to the old pre-war positions. No, their dissatisfaction is deeper than ever before, their hatred of the exploiters is fiercer. But at the same time they are politically disoriented, they do not see the paths of struggle, and therefore remain passively expectant – giving rise to the possibility of sharp swings to this or that side, depending on how the situation unfolds.

This big reservoir of the passive and the disoriented can, under a certain combination of circumstances, be widely utilized by the Dissidents against us.

23) In order to support the Communist Party, faith in the revolutionary cause, will to action and loyalty are needed. In order to support the Dissidents, disorientation and passivity are necessary and sufficient. It is perfectly natural for the revolutionary and dynamic section of the working class to effuse from its ranks a much larger proportion of members for the Communist Party than the passive and disoriented section is able to supply to the party of the Dissidents.

The same thing applies to the press. The elements of indifferentism read little. The insignificant circulation and content of *Le Populaire* mirrors the mood of a certain section of the working class. The fact that complete ascendancy of the professional intellectuals over the workers prevails in the party of the Dissidents runs nowise counter to our diagnosis and prognosis. Because the passive and partially disillusioned, partially disoriented worker-masses are an ideal culture medium, especially in France, for political cliques composed of attorneys and journalists, reformist witch-doctors and parliamentary charlatans.

24) If we regard the party organization as an operating army, and the unorganized mass of workers as the reserves, and if we grant that our operating army is three to four times stronger than the active army of

Dissidents, then, under a certain combination of circumstances, the reserves may prove to be divided between ourselves and the social-reformists in a proportion much less favourable to us.

25) The political atmosphere of France is pervaded with the idea of the "Left Bloc". After a new period of Poincaré-ism which represents the bourgeoisie's attempt to serve up to the people a warmed-over hash of the illusions of victory, a pacifist reaction may quite likely set in among broad circles of bourgeois society, i.e., first and foremost among the petty bourgeoisie. The hope for universal pacification, for agreement with soviet Russia, obtaining raw materials and payments from her on advantageous terms, cuts in the burden of militarism, and so on – in brief, the illusory program of democratic pacifism – can become for a while the program of a "Left Bloc", superseding the National Bloc.

From the standpoint of the development of the revolution in France, such a change of régimes will be a step forward only provided the proletariat does not fall prey to any extent to the illusions of petty-bourgeois pacifism.

26) Reformist-Dissidents are the agency of the "Left Bloc" within the working class. Their successes will be the greater, all the less the working class as a whole is seized by the idea and practice of the united front against the bourgeoisie. Layers of workers, disoriented by the war and by the tardiness of the revolution, may venture to support the "Left Bloc" as a lesser evil, in the belief that they do not thereby risk anything at all, or because they see no other road at present.

27) One of the most reliable methods of counteracting inside the working class the moods and ideas of the "Left Bloc", i.e., a bloc between the workers and a certain section of the bourgeoisie against another section of the bourgeoisie, is through promoting persistently and resolutely the idea of a *bloc between all the sections of the working class against the whole bourgeoisie.*

28) In relation to the Dissidents this means that we must not permit them to occupy with impunity an evasive, temporizing position on questions relating to the labour movement, and to use platonic declarations of sympathy for the working class as a cover for utilizing the patronage of the bourgeois oppressors. In other words, we can and must, in all suitable instances, propose to the Dissidents a specific form of joint aid to strikers, to locked-out workers, unemployed, war invalids, etc., etc., recording before the eyes of the masses their responses to our precise proposals, and in this way driving a wedge between them and certain sections of politically

indifferent or semi-indifferent masses on whom the reformists hope to lean for support under certain favourable conditions.

29) This kind of tactic is all the more important in view of the fact that the Dissidents are unquestionably bound up intimately with the reformist CGT and together with the latter constitute the two wings of the bourgeois agency inside the labour movement. We take the offensive both on the trade-union and political fields simultaneously against this twofold agency, applying the very same tactical methods.

30) The impeccable and agitationally extremely persuasive logic of our conduct is as follows: "You, the reformists of trade unionism and socialism," we say to them before the eyes of the masses, "have split the trade unions and the party for the sake of ideas and methods which we consider wrong and criminal. We demand that you at least refrain from placing a spoke in the wheel during the partial and un-postponable concrete tasks of the working-class struggle and that you make possible unity in action. In the given concrete situation we propose such and such a program of struggle."

31) The indicated method could be similarly employed and not without success in relation to parliamentary and municipal activities. We say to the masses, "The Dissidents, because they do not want the revolution, have split the mass of the workers. It would be insanity to count upon their helping the proletarian revolution. But we are ready, inside and outside the parliament, to enter into certain practical agreements with them, provided they agree, in those cases where one must choose between the known interests of the bourgeoisie and the definite demands of the proletariat, to support the latter in action. The Dissidents can be capable of such actions only if they renounce their ties with the parties of the bourgeoisie, that is, the 'Left Bloc' and its bourgeois discipline."

If the Dissidents were capable of accepting these conditions, then their worker-followers would be quickly absorbed by the Communist Party. Just because of this, the Dissidents will not agree to these conditions. In other words, to the clearly and precisely posed question whether they choose a bloc with the bourgeoisie or a bloc with the proletariat – in the concrete and specific conditions of mass struggle – they will be compelled to reply that they prefer a bloc with the bourgeoisie. Such an answer will not pass with impunity among the proletarian reserves on whom they are counting.

Internal Tasks of the Communist Party

32) The foregoing policy presupposes, naturally, complete organizational independence, ideological clarity and revolutionary firmness of the Communist Party itself.

Thus, for example, it would be impossible to conduct with complete success a policy aimed at making hateful and contemptible the idea of the "Left Bloc" among the working class, if in our own party ranks there are partisans of this "Left Bloc" bold enough openly to defend this projected program of the bourgeoisie. Unconditional and merciless expulsion in disgrace of those who come out in favour of the idea of the "Left Bloc" is a self-understood duty of the Communist Party. This will cleanse our policy of all elements of equivocation and unclarity; this will attract the attention of advanced workers to the acute character of the issue of the "Left Bloc" and will demonstrate that the Communist Party does not trifle with the questions which imperil the revolutionary unity in action of the proletariat against the bourgeoisie.

33) Those who seek to use the idea of the united front for agitating in favour of unification with the reformists and Dissidents must be mercilessly ejected from our party, inasmuch as they serve as the agency of the Dissidents in our ranks and are deceiving the workers concerning the reasons for the split and who is really responsible for it. Instead of correctly posing the question of the possibility of this or that co-ordinated, practical action with the Dissidents, despite their petty-bourgeois and essentially counter-revolutionary character, they are demanding that our own party renounce its Communist program and revolutionary methods. The ejection of such elements, mercilessly and in disgrace, will best demonstrate that the tactic of the workers' united front in no way resembles capitulation to or reconciliation with the reformists. The tactic of the united front demands from the party complete freedom in manoeuvring, flexibility and resoluteness. To make this possible, the party must clearly and specifically declare at every given moment just what its wishes are, just what it is striving for, and it must comment authoritatively, before the eyes of the masses, on its own steps and proposals.

34) Hence flows the complete inadmissibility for individual party members to issue on their own responsibility and risk political publications in which they counterpose their own slogans, methods of action and proposals to the slogans, methods of action and proposals of the party. Under the cover of the Communist Party and consequently also inside that milieu which is influenced by a Communist cover, i.e., in a workers' milieu, they spread from day to

day ideas hostile to us, or they sow confusion and scepticism which are even more pernicious than avowedly hostile ideologies. Periodicals of this type, together with their editors, must once and for all be placed outside the party and the entire working-class France must learn about this from articles which mercilessly expose the petty-bourgeois smugglers who operate under a Communist flag.

35) From what has been said, it likewise follows that it is completely inadmissible for the leading party publications to carry side by side with articles defending the basic concepts of Communism, other articles disputing these concepts or denying them. Absolutely impermissible is a continuation of a régime in the party press under which the mass of worker-readers find, in the guise of editorials in leading Communist periodicals, articles which try to turn us back to positions of tearful pacifism and which propagate among workers a debilitating hostility toward revolutionary violence in the face of the triumphant violence of the bourgeoisie. Under the guise of a struggle against militarism, a struggle is thus being conducted against the ideas of revolution.

If after the experience of the war and all the subsequent events, especially in Russia and Germany, the prejudices of humanitarian pacifism have still survived in the Communist Party; and if the party finds it advisable for the sake of completely liquidating these prejudices to open a discussion on this question, even in that case, the pacifists with their prejudices cannot come forward in such a discussion as an equal force but must be severely condemned by the authoritative voice of the party, in the name of its Central Committee. After the Central Committee decides that the discussion has been exhausted, all attempts to spread the debilitating ideas of Tolstoyanism and other varieties of pacifism must unquestionably bring expulsion from the party.

36) An objection might, however, be raised that so long as the work of cleansing the party of ancient prejudices and of attaining internal cohesion remains uncompleted, it would be dangerous to place the party in situations where it would come into close proximity with reformists and nationalists. But such a point of view is false. Naturally it is undeniable that a transition from broad propagandist activity to direct participation in the mass movement carries with it new difficulties and therefore dangers for the Communist Party. But it is completely wrong to suppose that the party can be prepared for all tests without directly participating in struggles, without directly coming in contact with enemies and adversaries. On the contrary, only in this way can a genuine, non-fictitious internal cleaning and fusing of the party be achieved. It is quite possible that some elements

in the party and in the trade-union bureaucracy will feel themselves drawn more closely to the reformists, from whom they have accidentally split than toward us. The loss of such camp-followers will not be a liability but an asset, and it will be compensated a hundredfold by the influx of those working men and women who still follow the reformists today. The party will in consequence become more homogeneous, more resolute and more proletarian.

Party Tasks in the Trade-Union Movement

37) Absolute clarity on the trade-union question is a task of first-rate importance, surpassing by far all the other tasks before the Communist Party of France.

Naturally the legend spread by the reformists that Plans are afoot to subordinate the trade unions organizationally to the party must be unconditionally denounced and exposed. Trade unions embrace workers of different political shadings as well as non-party men, atheists as well as believers, whereas the party unites political co-thinkers on the basis of a definite program. The party has not and cannot have any instrumentalities and methods for subjecting the trade unions to itself from the outside.

The party can gain influence in the life of the trade unions only to the extent that its members work in the trade unions and carry out the party point of view there. The influence of party members in the trade unions naturally depends on their numerical strength and especially on the degree to which they are able to apply party principles correctly, consistently and expediently to the needs of the trade-union movement.

The party has the right and the duty to aim to conquer, along the road above outlined, the *decisive influence* in the trade-union organization. It can achieve this goal only provided the work of the Communists in the trade unions is wholly and exclusively harmonized with the principles of the party and is invariably conducted under its control.

38) The minds of all Communists must therefore be completely purged of reformist prejudices, in accordance with which the party is regarded as a political parliamentary organization of the proletariat, and nothing more. The Communist Party is the organization of the proletarian vanguard for the ideological fructification of the labour movement and the assumption of leadership in all spheres – first and foremost in the trade unions. While the trade unions are not subordinate to the party but wholly autonomous organizations, the Communists inside the trade unions, on the other hand, cannot pretend to any kind of autonomy in their trade-union activity but

must act as the transmitters of their party's program and tactics. To be most severely condemned is the conduct of those Communists who not only fail to fight inside the trade unions for the influence of party ideas but actually counteract such a struggle in the name of a principle of "autonomy" which they apply absolutely falsely. As a matter of fact, they thus pave the way for the decisive influence in the trade unions of individuals, groups and cliques, bound neither by a definite program nor by party organization, and who utilize the formlessness of ideological groupings and relations in order to keep the organizational apparatus in their own hands and secure the independence of their own clique from any actual control by the workers' vanguard.

While the party, in its activity inside the trade unions, must show the greatest attentiveness and caution toward the non-party masses and their conscientious and honest representatives; while the party must, on the basis of joint work, systematically and tactically draw closer to the best elements of the trade-union movement – including the revolutionary anarchists who are capable of learning – the party can, on the contrary, no longer tolerate in its midst those pseudo-Communists who utilize the status of party membership only in order all the more confidently to promote anti-party influences in the trade unions.

39) The party through its own press, through its own propagandists and its members in the trade unions must submit to constant and systematic criticism the shortcomings of revolutionary syndicalism for solving the basic tasks of the proletariat. The party must tirelessly and persistently criticize the weak theoretical and practical sides of syndicalism, explaining at the same time to its best elements that the only correct road for securing the revolutionary influence on the trade unions and on the labour movement as a whole is the entry of revolutionary syndicalists into the Communist Party: their participation in working out all the basic questions of the movement, in drawing the balance sheet of experience, in defining new tasks, in cleansing the Communist Party itself and strengthening its ties with the working masses.

40) It is absolutely indispensable to take a census of all the members of the French Communist Party in order to determine their social status (workers, civil employees, peasants, intellectuals, etc.); their relations with the trade-union movement (do they belong to trade unions – do they participate in meetings of Communist and revolutionary syndicalists? do they carry out at these meetings the decisions of the party on the trade unions? etc.); their attitude toward the party press (what party publications do they read?), and so on.

The census must be so conducted that its chief aspects can be taken into account before the Fourth World Congress convenes.

March 2, 1922

Notes

1. The *Theses on the United Front*, were drafted by Trotsky for the enlarged Plenum of the ECCI which convened toward the end of February 1922.

2. *Le Populaire*, founded by Leon Blum, was the central publication of the French Socialist Party.

3. The CGT (*Confédération Générale du Travail* – General Confederation of Labor) was the central trade union organization of France. Formed in 1903 it embraced all the existing trade unions. Prior to World War I the CGT was the most revolutionary organization in France. But with the outbreak of war in 1914, the majority of the leaders, headed by Jouhaux, became nationalists. The official CGT leadership opposed the growing left wing movement, which grew after the war and came under Communist influence. They split, which led early in 1922 to the formation of the Unitarian General Confederation of Labor (*Confédération Générale du Travail Unitaire* or CGTU). This split was marked by a sharp decline in total union membership. In 1920 there were about 2,500,000 workers in the CGT. By 1923 the combined memberships of the CGT and CGTU fell under 100,000.

4. *La Ligue Civique* was a strikebreaking organization in France.

What Next?
Vital Questions for the German Proletariat.
Leon Trotsky

A Historical Review of the United Front

THE contentions regarding the policies of the united front take their origin from such fundamental and inexorable exigencies of the struggle of *class against class* (in the Marxist and not the bureaucratic sense of these words) that one cannot read the refutations of the Stalinist bureaucracy without a feeling of shame and indignation. It is one thing to keep on explaining, from day to day, the most rudimentary ideas to the most backward and benighted workers or peasants, One can do it without any feeling of exhaustion; for here it is a matter of enlightening fresh strata. But woe to him who is perforce obliged to explain and to prove elementary propositions to people whose brains have been flattened out by the bureaucratic steam roller. What can one do with "leaders" who have no logical arguments at their disposal and who make up for that by referring to the cyclopedia of international epithets? The fundamental propositions of Marxism they parry by one and the same epithet, "counter-revolution"! This word has become inordinately cheapened on the lips of those who have in no manner as yet proved their capacity to achieve a revolution. Still, what about the decisions passed by the first four Congresses of the Comintern? Does the Stalinist bureaucracy accept them, or not?*

The documents still survive and still preserve their significance to this day. Out of a large number, I have chosen the theses worked out by me, between the III and the IV Congresses; they relate to the French Communist Party; they were approved by the Politbureau of the CPSU and the Executive Committee of the Comintern and were published, in their time, in various foreign Communist publications. Below is reprinted verbatim that part of the theses which is devoted to the formulation and the defence of the policy of the united front:

It is quite obvious that the class life of the proletariat does not cease during the period preparatory to the revolution. Clashes with industrialists, with the bourgeoisie, with the state, at the initiative of

---

* These are three sections of *What Next*, a book on Germany first published in 1932. It was written in Russian and then translated immediately for distribution by German Left Oppositionists.

either side, occur with the self-same regularity. In these clashes, in so far as they involve the vital interests of the entire working class, or of its majority, or any part of it, the working masses realize the need for united action ...The party that mechanically counterposes itself to this need ... will be inevitably condemned in the minds of the workers.

"The problem of the united front-notwithstanding the inevitable split, in a given period, between the political organizations which lean upon the working class-originates in the urgent need to guarantee to the working class the possibility of the united front in its struggle against capitalism. For him who does not understand this problem, the party is a society for propaganda, and not the organization for mass action.

"Had not the Communist party broken definitely and irrevocably with the social democracy, it could have never become the party of the proletarian revolution. Had not the Communist party sought for organizational means to the end that, at each given moment, joint action, mutually agreed upon, be made possible between the Communist and non-Communist (including the social-democratic) working masses, it would have revealed thereby its incapacity – on the basis of mass action – to win over the majority of the working class.

"After dissociating the Communists from reformism, it is not enough to bind them by organizational discipline; it is also necessary that the organization be taught how to guide all collective activities of the proletariat, in all spheres of its living struggle. That is the second letter of the ABC of Communism.

"Is the united front to be extended so as to include only the working masses, or so as to include also opportunistic leaders? The very manner in which this question is posed is the outgrowth of a misconception. Were we able to simply unite the working masses around our banner ... by eliminating the reformist party, or trade union organizations – that, of course, would be the best way. But, in that case, the very question of the united front, in its present form, would be non-existent.

"We are interested, beyond all other considerations, in dragging the reformists from out of their lairs and in opposing them before the eyes of the struggling masses. With a correct tactic, we alone stand to gain thereby. The Communist who is dubious or afraid of this behaves after the fashion of a swimmer who, after approving the propositions as regards the best method of swimming, dares not risk jumping into the water.

"Upon entering into agreements with other organizations, we bind ourselves, of course, to a certain discipline of action. But this discipline must not take on an absolute character. In the event that the reformists begin applying the brake to the struggle, to the evident detriment of the movement and in counterpoise to the situation and the state of mind of the masses, we, as an independent organization, always reserve the right to lead the struggle to its conclusion without our temporary semi-allies.

"One can see in this policy a merger with the reformists only from the point of view of a journalist, who flatters himself that he is far removed from reformism because he criticizes it in the self-same pat phraseology, without leaving the editorial room, but who is leery of encountering it in the eyes of the working masses and thus giving them the opportunity to appraise the Communist and the reformist under the equal conditions of the mass struggle. Behind this ostensibly revolutionary dread of 'merger' there hides, in fact, a political passivity which yearns to maintain such an order of things as will allow both the Communists and the reformists to have their own sharply demarcated spheres of influence, their own audiences at meetings, and their own press – which all together creates the illusion of a serious political struggle.

"In the question of the united front, as it is raised, we observe a passive and wishy-washy tendency masked by verbal intransigence. At once, the following paradox hits one in the eye: the Right wing elements of the party, with their Centrist and pacifist tendencies... step forward as the most irreconcilable opponents of the united front. And on the other hand, those elements, which, during the most difficult moments held their position entirely on the grounds of the 3rd International, now step forward for the tactic of the united front. What is actually the case is that the supporters of the temporizing and passive tactic are now stepping forward behind the mask of pseudo-revolutionary intransigence." (Trotsky, *Five Years of the Comintern*, pp.375-378; Russian edition.)

Doesn't it seem as if these lines were written today against Stalin-Manuilsky-Thälmann-Neumann? Actually, they were written ten years ago, against Frossard, Cachin, Charles Rappaport, Daniel Renoult and other French opportunists disguising themselves with ultra-leftism. We put this question point blank to the Stalinist bureaucracy: Were the theses we quoted "counter-revolutionary" even during that time when they expressed the policies of the Russian Politbureau, with Lenin at its head, and when they defined the policy of the Comintern? We warn them duly not to attempt in answer to reply that conditions have changed since that period: the matter does not concern questions of conjuncture; but, as the text itself puts it, of the *A B C of Marxism.*

And so, ten years ago, the Comintern explained that the gist of the united front policy was in the following: the Communist party proves to the masses and their organizations its readiness in action to wage battle in common with them, for aims, no matter how modest, so long as they lie on the road of the historical development of the proletariat; the Communist party in this struggle takes into account the actual condition of the class at each given moment; it turns not to the masses only, but also to those organizations whose leadership. is recognized by the masses; it confronts the reformist organizations before the eyes of the masses with the real problems of the class struggle. The policy of the united front hastens the revolutionary development of the class by revealing in the open that the common struggle is undermined not by the disruptive acts of the Communist party but by the conscious sabotage of the leaders of the social democracy. It is absolutely clear that these conceptions could in no sense have become obsolete.

Then how explain the rejection of the policy of the united front by the Comintern? By the miscarriages and the failures of this policy in the past. Were these failures, the causes for which reside, not in the policy but in the politicians, examined and analyzed and studied in their time, the German Communist Party would be strategically and tactically excellently equipped for the present situation. But the Stalinist bureaucracy chose to behave like the near-sighted monkey in the fable; after adjusting the spectacles on its tail and licking them to no result, the monkey concluded that they were no good at all and dashed them against a rock. Put it as you please, but the spectacles are not at fault.

The mistakes made in the policy of the united front fall into two categories. In mot cases the leading organs of the Communist party approached the reformists with an offer of joining in a common struggle for radical slogans which were alien to the situation and which found no response in the masses. These proposals partook of the nature of blank shots. The masses remained indifferent; the reformist leaders interpreted these proposals of the Communists as a trick to destroy the social democracy. In each of these instances only a purely formal, declamatory application of the policy of united front was inaugurated; whereas, by its very nature, it can prove fruitful only on the basis of a realistic appraisal of the situation and of the condition of the masses. The weapon of "open letters" became outworn from too frequent and thereto, faulty application, and had to be given up.

The second type of perversion bore a much more fatal character. In the hands of the Stalinist bureaucracy, the policy of the united front became a hue and cry after allies at the cost of sacrificing the independence of the party. Backed by Moscow and deeming themselves omnipotent, the functionaries of the Comintern seriously esteemed themselves to be capable of laying down the law to the classes and of prescribing their itinerary; of checking the agrarian and strike movements in China; of buying an alliance with Chiang Kai-Shek at the cost of sacrificing the independent policies of the Comintern; of re-educating the trade union bureaucracy, the chief bulwark of British imperialism through educational courses at banquet tables in London, or in Caucasian resorts; of transforming Croatian bourgeois of Radich's type into Communists, etc., etc. All this was undertaken, of course, with the best of intentions, in order to hasten developments by accomplishing for the masses what the masses weren't mature enough to do for themselves. It's not beside the point to mention that in a number of countries, Austria in particular, the functionaries of the Comintern tried their hand, during the past period, at creating artificially and "from above" a "Left" social democracy-to serve as a bridge to Communism. Nothing but failures were produced by this tomfoolery likewise. Invariably these experiments and flubusterings ended catastrophically. The revolutionary movement in the world was flung back for many years.

Thereupon Manuilsky decided to break the spectacles; and as for Kuusinen – he, to avoid further mistakes, decreed everyone, except himself and his cronies, to be Fascists. Whereupon the matter was clarified and simplified, no more mistakes were possible. What kind of a united front can there be with "social Fascists" against National Fascists, or with the "Left social Fascists" against the "Rights"? Thus by describing over our heads an arc of 180°, the Stalinist bureaucracy found itself compelled to announce the decisions of the first four Congresses as counter-revolutionary.

Lessons of the Russian Experience

In one of our earlier pamphlets, we made reference to the Bolshevik experience in the struggle against Kornilov; the official leaders answered with bellows of disapproval. We shall recapitulate here once again the gist of the matter, in order to show more clearly and in greater detail how the Stalinist school draws lessons from the past. During July and August 1917, Kerensky, then head of the government, was in fact fulfilling the program of Kornilov, the commander-in-chief of the army. He reinstated at the front military court-martials and the death penalty. He deprived the duly elected soviets of all influence upon government matters; he repressed the peasants; he doubled the price of bread (under the state trade monopoly of the foodstuffs); he prepared for the evacuation of revolutionary Petrograd; with Kornilov's consent, he moved up counter-revolutionary troops towards the capital; he promised the Allies to initiate a new attack at the front, etc. Such was the general political background.

On August 26, Kornilov broke with Kerensky because of the latter's vacillation, and threw his army against Petrograd. The status of the Bolshevik Party was semi-legal. Its leaders from Lenin down were either hiding underground or committed to prison, being indicted for affiliation with the General Staff of the Hohenzollerns. The Bolshevik papers were being suppressed. These persecutions emanated from Kerensky's government, which was supported from the left by the coalition of Social Revolutionary and Menshevik deputies.

What course did the Bolshevik Party take? Not for an instant did it hesitate to conclude a practical alliance to fight against Kornilov with its jailers – Kerensky, Tseretelli, Dan, etc. Everywhere committees for revolutionary defense were organized, into which the Bolsheviks entered as a minority. This did not hinder the Bolsheviks from assuming the leading role: in agreements projected for revolutionary mass action, the most thoroughgoing and the boldest revolutionary party stands to gain always. The Bolsheviks were in the front ranks; they smashed down the barriers blocking them from the Menshevik workers and especially from the Social Revolutionary soldiers, and carried them along in their wake.

Perhaps the Bolsheviks took this course of action only because they were caught unawares? No. During the preceding months, the Bolsheviks tens and hundreds of times demanded that the Mensheviks join them in a common struggle against the mobilizing forces of the counterrevolution. Even on May 27, while Tseretelli was clamoring for repressions against Bolshevik sailors, Trotsky declared during the session of the Petrograd Soviet, "When the time comes and the counterrevolutionary general will try to slip the noose around the neck of the revolution, the Cadets will be busy soaping the rope, but the sailors of Kronstadt will come to fight and to die side by side with us." These words were fully confirmed. In the midst of Kornilov's campaign, Kerensky appealed to the sailors of the cruiser Aurora, begging them to assume the defense of the Winter Palace. These sailors were, without exception, Bolsheviks. They hated Kerensky. Their hatred did not hinder them from vigilantly guarding the Winter Palace. Their representatives came to the Kresty Prison for an interview with Trotsky, who was jailed there, and they asked, "Why not arrest Kerensky?" But they put the query half in jest: the sailors understood that it was necessary first to smash Kornilov and after that to attend to Kerensky. Thanks to a correct political leadership, the sailors of the *Aurora* understood more than Thälmann's Central Committee.

Die Rote Fahne refers to our historical review as "fraudulent." Why? Vain question. How can one expect reasoned refutations from these people? They are under orders from Moscow, on the pain of losing their jobs, to set up a howl at the mention of Trotsky's name. They fulfill the command, as best they can. Trotsky produced, in their words, "a fraudulent comparison" between the struggle of the Bolsheviks during Kornilov's reactionary mutiny, at the beginning of September 1917at the time when the Bolsheviks were righting with the Mensheviks for a majority within the soviets, immediately before an acutely revolutionary situation; at the time when the Bolsheviks, armed in the struggle against Kornilov, were simultaneously carrying on a flank attack on Kerensky – with the present "struggle" of Brüning "against" Hitler. "In this manner, Trotsky paints the support of Brüning and of the Prussian government as 'the lesser evil'." (*Die Rote Fahne*, December 22, 1931) It is quite a task to refute this barrage of words. A pretense is made that I compare the Bolshevik struggle against Kornilov with Brüning's struggle against Hitler. I don't overestimate the mental capacities of the editors of *Die Rote Fahne* – but these gentlemen could not be so stupid as not to understand what I meant. Brüning's struggle against Hitler I compared with Kerensky's struggle against Kornilov; the struggle of the Bolsheviks against Kornilov I compared with the struggle of the German Communist Party against Hitler. Wherein is this comparison "fraudulent"? The Bolsheviks, says *Die Rote Fahne*, were fighting at the time with the Mensheviks for the majority in the soviets. But the German Communist Party, too, is righting against the Social Democracy for the majority of the working class. In Russia they were faced with "an acute revolutionary situation." Quite true! If, however, the Bolsheviks had adopted Thälmann's position in August 1917, then instead of a revolutionary situation a counterrevolutionary situation could have ensued.

During the last days of August, Kornilov was crushed, in reality not by force of arms but by the singleness of purpose with which the masses were imbued. Then and there, after September 3, Lenin offered through the press to compromise with the Social Revolutionaries and the Mensheviks: you compose the majority in the soviets, he said to them. Take over the state; we shall support you against the bourgeoisie. Guarantee us complete freedom of agitation and we shall assure you of a peaceful struggle for the majority in the soviets. Such an opportunist was Lenin! The Mensheviks and the Social

Revolutionaries rejected the compromise, i.e., the new offer of a united front against the bourgeoisie. In the hands of the Bolsheviks, this rejection became a mighty weapon in preparation for the armed uprising, which within seven weeks swept away the Mensheviks and the Social Revolutionaries.

Up to now there has been only one victorious proletarian revolution in the world. I do not at all hold that we committed no errors on our road to victory; but nevertheless, I maintain that our experience has some value for the German Communist Party. I cite the closest and the most pertinent historical analogy. How do the leaders of the German Communist Party reply? With profanity.

Only the ultra-left group, *Der Rote Kaempfer*, attempted to refute our comparison "seriously," accoutred in the complete armor of erudition. It holds that the Bolsheviks behaved correctly in August, "because Kornilov was the standard-bearer of the Czarist counter-revolution, which means that he was waging the battle of the feudal reaction against the bourgeois revolution. Under these conditions the tactical coalition of the workers with the bourgeoisie and its Social Revolutionary Menshevik appendage was not only correct but necessary and unavoidable as well, because the interests of both classes coincided in the matter of repelling the feudal counter-revolution." But since Hitler represents not the feudal but the bourgeois counter-revolution, the Social Democracy which supports the bourgeoisie cannot take the field against Hitler. That's why the united front does not exist in Germany, and that's why Trotsky's comparison is erroneous.

All this has a very imposing sound. But coming down to actual facts, not a word of it is true. In August 1917, the Russian bourgeoisie was not at all opposed to the feudal reaction; all the landowners supported the Cadet Party, which fought against the expropriation of the landowners. Kornilov proclaimed himself a Republican, "the son of a peasant" and the supporter of agrarian reform and of the constitutional assembly. The entire bourgeoisie supported Kornilov. The alliance of the Bolsheviks with the Social Revolutionaries and Mensheviks was made possible only because the conciliationists broke with the bourgeoisie temporarily: they were compelled to, from fear of Kornilov. The representatives of these parties knew that the moment Kornilov was victorious the bourgeoisie would no longer need them, and would allow Kornilov to strangle them. Within these limits there is, as we see, a complete analogy with the interrelations between the Social Democracy and fascism.

The distinctions begin not at all where the theoreticians of *Der Rote Kaempfer* see them. In Russia, the masses of the petty bourgeoisie, above all the peasants, gravitated to the left and not to the right. Kornilov did not lean upon the petty bourgeoisie. And just because of this, his movement was not fascist. The counter-revolution was bourgeois – not at all feudal – in conspiracy with the generals. Therein lay its weakness. Kornilov leaned upon the moral support of the entire bourgeoisie and the military support of the officers and Junkers, i.e., the younger generation of the same bourgeoisie. This proved to be insufficient. But had Bolshevik policies been false, the victory of Kornilov was by no means excluded.

As we see, the arguments in *Der Rote Kaempfer* against the united front in Germany are based on the fact that its theoreticians understand neither the Russian nor the German situation. [3]

Since *Die Rote Fahne* doesn't feel secure on the slippery ice of Russian history, it attempts to tackle the question from the opposite direction. "To Trotsky, only the National Socialists are fascists. The declaration of the state of emergency, the dictatorial wage reductions, the effective prohibition of strikes ... all this is not fascism to Trotsky. All this our party must put up with." These people almost disarm one with the impotence of their spleen. When and where did I suggest anyone's "putting up with" Brüning's government? And just what does this "putting up with" mean? If it's a matter of parliamentary or extraparliamentary support of the Brüning regime, then you should be ashamed of even bringing up such a topic for discussion among Communists. But in another and a wider historical sense you, raucously bleating gentlemen, are nevertheless compelled to "put up with" Brüning's government, because you lack the thews and sinews to overthrow it

All the arguments which *Die Rote Fahne* musters against me in relation to the German situation might have been used with equal justification against the Bolsheviks in 1917. One might have said, "For Bolsheviks, Kornilovism begins only with Kornilov. But isn't Kerensky a Kornilovite? Aren't his policies aimed toward strangling the revolution? Isn't he crushing the peasants by means of punitive expeditions? Doesn't he organize lockouts? Doesn't Lenin have to hide underground? And all this we must put up with?"

So far as I recall, I can't think of a single Bolshevik rash enough to have advanced such arguments. But were he to be found, he would have been answered something after this fashion. "We accuse Kerensky of preparing for and facilitating the coming of Kornilov to power. But does this relieve us of the duty of rushing to repel Kornilov's attack? We accuse the gatekeeper of leaving the gates ajar for the bandit. But must we therefore shrug our shoulders and let the gates go hang?" Since, thanks to the toleration of the Social Democracy, Brüning's government has been able to push the proletariat up to its knees in capitulation to fascism, you arrive at the conclusion that up to the knees, up to the waist, or over the head isn't it all one thing? No, there is some difference. Whoever is up to his knees in a quagmire can still drag himself out Whoever is in over his head, for him there is no returning.

Lenin wrote about the ultra-lefts: "They say many flattering things about us Bolsheviks. At times one feels like saying, 'Please, praise us a little less, and try your hand a little more at investigating the tactics of the Bolsheviks, and become a little better acquainted with them.'"

Lessons of the Italian Experience

Italian fascism was the immediate outgrowth of the betray al by the reformists of the uprising of the Italian proletariat From the time the war ended, there was an upward trend in the revolutionary movement in Italy, and in September 1920, it resulted in the seizure of factories and industries by the workers. The dictatorship of the proletariat was an actual fact; au that was lacking was to organize it, and to draw from it all the necessary conclusions. The Social Democracy took fright and sprang back. After its bold and heroic exertions, the proletariat was left facing the void. The disruption of the revolutionary movement became the most important factor in the growth of fascism. In September, the revolutionary advance came to a standstill; and November already witnessed the firs major demonstration of the fascists (the seizure of Bologna). True, the proletariat even after the September catastrophe was capable of waging defensive battles. But the Social Democracy was concerned with only one thing: to withdraw the workers from under fire at the cost of one concession after the other. The Social Democracy hoped that the docile conduct of the workers would restore the "public opinion" of the bourgeoisie against the fascists. Moreover, the reformists even banked strongly upon the help of Victor Emmanuel. To the last hour, they restrained the workers with might and main from giving battle to Mussolini's bands. It availed them nothing. The Crown, along with the upper crust of the bourgeoisie swung over to the side of fascism. Convinced at the last moment that fascism was not to be checked by obedience, the Social Democrats issued a call to the workers for a general strike. But their proclamation suffered a fiasco. The reformists had dampened the powder so long, in their fear lest it should explode, that when they finally and with a trembling hand applied a burning fuse to it, the powder did not catch.

Two years after its inception, fascism was in power. It entrenched itself thanks to the fact that the first period of its overlordship coincided with a favorable economic conjuncture, which followed the depression of 1921-1922. The fascists crushed the retreating proletariat beneath the offensive power of the petty bourgeoisie. But this was not achieved at a single blow. Even after he assumed power, Mussolini proceeded on his course with due caution: he lacked as yet ready-made models. During the first two years, not even the constitution was altered. The fascist government took on the character of a coalition. In the meantime the fascist bands were busy at work with clubs, knives, and pistols. Thus, slowly, the fascist government was created that meant the complete strangulation of all independent mass organizations.

Mussolini attained this at the cost of bureaucratizing the fascist party itself. After utilizing the onrushing forces of the petty bourgeoisie, fascism strangled it within the vise of the bourgeois state. He couldn't have done otherwise, for the disillusionment of the masses he had united was transforming itself into the most immediate danger ahead. Fascism, become bureaucratic, approaches very closely to other forms of military and police dictatorship. It no longer possesses its former social support. The chief reserve of fascism – the petty bourgeoisie – has been spent. Only historical inertia enables the fascist government to keep the proletariat in a state of dispersion and helplessness. The correlation of forces is changing automatically in favor of the proletariat. This change must lead to a revolution. The downfall of fascism will be one of the most catastrophic events in European history. But all these processes, as the facts bear out, need time. The fascist government has maintained itself for ten years already. How much longer will it hold on? Without venturing into the risky business of setting dates, one can still say with assurance that Hitler's victory in Germany would mean a new and a long lease of life for Mussolini. Hitler's crash will mean the beginning of the end for Mussolini.

In its politics as regards Hitler, the German Social Democracy has not been able to add a single word: all it does is repeat more ponderously whatever the Italian reformists in their own time performed with greater flights of temperament The latter explained fascism as a post war psychosis; the German Social Democracy sees in it a "Versailles" or crisis psychosis. In both instances, the reformists shut their eyes to the organic character of fascism as a mass movement growing out of the collapse of capitalism.

Fearful of the revolutionary mobilization of the workers, the Italian reformists banked all their hopes on "the state. " Their slogan was,

"Victor Emmanuel! Help! Intervene!" The German Social Democracy lacks such a democratic bulwark as a monarch loyal to the constitution. So they must be content with a president. "Hindenburg! Help! Intervene!"

While waging battle against Mussolini, that is, while retreating before him, Turati let loose his dazzling motto, "One must have the manhood to be a coward." The German reformists are less frisky with their slogans. They demand, "Courage under unpopularity (*Mut zur Unpopularität*)." Which amounts to the same thing. One must not be afraid of the unpopularity which has been aroused by one's own cowardly temporizing with the enemy.

Identical causes produce identical effects. Were the march of events dependent upon the Social Democratic Party leadership, Hitler's career would be assured.

One must admit, however, that the German Communist Party has also learned little from the Italian experience.

The Italian Communist Party came into being almost simultaneously with fascism. But the same conditions of revolutionary ebb tide which carried the fascists to power served to deter the development of the Communist Party. It did not take account of the full sweep of the fascist danger; it lulled itself with revolutionary illusions; it was irreconcilably antagonistic to the policy of the united front; in short, it called from all the infantile diseases. Small wonder! It was only two years old. In its eyes fascism appeared to be only "capitalist reaction." The particular traits of fascism which spring from the mobilization of the petty bourgeoisie against the proletariat, the Communist Party was unable to discern. Italian comrades inform me that with the sole exception of Gramsci, the Communist Party wouldn't even allow of the possibility of the fascists' seizing power. Once the proletarian revolution had suffered defeat and capitalism had kept its ground, and the counter-revolution had triumphed, how could there be any further kind of counter-revolutionary upheaval? The bourgeoisie cannot rise up against itself! Such was the gist of the political orientation of the Italian Communist Party. Moreover, one must not let out of sight the fact that Italian fascism was then a new phenomenon, and only in the process of formation; it wouldn't have been an easy task even for a more experienced party to distinguish its specific traits.

The leadership of the German Communist Party reproduces today almost literally the position from which the Italian Communists took their point of departure: fascism is nothing else but capitalist reaction; from the point of view of the proletariat the differences between divers types of capitalist reaction are meaningless. This vulgar radicalism is the less excusable because the German party is much older than the Italian was at a corresponding period; and in addition, Marxism has been enriched now by the tragic experience in Italy. To insist that fascism is already here, or to deny the very possibility of its coming to power – amounts politically to one and the same thing. By ignoring the specific nature of fascism, the will to fight against it becomes inevitably paralyzed,

The brunt of the blame must be borne, of course, by the leadership of the Comintern. Italian Communists above all others were duty-bound to raise their voices in alarm. But Stalin, with Manuilsky, compelled them to disavow the most important lessons of their own annihilation. We have already observed with what diligent alacrity Ercoli switched over to the position of social fascism, i.e., to the position of passively waiting for the fascist victory in Germany.

For a long time, the international Social Democracy solaced itself with the notion that Bolshevism was conceivable only in a backward country. It found refuge in the same solace afterwards as regards fascism. The German Social Democracy is now compelled to experience on its own back the falseness of this comforting notion: its fellow travelers from the petty bourgeoisie have gone and are going over to the fascist camp; the workers are leaving it for the Communist Party. Only these two groups are growing in Germany: fascism and Bolshevism. Even though Russia on the one hand and Italy on the other are countries incomparably more backward than Germany, nevertheless they have both served as arenas for the development of political movements which are inherent in imperialist capitalism as such. Advanced Germany must recapitulate the processes which reached their fulfillment in Russia and Italy. The fundamental problem of German development may be at present formulated thus: which way out the way of Russia, or the way of Italy?

Obviously this does not mean that the highly developed social structure is of no significance from the point of view of the development of the destinies of Bolshevism and fascism. Italy is a petty-bourgeois and peasant country to a much greater degree than Germany. One need only recall that to 9.8 million engaged in farming and forestry in Germany there are 18.5 million employed in industry and trade; that is, almost twice as many. Whereas, in Italy, to 10.3 million engaged in farming and forestry there are 6.4 million employed in industry and trade. These bare totals do not by far give an adequate representation of the preponderant relative weight of the proletariat in the life of the German nation. Even the tremendous number of the unemployed is only a proof, turned inside out, of the social might of the German proletariat. The whole question consists in how to translate this might into the language of revolutionary politics.

The last major defeat of the German party, which can be placed on the same historical board with the September days in Italy, dates back to 1923. During the more than eight years that have elapsed since, many wounds have been healed, and a new generation has risen to its feet. The German party represents an incomparably greater force than did the Italian Communists in 1922. The relative weight of the proletariat; the considerable time elapsed since its last defeat; the considerable strength of the Communist Party – these are the three advantages, which bear a great significance for the general summation of the background and of the perspectives.

But to make the best of one's advantages, one must understand them. That is lacking. Thälmann's position in 1932 reproduces Bordiga's in 1922. In this direction, the danger takes on a particularly acute character. But here too there exists one supplementary advantage which was nonexistent ten years ago. Within the revolutionary ranks in Germany there is a Marxist opposition, which leans upon the experience of the preceding decade. This opposition is weak numerically, but the march of events adds extraordinary strength to its voice. Under certain conditions a slight shock may bring down an avalanche. The critical shock of the Left Opposition can aid in bringing about a timely change in the politics of the proletarian vanguard. In this lies our task at present

Through the United Front - To the Soviets as the Highest Organs of the United Front

Verbal genuflections before the soviets are equally as fashionable in the "left" circles as the misconception of their historical function. Most often the soviets are defined as the organs of struggle for power, as the organs of insurrection, and finally, as the organs of dictatorship. Formally these definitions are correct. But they do not at all exhaust the historical function of the soviets. First of all they do not explain why, in the struggle for power, precisely the soviets are necessary. The answer to this question is: just as the trade union is the rudimentary form of the united front in the economic struggle, so *the soviet is the highest form of the united front* under the conditions in which the proletariat enters the epoch of fighting for power.

The soviet in itself possesses no miraculous powers. It is the class representation of the proletariat, with all of the latter's strong and weak points. But precisely and only because of this does the soviet afford to the workers of divers political trends the organizational opportunity to unite their efforts in the revolutionary struggle for power. In the present pre-revolutionary environment it is the duty of the most advanced German workers to understand most clearly the historical function of the soviets as the organs of the united front.

Could the Communist Party succeed, during the preparatory epoch, in pushing all other parties out of the ranks of the workers by uniting under its banner the overwhelming majority of the workers, then there would be no need whatever for soviets. But historical experience bears witness to the fact that there is no basis whatever for the expectation that in any single country – in countries with an old capitalist culture even less than in the backward ones – the Communist Party can succeed in occupying such an undisputed and absolutely commanding position in the workers' ranks, prior to the proletarian overturn.

Precisely in Germany today are we shown that the proletariat is faced with the task of a direct and immediate struggle for power, long before it has been completely united under the banner of the Communist Party. The revolutionary situation itself, if approached on the political plane, arises from the fact that all groups and layers of the proletariat, or at least their overwhelming majority, are seized with the urge to unite their efforts in changing the existing regime. This does not mean, however, that they all understand how to do it; and still less that they are ready at the very moment to break with their parties and to join the ranks of the Communists. The political conscience of the class does not mature so methodically and uniformly; deep inner divergences remain even in the revolutionary epoch, when all processes develop by leaps and bounds. But, at the same time, the need for an organization above parties and embracing the entire class becomes extremely urgent. To crystallize this need into a form – that is the historic destiny of the soviets. That is their great function. Under the conditions of a revolutionary situation they arise as the highest organized expression of proletarian unity. Those who haven't understood this, have understood nothing in matters relating to the problem of the soviets. Thälmann, Neumann, and Remmele may keep on writing articles and uttering speeches about the future "Soviet Germany" without end. By their present policies they are sabotaging the inception of the soviets in Germany.

Removed from the actual sphere of action, unable to gather direct impressions from the masses or to place a hand daily on the pulse of the working class, it is very difficult to forecast the transitional forms which will lead in Germany to the creation of soviets. In another connection I offered the hypothesis that the German soviets may arise as an expanded form of the factory committees: in this, I leaned chiefly on the experience in 1923. But of course that is not the only way. Under the pressure of want and unemployment on the one hand and the onset of the fascists on the other, the need for revolutionary unity may all at once come to the surface in the form of soviets, skipping the factory committees. But whichever way the soviets arise, they cannot become anything save the organizational expression of the strong and weak sides of the proletarian of its inner contradictions and the general urge to overcome them; in short, the organs of the united front

The Social Democracy and the Communist Party divide in Germany the influence over the working class. The Social Democratic leadership does its best to repel the workers from itself. The leadership of the Communist Party strives with all its might to counteract the influx of the workers. As a consequence we get the formation of a third party and a comparatively slow change in the correlation of forces in favor of the Communists. But even if Communist Party policies were entirely correct, the workers' need for a revolutionary unification of the class would have grown incomparably faster than the preponderance of the Communist Party within the class. The need of creating soviets would thus remain in its full scope.

The creation of the soviets presupposes that the different parties and organizations within the working class, beginning with the factories, become agreed, both as regards the very necessity for the soviets and as regards the time and methods Of their formation. Which means: since the soviets, in themselves, represent the highest form of the united front in the revolutionary epoch, therefore their inception must be preceded by the policy of the united front in the preparatory period.

Is it necessary to recall once again that in the course of six months in 1917, the soviets in Russia had a conciliationist Social Revolutionary-Menshevik majority? Without renouncing for one moment its revolutionary independence as a party, the Bolshevik Party observed, within the framework of soviet activities, discipline in relation to the majority. There isn't the slightest doubt that in Germany, from the very first day on which the first soviet is formed, the Communist Party will occupy in it a place much more important than that of the Bolsheviks in the soviets of March 1917. Nor is the possibility excluded that the Communists would very shortly receive the majority in the soviets. This would not in any way deprive the soviets of their significance as the apparatus of the united front, because the minority – the Social Democratic, non-party, Catholic workers, etc. –

would at first still number millions; and any attempt to hurdle such a minority is the best conceivable method of breaking one's neck under the most revolutionary conditions obtainable. But this is all the music of the future. Today, the Communist Party is in the minority. And that must serve as our point of departure.

What has been said above doesn't mean, of course, that the infallible means of achieving the soviets lies in preliminary agreements with Wels, Hilferding, Breitscheid, etc. If in 1918 Hilferding cudgeled his brain for ways of including the soviets in the Weimar Constitution without injuring the latter, then one must assume that his brain is now at work over the problem of how to include fascist barracks in the Weimar Constitution without damaging the Social Democracy ... One must begin creating the soviets at the moment when the general condition of the proletariat permits soviets to be created, even against the will of the upper crust of the Social Democracy. But to do so, it is necessary to tear away the Social Democratic mass from the leading clique; and the way to do that is not by pretending it is already done. In order to separate the millions of Social Democratic workers from their reactionary leaders we must begin by showing these workers that we are ready to enter the soviets even with these "leaders."

One must not, however, discount entirely beforehand the possibility that top layers of the Social Democracy will be once again compelled to venture into the red-hot atmosphere of the soviets in order to try to repeat the maneuver of Ebert, Scheidcmann, Haase, etc., in 1918-1919: here the outcome will depend not so much on the bad faith of these gentlemen as upon the degree and manner in which history will seize them in its vise.

The formation of the first important local soviet in which the Communist and Social Democratic workers would represent not individuals but organizations, would have an enormous effect upon the entire German working class. Not only Social Democratic and nonparty workers but also the Catholic and liberal workers would be unable long to resist the pull of the centripetal force. All the sections of the German proletariat most adapted to and capable of organization would be drawn to the soviets, as are iron filings to the poles of a magnet. Within the soviets, the Communist Party would obtain a new and exceptionally favorable arena for fighting for the leading role in the proletarian revolution. One may hold absolutely incontrovertible the statement that even today the overwhelming majority of the Social Democratic workers and even a considerable part of the Social Democratic apparatus would be participating within the framework of soviets, had not the leadership of the Communist

Party so zealously aided the Social Democratic leaders in paralyzing the pressure of the masses.

If the Communist Party holds inadmissible any agreement on a program of definite practical tasks with Social Democratic, trade-union and other organizations, then this means nothing else but that it holds inadmissible the joint creation of the soviets together with the Social Democracy. And since there cannot be purely Communist soviets, and since, indeed, there wouldn't be any need of them in that case, then *the refusal by the Communist Party to make agreements and take joint action with other parties within the working class means nothing else but the refusal to create soviets.*

Die Rote Fahne will doubtless answer this deduction with a volley of curses, and proceed to prove that just as two times two are four, so am I surely Brüning's campaign agent, Wels's secret ally, etc. I am ready to stand indicted under all these charges, but under one condition: that *Die Rote Fahne* on its part undertakes to explain to the German workers when and in what manner the soviets may be organized in Germany without accepting the policies of the united front in relation to other workers' organizations.

Just to clarify the question of the soviets as the organs of the united front, the opinions expressed on this subject by one of the provincial Communist papers, *Der Klassenkampf* of Halle-Merseburg, are extremely instructive. "All workers' organizations," says this paper ironically, "in their present form, with all their faults and weaknesses, must be combined into great anti-fascist defensive unions. What does this mean? We may dispense with lengthy theoretic explanations; history itself proved a severe teacher in these questions to the German working class: the formless hodge-podge united front of all workers, organizations was paid for by the German working class at the price of the lost revolution in 1918-1919." In truth, an unsurpassable sample of superficial verbiage!

In 1918-1919, the united front was realized primarily through the soviets. Should the Spartacists have entered the soviets or shouldn't they? According to the exact meaning of the passage cited, they should have remained apart from the soviets. But since the Spartacists represented only a small minority of the working class, and since they could in no way substitute for the Social Democratic soviets their own, then their isolation from the soviets would have meant simply their isolation from the revolution. If the united front was "formless" and a "hodge-podge," the fault lay not with the soviets, as the organs of the united front, but with the political condition of the working class itself; with the weakness of the Spartakusbund; and with the extreme power of the Social Democracy. The united front, in general, is never a substitute for a strong revolutionary party; it can only aid the latter to become stronger. This applies fully to the soviets. The weak Spartakusbund, by its fear to let slip the extraordinary occasion, was pushed into taking ultra-left courses and premature demonstrations. Had the Spartacists kept apart from the united front, that is, the soviets, these negative traits would undoubtedly have been yet more sharply pronounced.

Can it be possible that these people have gathered nothing at all from the experience of the German revolution in 1918-1919? Have they at least read *Left-Wing Communism*? Truly, the Stalinist regime has caused a mental havoc that is horrifying! After bureaucratizing the soviets in the USSR, the epigones look upon them as a technical weapon in the hands of the party apparatus. Forgotten is the fact that the soviets were founded as workers' parliaments and that they drew the masses because they offered the possibility of welding together all sections of the proletariat, independently of party distinctions; forgotten is the fact that therein precisely lay the great educational and revolutionary power of the soviets. Everything is forgotten; everything is jumbled and distorted. O, thrice-cursed epigonism!

The question of the interrelationship between the party and the soviets is of decisive importance for revolutionary policy. While the present course of the party is in fact directed towards supplanting the soviets by the party, Hugo Urbahns, loath to miss the opportunity to add to the confusion, is preparing to supplant the party by the soviets. According to a *Sozialistische Arbeiter Zeitung* dispatch, Urbahns, in refuting the pretension of the Communist Party to the leadership of the working class, said at a meeting in Berlin, in January, "The leadership will be kept in the hands of the soviets, elected by the masses themselves and not in accordance with the desires or at the discretion of the one and only party. (*Violent applause*)" One can easily understand that by its ultimatism the Communist Party irritates the workers, who are ready to applaud every protest against bureaucratic presumption. But this does not alter the fact that Urbahns in this question as well has nothing in common with Marxism. No one will gainsay that the workers will elect the soviets "themselves." But the whole question lies in whom they will elect. We must enter the soviets together with all other organizations such as they are, "with all their faults and weaknesses." But to avow that the soviets "by themselves" are capable of leading the struggle of the proletariat for power – is only to sow abroad vulgar soviet fetishism. Everything depends upon the party that leads the soviets. Therefore, in contradistinction to Urbahns, the Bolshevik-Leninists do not at all deny the Communist Party the right to lead the soviets; on the contrary, they say, "Only on the basis of the united front, only through the mass organizations, can the KPD *conquer* the leading position within the future soviets and lead the proletariat to the conquest of power."

The United Front for Defence: A Letter to a Social Democratic Worker.
Leon Trotsky

This pamphlet addresses itself to the Social Democratic workers, even though personally the author belongs to another party. * The disagreements between Communism and Social Democracy run very deep. I consider them irreconcilable. Nevertheless, the course of events frequently puts tasks before the working class which imperatively demand the joint action of the two parties. Is such an action possible? Perfectly possible, as historical experience and theory attest: everything depends upon the conditions and the character of the said tasks. Now, it is much easier to engage in a joint action when the question before the proletariat is not one of taking the offensive for the attainment of new objectives, but of defending the positions already gained.

That is how the question is posed in Germany. The German proletariat is in a situation where it is retreating and giving up its positions. To be sure, there is no lack of windbags to cry that we are allegedly in the presence of a revolutionary offensive. These are people who obviously do not know how to distinguish their right from their left There is no doubt that the hour of the offensive will strike. But today the problem is to arrest the disorderly retreat and to proceed to the regrouping of the forces for the defensive. In politics as in the military art to understand a problem clearly is to facilitate its solution. To get intoxicated by phrases is to help the adversary. One must see clearly what is happening: the class enemy, that is, monopoly capital and large feudal property, spared by the November Revolution, is attacking along the whole front. The enemy is utilizing two means with a different historical origin: first, the military and police apparatus prepared by all the preceding governments which stood on the ground of the Weimar Constitution; second, National Socialism, that is, the troops of the petty-bourgeois counter-revolution that finance capital arms and incites against the workers.

The aim of capital and of the landowning caste is clear: to crush the organizations of the proletariat, to strip them of the possibility not only of taking the offensive but also of defending themselves. As can be seen, twenty years of collaboration of the Social Democracy with the bourgeoisie have not softened by one iota the hearts of the

---

* Written in exile in Turkey, February 23, 1933. Translated for *The Militant*, April 1 and 15, 1933.

capitalists. These individuals acknowledge but one law: the struggle for profit. And they conduct this struggle with a fierce and implacable determination, stopping at nothing and still less at their own laws.

The class of exploiters would have preferred to disarm and atomize the proletariat with the least possible expense, without civil war, with the aid of the military and police of the Weimar Republic. But it is afraid, and with good reason, that "legal" means by themselves would prove to be insufficient to drive the workers back into a position where they will no longer have any rights. For this, it requires fascism as a supplementary force. But Hitler's party, fattened by monopoly capital, wants to become not a supplementary force, but the sole governing force in Germany. This situation occasions incessant conflicts between the governmental allies, conflicts which at times take on an acute character. The saviors can afford the luxury of engaging mutually in intrigues only because the proletariat is abandoning its positions without battle and is beating the retreat without plan, without system, and without direction. The enemy is unleashed to such a point that it does not constrain itself from discussing right in public where and how to strike the next blow: by frontal attack; by bearing down on the Communist left flank; by penetrating deeply at the rear of the trade unions and cutting off communications, etc. ... The exploiters whom it has saved discourse on the Weimar Republic as if it were some worn-out bowl; they ask themselves if it should still be utilized for a while or be thrown into the discard right away.

The bourgeoisie enjoys full freedom of maneuver, that is, the choice of means, of time, and of place. Its chiefs combine the arms of the law with the arms of banditry. The proletariat combines nothing at all and does not defend itself. Its troops are split up, and its chiefs discourse languidly on whether or not it is at all possible to combine forces. Therein lies the essence of the interminable discussions on the united front: If the vanguard workers do not become conscious of the situation and do not intervene peremptorily in the debate, the German proletariat may find itself crucified for years on the cross of fascism.

Is It Not Too Late?

It may be that here my Social Democratic interlocutor interrupts me and says, "Don't you come too late to propagate the united front? What did you do before this?"

This objection would not be correct. This is not the first time that the question of a united front of defense against fascism is raised. I permit myself to refer to what I had the occasion to say on this subject in September 1930, after the first great success of the National Socialists. Addressing myself to the Communist workers, I wrote:

"The Communist Party must call for the defense of those material and moral positions which the working class has managed to win in the German state. This most directly concerns the fate of the workers' political organizations, trade unions, newspapers, printing plants, clubs, libraries, etc. Communist workers must say to their Social Democratic counterparts: 'The policies of our parties are irreconcilably opposed; but if the fascists come tonight to wreck your organization's hall, we will come running, arms in hand, to help you. Will you promise us that if our organization is threatened you will rush to our aid?' This is the quintessence of our policy in the present period. All agitation must be pitched in this key.

"The more persistently, seriously, and thoughtfully ... we carry on this agitation, the more we propose serious measures for defense in every factory, in every working-class neighborhood and district the less the danger that a fascist attack will take us by surprise, and the greater the certainty that such an attack will cement rather than break apart the ranks of the workers."

The pamphlet from which I take this extract was written two and a half years ago. There is not the slightest doubt today that if this policy had been adopted in time, Hitler would not be Chancellor at the present time and the positions of the German proletariat would be unassailable. But one cannot return to the past. As a result of the mistakes which were committed and the time which was allowed to pass, the problem of defense is posed today with infinitely greater difficulty: but the task remains just as before. Even right now it is possible to alter the relation of forces in favor of the proletariat. Towards this end, one must have a plan, a system, a combination of forces for the defense. But above all, one must have the will to defend himself. I hasten to add that he alone defends himself well who does not confine himself to the defensive but who, at the first occasion, is determined to pass over to the offensive.

What attitude does the Social Democracy adopt towards this question?

A Non-Aggression Pact

The Social Democratic leaders propose to the Communist Party to conclude a "non-aggression pact." When I read this phrase for the first time in the *Vorwärts*, I thought it was an incidental and not very happy pleasantry. The formula of the non-aggression pact, however, is today in vogue and at the present time it is at the center of all the discussions. The Social Democratic leaders are not lacking in tried-out and skillful policies. All the more reason for asking how they could have chosen such a slogan, which runs counter to their own interests.

The formula has been borrowed from diplomacy. The meaning of this type of pact is this: two states which have sufficient causes for war engage themselves for a determined period not to resort to the force of arms against each other. The Soviet Union, for example, has signed such a rigorously circumscribed pact with Poland. Assuming that a war were to break out between Germany and Poland, the said pact would in no way obligate the Soviet Union to come to the aid of Poland. Non-aggression and nothing more. In no way does it imply common action for defense; on the contrary, it excludes this action: without this, the pact would have a quite different character and would be called by a quite different name.

What sense then do the Social Democratic leaders give to this formula? Do the Communists threaten to sack the Social Democratic organizations? Or else is the Social Democracy disposed to undertake a crusade against the Communists? As a matter of fact something entirely different is in question. If one wants to use the language of diplomacy, it would be in place to speak not of a nonaggression pact, but of a defensive alliance against a third party, that is, against fascism. The aim is not to halt or to exorcise an armed struggle between Communists and Social Democrats – there could be no question of a danger of war – but of combining the forces of the Social Democrats and the Communists against the attack with arms in hand that has already been launched against them by the National Socialists.

Incredible as it may seem, the Social Democratic leaders are substituting for the question of genuine defense against the armed actions of fascism, the question of the political controversy between Communists and Social Democrats. It is exactly as if one were to substitute for the question of how to prevent the derailment of a train, the question of the need for mutual courtesy between the travelers of the second and third classes.

The misfortune, in any case, is that the ill-conceived formula of a "non-aggression pact" will not even be able to serve the inferior aim in whose name it is dragged in by the hair. The engagement assumed by two states not to attack each other in no way eliminates their struggle, their polemics, their intrigues, and their maneuvers. The semiofficial Polish journals, in spite of the pact, foam at the mouth when they speak of the Soviet Union. For its part, the Soviet press is far from making compliments to the Polish regime. The fact of the matter is that the Social Democratic leaders have steered a wrong course in trying to substitute a conventional diplomatic formula for the political tasks of the proletariat.

Organize the Defense Jointly; Do Not Forget the Past; Prepare for the Future

More prudent Social Democratic journalists translate their thought in this sense: they are not opponents of a "criticism based upon facts," but they are against suspicions, insults, and calumnies. A very laudable attitude! But how is the limit to be found between permitted criticism and inadmissible campaigns? And where are the impartial judges? As a general rule, the criticism never pleases the criticized, above all when he can raise no objection to the essence of it.

The question of whether or not the criticism of the Communists is good or bad is a question apart. If the Communists and the Social Democrats had the same opinion on this subject, there wouldn't be two parties in the world, independent from each other. Let us concede that the polemic of the Communists is not worth much. Does that fact lessen the mortal danger of fascism or do away with the need for joint resistance?

However, let us look at the other side of the picture: the polemic of the Social Democracy itself against Communism. The *Vorwärts* (I am simply taking the first copy at hand) publishes the speech which Stampfer [1] delivered on the subject of the non-aggression pact. In this same issue a cartoon has as its caption: *The Bolsheviks are signing a nonaggression pact with Pilsudski, but they refuse to draw up a similar pact with the Social Democracy.* Now, a cartoon is also a polemical "aggression," and it so happens that this particular one is most unfortunate. The *Vorwärts* completely forgets the fact that a non-aggression treaty existed between the Soviets and Germany during the period when the Social Democrat Müller was at the head of the Reich government.

The *Vorwärts* of February 15, on the same page, defends in the first column the idea of a non-aggression pact, and in the fourth column makes the accusation against the Communists that their factory committee at the Aschinger Company betrayed the interests of the workers during negotiations for the new wage scale. They openly use the word "betrayed." The secret behind this polemic (is it a criticism based on facts or a campaign of slander?) is very simple: new elections to the factory committee of the Aschinger Company were to take place at this time. Can we, in the interests of the united front asks the *Vorwärts*, put an end to attacks of this sort? In order for that to happen, the *Vorwärts* would have to stop being itself, that is, a Social Democratic journal. If the *Vorwärts* believes what it prints on the subject of the Communists, its first duty is to open the eyes of the workers to the faults, crimes, and "betrayals" of the latter. How could it be otherwise? The need for a fighting agreement flows from the existence of two parties, but it does not do away with the fact. Political life goes on. Each party, even though it adopts the frankest attitude on the question of the united front cannot help thinking of its own future.

Adversaries Close Ranks in the Face of the Common Danger

Let us assume for the moment that a Communist member of the Aschinger Company factory committee declares to the Social Democratic member: "Because the *Vorwärts* characterized my attitude on the question of the wage scale as an act of treason, I do not want to defend, together with you, my head and your neck from the fascist bullets." No matter how indulgently we wanted to view this action, we could only characterize the reply as utterly insane.

The intelligent Communist the serious Bolshevik, will say to the Social Democrat: "You are aware of my enmity to the views expressed by the *Vorwärts*. I am devoting and shall devote all my energy to undermining the dangerous influence which this paper has among the workers. But I am doing that and shall do it by my speeches, by criticism and persuasion. But the fascists want to do away arbitrarily with the existence of the *Vorwärts*. I promise you that jointly with you I will defend your paper to the utmost of my ability, but I am waiting for you to say that at the first appeal you will likewise come to the defense of *Die Rote Fahne* regardless of your attitude towards its views." Is this not an irreproachable way of posing the question? Does not this method correspond with the fundamental interests of the whole of the proletariat?

The Bolshevik does not ask the Social Democrat to alter the opinion he has of Bolshevism and of the Bolshevik press. Moreover, he does not demand that the Social Democrat make a pledge for the duration of the agreement to keep silent on his opinion of Communism. Such a demand would be absolutely inexcusable. "So long," says the Communist "as I have not convinced you and you have not convinced me, we shall criticize each other with full freedom, each using the arguments and expressions he deems necessary. But when the fascist wants to force a gag down our throats, we will repulse him together!"

Can an intelligent Social Democratic worker counter this proposal with a refusal?

The polemic between Communist and Social Democratic newspapers, no matter how bitter it may be, cannot prevent the compositors of the papers from forming a fighting agreement to organize a joint defense of their presses from attacks of the fascist bands. The Social Democratic and Communist deputies in the Reichstag and the Landtags, the municipal counselors, etc., are compelled to come to the physical defense of each other when the Nazis resort to loaded canes and chairs. Are more examples needed?

What is true in each particular case is also true as a general rule: the inevitable struggle in which Social Democracy and Communism are engaged for the leadership of the working class cannot and must not prevent them from closing their ranks when blows threaten the whole working class. Isn't this obvious?

Two Weights and Two Scales

The *Vorwärts* is indignant because the Communists accuse the Social Democrats (Ebert, Scheidemann, Noske, Hermann Müller, Grzesinsky) of paving the road for Hitler. The *Vorwärts* has a legitimate right to indignation. But this remark is too much: how can we, it cries out, make a united front with such slanderers? What have we here: sentimentalism? Prudish sensitiveness? No, that really smacks of hypocrisy. As a matter of fact, the leaders of the German Social Democracy cannot have forgotten that Wilhelm Liebknecht and August Bebel [2] often asserted that the Social Democracy was ready, for the sake of definite objectives, to come to an agreement with the devil and his grandmother. The founders of the Social Democracy certainly did not demand that during this occasion the devil should check his horns in the museum and that his grandmother should become converted to Lutheranism. Whence then comes this prudish sensitiveness among the Social Democratic politicians who, since 1914, have made united fronts with the Kaiser, Ludendorff, Gröner, Brüning, Hindenburg? Whence come these two weights and two scales: one for the bourgeois parties, the other for the Communists?

The leaders of the Center consider that every infidel who denies the dogmas of the Catholic Church, the only Savior, is one of the damned and shortly destined for eternal torments. That did not prevent Hilferding, who has no particular reason for believing in the Immaculate Conception, from establishing a united front with the Catholics in the government and in parliament. Together with the

Center the Social Democrats set up the "Iron Front" However, not for a single instant did the Catholics cease their unbearable propaganda and their polemics in the churches. Why these demands on Hilferding's part with regard to the Communists? Either a complete cessation of mutual criticism, that is, of the struggle of tendencies within the working class, or a rejection of all joint action. "All or nothing!" The Social Democracy has never put such ultimatums to bourgeois society. Every Social Democratic worker should reflect upon these two weights and two measures.

Suppose at a meeting, even today, someone should ask Weis how it happens that the Social Democracy, which gave the republic its first Chancellor and its first president, has led the country to Hitler. Wels will surely reply that to a large extent it is the fault of Bolshevism. Surely the day hasn't passed that the *Vorwärts* has failed to repeat this explanation *ad nauseam*. Do you think that in the united front with the Communists it will forego its right and its duty to tell the workers what it considers to be truth? The Communists certainly have no need of that. The united front against fascism is only one chapter in the book of the struggle of the proletariat. The chapters that went before cannot be effaced. The past cannot be forgotten. We must build on it. We preserve the memory of Ebert's alliance with Gröner and of Noske's role. We remember under what conditions Rosa Luxemburg and Karl Liebknecht died. We Bolsheviks have taught the workers to forget nothing. We do not ask the devil to cut off his tail: that would hurt him and we would not profit by it. We accept the devil just as nature has created him. We have no need of the repentance of the Social Democratic leaders or of their loyalty to Marxism; but we do need the will of the Social Democracy to struggle against the enemy which actually threatens it with death. For our part, we are ready to carry out in the joint struggle all the promises which we have made. We promise to fight courageously and to carry the fight to a finish. That is quite enough for a fighting agreement.

Your Leaders Don't Want to Fight!

However, it still remains to be known why the Social Democratic leaders speak at all regarding polemics, non-aggression pacts, and the disgusting manners of the Communists, instead of answering this simple question: In what way shall we fight the fascists? For the simple reason that the Social Democratic leaders do not want to fight. They cherished the hope that Hindenburg would save them from Hitler. Now they are waiting for some other miracle. They do not want to fight. They lost the habit of fighting long ago. The struggle frightens them.

Stampfer wrote regarding the actions of the fascist banditry at Eisleben [3]: "Faith in right and justice has not yet died in Germany" (*Vorwärts*, February 14).

It is impossible to read these words without being revolted. Instead of a call for a fighting united front, we get the consoling words: "Faith in justice has not died." Now, the bourgeoisie has its justice, and the proletariat its own, too. Armed injustice always comes out on top of disarmed justice. The whole history of humanity proves this. Whoever makes an appeal to this obvious phantom of justice is deceiving the workers. Whoever wants the victory of proletarian justice over fascist violence must agitate for the struggle and set up the organs of the proletarian united front.

In the entire Social Democratic press it is impossible to find a single line indicating genuine preparation for the struggle. There is not a single thing, merely some general phrases, postponements to some indefinite future, nebulous consolations. "Only let the Nazis start something, and then ..." And the Nazis started something. They march forward step by step; they tranquilly take over one position after another. These petty-bourgeois reactionary malefactors do not care for risks. Now, they do not need to risk anything at all: they are sure in advance that the enemy will retreat without a fight. And they are not mistaken in their calculations.

Of course, it often occurs that a combatant must retreat in order to get a good start for a leap forward. But the Social Democratic leaders are not inclined to make the leap forward. They do not want to leap. And all their dissertations are made in order to conceal this fact Just a short time ago they kept asserting that so long as the Nazis do not quit the ground of legality, there is no room for a fight. Now we get a good look at what this legality was: a series of promissory notes on the *coup d'état*. Still, this *coup d'état* is possible only because the Social Democratic leaders lull the workers to sleep with phrases about the legality of the *coup d'état* and console them with hope of a new Reichstag yet more impotent than those that preceded it. The fascists can ask for nothing better.

Today the Social Democracy has even ceased speaking of struggles in the indefinite future. On the subject of the destruction of the working-class organizations and press, already begun, the *Vorwärts* "reminds" the government not to forget that "in a developed capitalist country the conditions of production group the workers in factories." These words indicate that the leadership of the Social Democracy accepts in advance the destruction of the political, economic, and cultural organizations created by three generations of the proletariat. "In spite of this" the workers will remain grouped by the industries themselves. Well then, what good are proletarian organizations if the question can be solved so simply?

The leaders of the Social Democracy and the trade unions wash their hands, and relegate themselves to the sidelines while waiting. If the workers themselves, "grouped together by industries," break the bonds of discipline and begin the struggle, the leaders, obviously, will intervene as they did in 1918, in the role of pacifiers and mediators, and will force themselves onto the workers' backs to reestablish the positions they have lost.

The leaders conceal from the eyes of the masses their refusal to fight and their dread of the struggle by means of hollow phrases about nonaggression pacts. Social Democratic workers, your leaders do not want to fight!

Then Is Our Proposal a Maneuver?

Here the Social Democrat will again interrupt us to say. "Since you do not believe in our leaders" desire to fight against fascism, isn't your proposal for a united front an obvious maneuver?" Even more, he will repeat the reflections printed in the *Vorwärts* to the effect that the workers need unity and not "maneuvers."

This type of argument has quite a convincing sound. In actuality it is an empty phrase. Yes, we Communists are positive that the Social Democratic and trade-union functionaries will continue to evade the struggle to the best of their ability. At the critical moment a large segment of the working-class bureaucracy will pass directly over to the fascists. The other segment, which succeeds in exporting its carefully hoarded financial resources to some other country, will emigrate at the opportune moment. All these actions have already begun, and their further development is inevitable. But we do not confuse this segment today the most influential in the reformist bureaucracy, with the Social Democratic Party or the entirety of the trade unions. The proletarian nucleus of the party will fight with sure blows, and it will carry behind it a good-sized section of the apparatus. Exactly where will the line of demarcation pass between the turncoats, traitors, and deserters, on one side, and those who want to fight, on the other? We can only find this out through experience. That is why, without possessing the slightest confidence in the Social Democratic bureaucracy, the Communists cannot abstain from addressing themselves to the whole party. Only in this manner will it be possible to separate those who want to fight from those who want to desert. If we are mistaken in our estimation of Wels, Breitscheid, Hilferding, Crispien [4], and the rest, let them prove that we are liars by their actions. We will declare a mea culpa on the public squares. If all this is merely a "maneuver" on our part, it is a correct and necessary maneuver which serves the interests of the cause.

You Social Democrats remain in your party because you have faith in its program, in its tactics, and in its leadership. This is a fact with which we reckon. You regard our criticism as false. That is your privilege. You are by no means obliged to believe the Communists on faith, and no serious Communist will demand this of you. But on their side the Communists have the right to put no confidence in the functionaries of the Social Democracy and not to consider the Social Democrats as Marxists, revolutionists, and genuine socialists. Otherwise, the Communists would have had no need to create a separate party and International. We must take the facts as they are. We must build the united front not in the clouds, but on the foundation which all the previous development has laid down. If you sincerely believe that your leadership will lead the workers to struggle against fascism, what Communist maneuver can you distrust? Then what is this maneuver of which the *Vorwärts* is continually speaking? Think it out carefully. Is this not a maneuver on the part of your leaders who want to frighten you with the hollow word "maneuver" and thus keep you away from the united front?

The Tasks and Methods of the United Front

The united front must have its organs. There is no need to imagine what these may be: the situation itself is dictating the nature of these organs. In many localities, the workers have already suggested the form of organization of the united front, as a species of defense cartels basing themselves on all the local proletarian organizations and establishments. This is an initiative which must be grasped, deepened, consolidated, extended to cover the industrial centers with cartels, by linking them up with each other and by preparing a German workers' congress of defense.

The fact that the unemployed and the employed workers are becoming increasingly estranged from each other bears within itself a deadly danger not only for the collective-bargaining agreements, but also for the trade unions, without even any need for a fascist crusade. The united front between Social Democrats and Communists means first of all a united front of the employed and unemployed workers. Without that, any serious struggle in Germany is quite unthinkable.

The RGO must enter into the Free Trade Unions as a Communist fraction. That is one of the principal conditions for the success of the united front The Communists within the trade unions must enjoy the rights of workers' democracy and, in the first place, full freedom of criticism. On their part they must respect the statutes of the trade unions and their discipline.

Defense against fascism is not an isolated thing. Fascism is only a cudgel in the hands of finance capital. The aim of the crushing of proletarian democracy is to raise the rate of exploitation of labor power. There lies an immense field for the united front of the proletariat: the struggle for daily bread, extended and sharpened, leads directly under present conditions to the struggle for workers' control of production.

The factories, the mines, the large estates fulfill their social functions thanks only to the labor of the workers. Can it be that the latter have not the right to know whither the owner is directing the establishment why he is reducing production and driving out the workers, how he is fixing prices, etc.? We will be answered: "Commercial secrets." What are commercial secrets? A plot of the capitalists against the workers and the people as a whole. Producers and consumers, the workers in this twofold capacity must conquer the right to control all the operations of their establishments, unmasking fraud and deceit in order to defend their interests and the interests of the people as a whole, facts and figures in hand. The struggle for workers' control of production can and should become the slogan of the united front.

With regard to organization, the forms necessary for cooperation between Social Democratic workers and Communist workers will be found without difficulty: it is only necessary to pass over from words to deeds.

The Irreconcilable Character of the Social Democratic and the Communist Parties

Now, if a common defence against the attack of capital is possible, can we not go still farther and form a genuine bloc of the two parties on all the questions? Then the polemic between the two would take on an internal, pacific, and cordial character. Certain left Social Democrats, of the type of Seydewitz, as is known, even go so far as to dream of a complete union of the Social Democracy and the Communist Party. But all this is a vain dream! What separates the Communists from the Social Democracy are antagonisms on fundamental questions. The simplest way of translating the essence of their disagreements is this: the Social Democracy considers itself the democratic doctor of capitalism, we are its revolutionary gravediggers.

The irreconcilable character of the two parties appears with particular clearness in the light of the recent evolution of Germany. Leipart laments that in calling Hitler to power the bourgeois classes have disrupted the "integration" of the workers into the State and he warns the bourgeoisie against the "dangers" flowing from it (*Vorwärts*, February 15, 1933). Leipart thus makes himself the watchdog of the bourgeois state by desiring to preserve it from the proletarian revolution. Can we even dream of union with Leipart?

The *Vorwärts* prides itself every day on the fact that hundreds of thousands of Social Democrats died during the war "for the ideal of a finer and freer Germany" ... It only forgets to explain why this finer Germany turned out to be the Germany of Hitler-Hugenberg. In reality, the German workers, like the workers of the other belligerent countries, died as cannon fodder, as slaves of capital. To idealize this fact is to continue the treason of August 4, 1914.

The *Vorwärts* continues to appeal to Marx, to Engels, to Wilhelm Liebknecht, to Bebel, who from 1848 to 1871 spoke of the struggle for the unity of the German nation. Lying appeals! At that time, it was a question of completing the bourgeois revolution. Every proletarian revolutionist had to fight against the particularism and provincialism inherited from feudalism. Every proletarian revolutionist had to fight against this particularism and provincialism in the name of the creation of a national state. At the present time, such an objective is invested with a progressive character only in China, in Indochina, in India, in Indonesia, and other backward colonial and semicolonial countries. For the advanced countries of Europe, the national frontiers are exactly the same reactionary chains as were the feudal frontiers at one time.

"The nation and democracy are twins," the *Vorwärts* says again. Quite true! But these twins have become aged, infirm, and have fallen into senility. The nation as an economic whole, and democracy as a form of the domination of the bourgeoisie, have been transformed into fetters upon the productive forces and civilization. Let us recall Goethe once again: "All that is born is doomed to perish."

A few more millions may be sacrificed for the "corridor," for Alsace-Lorraine, for Malmedy. [5] These disputed bits of land may be covered with three, five, ten tiers of corpses. All this may be called national defense. But humanity will not progress because of it; on the contrary, it will fall on all fours backward into barbarism. The way out is not in the "national liberation" of Germany, but in the liberation of Europe from national barriers. It is a problem which the bourgeoisie cannot resolve, any more than the feudal lords in their time were able to put an end to particularism. Hence the coalition with the bourgeoisie is doubly reprehensible. A proletarian revolution is necessary. A federation of the proletarian republics of Europe and the whole world is necessary.

Social patriotism is the program of the doctors of capitalism; internationalism is the program of the gravediggers of bourgeois society. This antagonism is irreducible.

Democracy and Dictatorship

The Social Democrats consider the democratic constitution to be above the class struggle. For us, the class struggle is above the democratic constitution. Can it be that the experience undergone by postwar Germany has passed without leaving a trace, just as the experiences undergone during the war? The November Revolution brought the Social Democracy to power. The Social Democracy spurred the powerful movement of the masses along the road of "right" and the "constitution." The whole political life which followed in Germany evolved on the bases and within the framework of the Weimar Republic.

The results are at hand: bourgeois democracy transforms itself legally, pacifically, into a fascist dictatorship. The secret is simple enough: bourgeois democracy and fascist dictatorship are the instruments of one and the same class, the exploiters. It is absolutely impossible to prevent the replacement of one instrument by the other by appealing to the Constitution, the Supreme Court at Leipzig, new elections, etc. What is necessary is to mobilize the revolutionary forces of the proletariat. Constitutional fetishism brings the best aid to fascism. Today this is no longer a prognostication, a theoretical affirmation, but the living reality. I ask you, Social Democratic worker: if the Weimar democracy blazed the trail for the fascist dictatorship, how can one expect it to blaze the trail for socialism?

"But can't we Social Democratic workers win the majority in the democratic Reichstag?"

That you cannot. Capitalism has ceased to develop; it is putrefying. The number of industrial workers is no longer growing. An important section of the proletariat is being degraded in continual unemployment. By themselves, these social facts exclude the possibility of any stable and methodical development of a labor party in parliament as before the war. But even if, against all probability, the labor representation in parliament should grow rapidly, would the bourgeoisie wait for a peaceful expropriation? The governmental machinery is entirely in its hands! Even admitting that the bourgeoisie allows the moment to pass and permits the proletariat to gain a parliamentary representation of 51 percent, wouldn't the Reichswehr, the police, the Stahlhelm, and the fascist storm troops disperse this parliament in the same way that the camarilla today disperses with a stroke of the pen all the parliaments which displease it?

"Then, down with the Reichstag and elections?"

No, that's not what I mean. We are Marxists and not anarchists. We are supporters of the utilization of parliament: it is not an instrument for transforming society, but a means of rallying the workers. Nevertheless, in the development of the class struggle, a moment arrives when it is necessary to decide the question of who is to be master of the country: finance capital or the proletariat. Dissertations on the nation and on democracy in general constitute, under such conditions, the most impudent lying. Under our eyes, a small German minority is organizing and arming, as it were, half of the nation to crush and strangle the other half. It is not a question today of secondary reforms, but of the life or death of bourgeois society. Never have such questions been decided by a vote. Whoever appeals today to the parliament or to the Supreme Court at Leipzig, is deceiving the workers and in practice is helping fascism.

There Is No Other Road

"What is to be done under such conditions?" my Social Democratic interlocutor will ask.
The proletarian revolution.
"And then?"
The dictatorship of the proletariat.
"As in Russia? The privations and the sacrifices? The complete stifling of freedom of opinion? No, not for me."

It is precisely because you are not disposed to tread the road of the revolution and the dictatorship that we cannot form one single party together. But nevertheless allow me to tell you that your objection is not worthy of a conscious proletarian. Yes, the privations of the Russian workers are considerable. But in the first place, the Russian workers know in the name of what they are making these sacrifices. Even if they should undergo a defeat humanity would have learned a great deal from their experience. But in the name of what did the German working class sacrifice itself in the years of the imperialist war? Or again, in the years of unemployment? To what do these sacrifices lead, what do they yield, what do they teach? Only those sacrifices are worthy of man which blaze the trail to a better future.

That's the first objection I heard you make; the first, but not the only one.

The sufferings of the Russian workers are considerable because in Russia, as a consequence of specific historical factors, was born the first proletarian state, which is obliged to raise itself from extreme poverty by its own strength. Do not forget that Russia was the most backward country of Europe. The proletariat there constituted only a tiny part of the population. In that country, the dictatorship of the proletariat necessarily had to assume the harshest forms. Thence the consequences which flowed from it: the development of the bureaucracy which holds power, and the chain of errors committed by the political leadership which has fallen under the influence of this bureaucracy. If at the end of 1918, when power was completely in its hands, the Social Democracy had entered boldly upon the road to socialism and had concluded an indissoluble alliance with Soviet Russia, the whole history of Europe would have taken another direction and humanity would have arrived at socialism in a much shorter space of time and with infinitely less sacrifice. It is not our fault that this did not happen.

Yes, the dictatorship in the Soviet Union at the present time has an extremely bureaucratic and distorted character. I have personally criticized more than once in the press the present Soviet regime which is a distortion of the workers' state. Thousands upon thousands of my comrades fill the prisons and the places of exile for having fought against the Stalinist bureaucracy. However, even when judging the negative sides of the present Soviet regime, it is necessary to preserve a correct historical perspective. If the German proletariat much more numerous and more civilized than the Russian proletariat, were to take the power tomorrow, this would not only open up immense economic and cultural perspectives but would also lead immediately to a radical attenuation of the dictatorship in the Soviet Union.

It must not be thought that the dictatorship of the proletariat is necessarily connected with the methods of Red terror which we had to apply in Russia. We were the pioneers. Covered with crime, the Russian possessing classes did not believe that the new regime would last. The bourgeoisie of Europe and America supported the Russian counterrevolution. Under these conditions, one could hold on only at the cost of terrific exertion and the implacable punishment of our class enemies. The victory of the proletariat in Germany would have quite a different character. The German bourgeoisie, having lost the power, would no longer have any hope of retaking it. The alliance of Soviet Germany with Soviet Russia would multiply, not twofold but tenfold, the strength of the two countries. In all the rest of Europe, the position of the bourgeoisie is so compromised that it is not very likely that it would be able to get its armies to march against proletarian Germany. To be sure, the civil war would be inevitable: there are enough fascists for that But the German proletariat, armed with state power and having the Soviet Union behind it, would soon bring about the atomization of fascism by drawing to its side substantial sections of the petty bourgeoisie. The dictatorship of the proletariat in Germany would have incomparably more mild and more civilized forms than the dictatorship of the proletariat in Russia.

"In that case, why the dictatorship?"

To annihilate exploitation and parasitism; to crush the resistance of the exploiters; to end their inclination to think about a reestablishment of exploitation; to put all the power, all the means of production, all the resources of civilization into the hands of the proletariat; and to permit it to utilize all these forces and means in the interest of the socialist transformation of society: there is no other road.

The German Proletariat Will Have the Revolution in German and Not in Russian

"Still, it often happens that our Communists approach us Social Democrats with this threat: just wait, as soon as we will get into power, we'll put you up against the wall."

Only a handful of imbeciles, windbags, and braggarts, who are a safe bet to decamp at the moment of danger, can make such threats. A serious revolutionist, while acknowledging the inescapability of revolutionary violence and its creative function, understands at the same time that the application of violence in the socialist transformation of society has well-defined limits. The Communists cannot prepare themselves save by seeking mutual understanding and a rapprochement with the Social Democratic workers. The revolutionary unanimity of the overwhelming majority of the German proletariat will reduce to a minimum the repression which the revolutionary dictatorship will exercise. It is not a question of slavishly copying Soviet Russia, of making a virtue of each of its necessities. That is unworthy of Marxists. To profit by the experience of the October Revolution does not mean that it should be copied blindly. One must take into account differences among nations, in the social structure and above all in the relative importance and the cultural level of the proletariat. To assume that one can make the socialist revolution in a presumably constitutional, peaceful manner, with the acquiescence of the Supreme Court at Leipzig – that can be done only by incurable philistines. The German proletariat will be unable to walk around the revolution. But in its revolution, it will speak in German and not in Russian. I am convinced that it will speak much better than we did.

What Shall We Defend?

"Very good, but we Social Democrats propose nevertheless to come to power by democracy. You Communists consider that an absurd utopia. In that case, is the united front of defense possible? For it is necessary to have a clear idea of what there is to defend. If we defend one thing and you another, we will not end up with common actions. Do you Communists consent to defend the Weimar Constitution?"

The question is a fitting one and I will try to answer it candidly. The Weimar Constitution represents a whole system of institutions, of rights and of laws. Let us commence from the top. The republic has at its head a president. Do we Communists consent to defend Hindenburg against fascism? I think that the need for that doesn't make itself felt, Hindenburg having called the fascists to power. Then comes the government presided over by Hitler. This government does not need to be defended against fascism. In the third place comes the parliament. When these lines appear, the sort of parliament emerging from the elections of March 5 will probably have been determined. But even at this juncture one can say with certainty that if the composition of the Reichstag proves to be hostile to the government; if Hitler takes it into his head to liquidate the Reichstag and if the Social Democracy shows a determination to fight for the latter, the Communists will help the Social Democracy with all their strength.

We Communists cannot and do not want to establish the dictatorship of the proletariat against you or without you, Social Democratic workers. We want to come to this dictatorship together with you. And we regard the common defense against fascism as the first step in this sense. Obviously, in our eyes, the Reichstag is not a capital historical conquest which the proletariat must defend against the fascist vandals. There are more valuable things. Within the framework of bourgeois democracy and parallel to the incessant struggle against it, the elements of proletarian democracy have formed themselves in the course of many decades: political parties, labor press, trade unions, factory committees, clubs, cooperatives, sports societies, etc. The mission of fascism is not so much to complete the destruction of bourgeois democracy as to crush the first outlines of proletarian democracy. As for our mission, it consists in placing those elements of proletarian democracy, already created, at the foundation of the soviet system of the workers' state. To this end, it is necessary to break the husk of bourgeois democracy and free from it the kernel of workers' democracy. Therein lies the essence of the proletarian revolution. Fascism threatens the vital kernel of workers' democracy. This itself clearly dictates the program of the united front. We are ready to defend your printing plants and our own, but also the democratic principle of freedom of the press; your meeting halls and ours, but also the democratic principle of the freedom of assembly and association. We are materialists and that is why we do not separate the soul from the body. So long as we do not yet have the strength to establish the soviet system, we place ourselves on the terrain of bourgeois democracy. But at the same time we do not entertain any illusions.

As to Freedom of the Press

"And what will you do with the Social Democratic press if you should succeed in seizing power? Will you prohibit our papers as the Russian Bolsheviks prohibited the Menshevik papers?"

You put the question badly. What do you mean by "our" papers? In Russia the dictatorship of the proletariat proved possible only after the overwhelming majority of the worker-Mensheviks passed over to the side of the Bolsheviks, whereas the petty-bourgeois debris of Menshevism undertook to help the bourgeoisie fight for the restoration of "democracy," that is, of capitalism. However, even in Russia we did not at all inscribe upon our banner the prohibition of the Menshevik papers. We were led to do this by the incredibly harsh conditions of the struggle that had to be conducted to save and maintain the revolutionary dictatorship. In Soviet Germany, the situation will be, as I have already said, infinitely more favorable; and the regime of the press will necessarily feel the effects of it. I do not think that in this field the German proletariat needs to resort to repression.

To be sure, I do not want to say that the workers' state will tolerate even for a day the regime of "(bourgeois) freedom of the press," that is, the state of affairs in which only those who control the printing plants, the paper companies, the bookstores, and so on, that is, the capitalists, can publish papers and books. Bourgeois "freedom of the press" signifies a monopoly for finance capital to impose capitalist prejudices upon the people by means of hundreds and thousands of papers charged with disseminating the virus of lies in the most perfect technical form. Proletarian freedom of the press will mean the nationalization of the printing plants, the paper companies, and the bookstores in the interest of the workers. We do not separate the soul from the body. Freedom of the press without linotypes, without printing presses, and without paper is a miserable fiction. In the proletarian state the technical means of printing will be put at the disposal of groups of citizens in accordance with their real numerical importance. How is this to be done? The Social Democracy will obtain printing facilities corresponding to the number of its supporters. I do not think that at that time this number will be very high: otherwise the very regime of the dictatorship of the proletariat would be impossible. Nevertheless, let us leave it to the future to settle this question. But the principle itself, of distributing the technical means of printing, not according to the thickness of the checkbook, but according to the number of supporters of a given program, of a given current, of a given school, is, I hope, the most honest, the most democratic, the most authentically proletarian principle. Isn't that so?

"Maybe."

Then shall we shake hands on it? "I'd like to think it over a bit."

I ask for nothing else, my dear friend: the aim of all my reflections is to have you meditate once more upon all the great problems of proletarian policy.

Some Comments on Party Policy and Tactics in the Antiwar Movement.
Tom Kerry

Just what is the character of the formation that has arisen in the course of development of the antiwar movement and what is our relation to it?* It can be said at the outset that even if we grant there is nothing unique about some aspects of the antiwar movement, the formation itself is decidedly unique; i.e., nothing like it has been seen before in this country. When comrades cast about to find some analogous experience in the history of the party they find none to serve as a secure mooring upon which to anchor our tactical approach.

Obviously, the so-called "classical" form under which the united front tactic was applied in the past does not appear relevant to the existent formation. If not a united front then what is it? A coalition, a bloc, an alliance, a confederation, or some combination of these, just what is it? Unfortunately, like with some other things, language does not keep pace with the historical development. There just is no new word, that I know of, to adequately define this new phenomenon, it would certainly simplify matters if there were, terminology-wise (in Madison Avenue jargon) if not otherwise.

For the simon-pure sectarian this poses no problem. Looking back in history, he "discovers" that the united front tactic as projected by the Bolsheviks was intended to apply to agreements between mass organizations. Finding no replica of the past in present day reality he washes his hands of the whole mess and takes refuge in the limbo of infantile leftism there to await the day when history finally catches up with doctrinaire prescription. A prime example of this type of sectarian approach is Gerry Healy, general secretary of the British Socialist Labour League.

Writing a series of two lengthy articles in *The Newsletter*, Jan. 7 and Feb. 11, 1967, under the general title: "The Real Meaning of the United Front," Healy explains why the SLL will have no part of any

---

* Tom Kerry, a leader of the Fourth Internationalists in the USA, wrote this in answer to an article by David Fender entitled "Remarks on the Antiwar Movement". Both appeared in the SWP Discussion Bulletin Volume 26 during October 1967.

"united front" antiwar movement in Great Britain. "The united front tactic," he affirms, "was developed in order to deal with a situation where you had a mass communist party and a mass reformist organization," Here we have stated the alleged "classical" formula for the united front tactic. (I say "alleged" because it is an extremely oversimplified definition, but let it pass for the moment.)

Healy then proceeds to elaborate on this theme. The united front, he avers, "was essentially conceived of as a tactic governing relations between mass organizations and not groups or small parties who did not represent the mass of the working class," As the Labor Party, which includes the trade unions, is the only mass working class organization in Great Britain, you can readily see how this effectively rules out any "united front" antiwar action. A rather dreary outlook. But hold, there is yet hope! In a second article in *The Newsletter*, under the title: "How NOT to Defend the Vietnamese Revolution," (a very appropriate title, I thought) Healy offers a straw to cling to:

"If," he blandly assures his constituents, "the Socialist Labour League was a mass organization it would endeavour to involve the Labour Party in a joint campaign against the war in Vietnam, but this is not the case." And in the meantime?

"The Socialist Labour League," he concludes, "is, therefore, forced to confine itself to a propaganda political preparation for the struggle in defence of the Vietnamese people." If everyone will just be patient enough to mark time until Healy's SLL develops into a mass communist party so that he could then enter into a united front pact with the mass reformist Labor Party the whole problem will be neatly solved. What tripe! We expect the Vietnam war to go on for a long time --but not THAT long!

Meanwhile, the British working class is not reconciled to waiting for Healy's "mass communist party" to materialize. Their impatience was expressed at the recent Labor Party conference, voting a resolution, 2,752,000 to 2,633,000, calling upon the Labor Government to "dissociate itself completely," from U.S. policy in Vietnam. The *N.Y. Times,* Oct. 7, reports that: "The audience cheered a number of highly critical speeches on Vietnam. Alan Campbell McLean, a Scottish delegate, compared the United States action in Vietnam to the German bombing of Stalingrad in World War II. He said that American troops had 'no legal or political or moral right' to be in Vietnam."

The vote is indicative, but not truly representative of the feelings of the British working class who, in their overwhelming number support the sentiment expressed by the majority resolution voted by their representatives at the Labor Party conference. This is good so far as it goes. True, it is no substitute for effective action. But it does present the antiwar forces in Great Britain with an opening to press for implementing actions by the trade unions and Labor Party constituency groups. And it is at least one thousand times more effective "propaganda" than all of Healy's ultraleftist gibberish.

Healy's defense of the "classical" form of the united front against "revisionist" corruption is a prime expression of the tendency of infantile leftism to use the cover of "Marxist nomenclature" to cloak a policy of abstention from the real struggle. Or, as Lenin put it: "The surest way of discrediting and damaging a new political (and not only political) idea is to reduce it to absurdity on the plea of defending it." This is precisely what Healy does to the idea of the United Front.

Let us examine the idea of the united front from the viewpoint of "terminology" or "nomenclature" if you will. It may come as a surprise to many comrades to learn that the "nomenclature" came some time after the idea had been long in practice. In a speech to the Executive Committee of the Communist International held in November 1922, Zinoviev pointed out that: "The slogan of the United Front [was] first formulated by our Executive in December, 1921," when a united front campaign was launched on an international scale.

The theses on the united front were formally adopted by the Fourth Congress of the Comintern. (Comrades will find the text of the theses, which were drafted by Trotsky for consideration by the Feb. 1922 plenum of the ECCI, on page 91 in volume 2 of *The First Five Years of the Communist International* .) But, as pointed out above, the idea of the united front had been part of the tactical arsenal of Bolshevism for some time before.

Lenin's important treatise on communist (Bolshevik) tactics, *Left Wing Communism, an Infantile Disorder*, published in 1920, never once employs the term, united front. Yet, in this classical polemic against the disease of ultraleftism, is contained a rich exposition of the united front idea as applied throughout the whole history of Bolshevism dating back to its very inception at the turn of the century. Consistent with his whole method, Lenin pinpoints those social, class and political divisions which capitalism engenders, which make necessary the application of the united front tactic, although he does not call it that:

"Capitalism would not be capitalism if the 'pure' proletariat were not surrounded by a large number of exceedingly motley types intermediate between the proletarian and the semiproletarian (who earns his livelihood in part by the sale of his labor power), between the semiproletarian and the small peasant (and petty artisan, handicraft worker and small master in general), between the small peasant and the middle peasant, and so on, and if the proletariat itself were not divided into more developed and less developed strata, if it were not divided according to territorial origin, trade, sometimes according to religion, and so on. And from all this follow the necessity, the absolute necessity, for the vanguard of the proletariat, for its class-conscious section, for the Communist Party, to resort to manoeuvres, agreements and compromises with the various groups of proletarians, with the various parties of the workers and small masters.

"The whole point lies in *knowing how* to apply these tactics in order to *raise*, and not lower, the *general* level of proletarian class consciousness, revolutionary spirit, and ability to fight and win, Incidentally, it should be noted that the victory of the Bolsheviks over the Mensheviks demanded the tactics of manoeuvres, agreements and compromises not only before *but also after* the October Revolution of 1917, but such manoeuvres and compromises, of course, as would assist, accelerate, consolidate and strengthen the Bolsheviks at the expense of the Mensheviks. The petty-bourgeois democrats (including the Mensheviks) inevitably vacillate between the bourgeoisie and the proletariat, between bourgeois democracy and the Soviet system, between reformism and revolutionism, between love-for-the-workers and fear of the proletarian dictatorship, etc. The proper tactics for the Communists must be to *utilize* these vacillations, not to ignore them; and utilizing them calls for concessions to those elements which are turning toward the proletariat—whenever and to the extent that they turn towards the proletariat- in addition to fighting those who turn toward the bourgeoisie. The result of the application of correct tactics is that Menshevism has disintegrated, and is disintegrating more and more in our country, that the stubbornly opportunist leaders are being isolated and that the best elements among the petty-bourgeois democrats are being brought into our camp." (All emphasis by author.)

In another section, Lenin declares that "the whole history of Bolshevism, both before and after the October Revolution, is full of instances of manoeuvring, making agreements and compromises with other parties, bourgeois parties included.

"To carry on a war for the overthrow of the international bourgeoisie, a war which is a hundred times more difficult, protracted and complicated than the most stubborn of ordinary wars between states, and to refuse beforehand to manoeuvre, to utilize the conflict of interests (even though temporary) among one's enemies, to refuse to agree and compromise with possible (even though temporary, unstable, vacillating and conditional) allies is not this ridiculous in the extreme?" (Emphasis by author.)

Lenin uses the terms bloc, alliance, agreements, etc., interchangeably throughout his work, in content synonymous with the tactic of the united front, though the latter term had not yet come into common usage. And nowhere does he suggest that the tactic was intended to apply only where there existed rival mass communist and mass reformist parties. In fact, prior to 1917, there were no such mass formations in Russia. Further, even in the early 1920's, after the first spontaneous revolutionary surge in Western Europe failed to conquer power and the Comintern, under the prodding of Lenin and Trotsky, was constrained to sound the call for a temporary retreat, such mass formations existed in only a few countries.

Yet, when the Comintern launched its campaign for application of the united front tactic, it was specifically designated as an "international campaign." For example, in the above mentioned speech by Zinoviev to the Nov. 22, 1922 meeting of the ECCI, he declared: "The United Front was really the first international campaign which the International attempted on a large scale." As such it was to be applied in consonance with the relationship of forces in each country, taking all subjective and objective factors into consideration.

Tactics are always concrete. Or, as Lenin observes in his work on "Left Wing" Communism: "Tactics must be based on a sober and strictly objective appraisal of *all* the class forces of the particular state (and of the states surrounding it, and of all states the world over) as well as of the experience of revolutionary movements." (Emphasis in original.)

So much for Healyite historiography. To return for a moment to our young critic from afar. He is upset no end about the interchangeable application of the terms "coalition, united front and bloc," and what is worse, of "even combining them- 'broad united front type coalition' (!)." (The parenthetical bang is his, not mine.) He considers it highly improper to take such liberties with "traditional" Marxist nomenclature. The word "coalition," we are scolded, is "traditionally" applied exclusively to "coalition politics." Does this mean that we are no longer opposed to coalition politics? Or as he puts it with another of his loaded "questions": "Is it still proper for us to denounce coalition politics?" Off hand, I would say yes, it is. For, if memory serves me, it seems that *The Militant* does just that in almost every issue and no one, to my knowledge, has yet registered an objection.

Where is it written that the word "coalition" must be expunged from our political lexicon unless it applies exclusively to "coalition politics?" Why this ritual genuflection to linguistic dogma? According to my copy of Webster's Collegiate dictionary, the word coalition is defined as, "a temporary alliance for joint action." The same can be said of our "traditional concept," the united front. It seems to me that the word "coalition" as defined by Webster, an acknowledged authority on such matters, is quite appropriate.

I am afraid that our critic suffers from the affliction that Trotsky once diagnosed as "philological scholasticism." What a dismal method, this juggling of words, this twisting and distorting of words, phrases and sentences to laboriously set up spurious straw men to serve as a substitute target for the real thing; this use of the loaded question which is no real question but is designed to absolve the questioner of responsibility for an affirmative statement; etc., etc., etc. And all in the name of "clarity, precision and firmness."

Which of these terms shall we employ in defining our tactic within the antiwar movement? Any and all, either separately or in combination, interchangeably or together, so long as we are certain that our objective appraisal of the phenomenon is correct. The forms it assumes are complex because the movement is unique. There does not exist in this country a mass communist party and a mass reformist party so the so-called "classical" form of the united front tactic obviously does not apply. That is, it is not based on formal agreement between formally constituted organizations, mass or otherwise.

The antiwar formation is composed of diverse organizations, groups and individuals, always shifting, rarely the same, knit together at moments of action in a temporary coalition for a limited objective. After each major action the centrifugal tendency inherent in so heterogeneous a formation threatens to make it fly apart. The cement that holds it together is common opposition to U.S. administration policy in. the Vietnam war. How long it will endure in its present form is anyone's guess.

Neither of the two "major" contending working class tendencies, Stalinism and Trotskyism, are in a position to establish their unchallenged hegemony over the movement. The organized Social Democrats remain outside and hostile. It is this "stalemate" which permits accidental figures with little or no organization following or support to play so prominent a part in the leadership of the movement. What is amazing about this patchwork formation is that it is held together at all. I believe that the SWP-YSA can claim a large part of the credit for this achievement. For despite the meagerness of our forces, our influence has exercised an important and often a decisive role in holding it together. And I speak of our influence not only in the organization but in the political sense, which is testimony to the correctness of our general line, both as regards slogans advanced, single issue character, and thrust toward massive national demonstration actions in the streets.

And so far as tactics are concerned, it is *our* concept of the united front tactic that has prevailed, as against those who sought to narrow and cripple the movement by imposing a programmatic character upon it. For when it comes to *that* question there is no one with whom we can come to agreement outside of a narrow circle of our sympathizers and supporters. The correctness of our line has been abundantly confirmed by experience. There is no reason to alter it in any of its basic essentials- let along throwing it overboard as our philological critic exhorts us to do. And I have not a single doubt that we will have the necessary tactical flexibility to meet whatever exigencies may arise in the future.

PART 2
THE TRANSITIONAL PROGRAM
& HOW TO USE IT

On transitional demands, the United Front and the fight against Fascism.
Daniel Bensaïd

The questions put in the light of the Russian revolution were: how to mobilise the greatest possible numbers; how to raise the level of consciousness through action; and how to create the most effective alliance of forces for the inescapable confrontation with the ruling classes. This is what the Bolsheviks had known how to do in 1917 around the vital questions of bread, peace, land. It was a question of moving beyond abstract discussion of the intrinsic virtue of the claims, whether reformist by nature (because compatible with the established order) or revolutionary by nature (because incompatible with this order). The appropriateness of the demands depends on their mobilising value in connection with a concrete situation, and on their educational value for those who enter into struggle. The concept of 'transitional demands' overcomes sterile antinomies between a reformist gradualism which believes in changing society without revolutionising it, and a fetishism of the 'glorious day' which reduces revolution to its climactic moment, to the detriment of the patient work of organisation and education.*

This debate is directly related to the one at the centre of strategic discussions on the program of the Fifth and the Sixth Congresses of the Communist International. Reporting on the question in 1925, Bukharin reaffirmed the validity of 'the tactics of the offensive' of the beginning of the 1920s. On the other hand, at the Fifth Congress, the German representative Thalheimer supported the idea of the united front and transitional demands. He argued in particular:

"One only has to look at the history of the Second International and its disintegration to recognise that it is precisely the separation between day-to-day questions and broad objectives which constituted the starting point of its descent into opportunism [...] The specific difference between us and the reformist socialists lies not in the fact that we want to eliminate from our program demands for reform, by

---

* This translation first appeared in *100 Years of Permanent Revolution*, edited by Bill Dunn and Hugo Radice, and appears with their kind permission. It is an extract of a longer work, also published by the IIRE, in issue 42/43 of the Notebooks for Study and Research: *Strategies of Resistance: 'Who are the Trotskyists'*, 2009.

whatever name we give them, in order to distance ourselves from them. Rather, it consists in the fact that we locate these transitional demands in the closest relationship to our principles and our aims".

The question was again on the agenda of the Sixth Congress of 1928, under profoundly different conditions. Exiled in Turkey since 1929, Trotsky benefited from his enforced retreat to assess more deeply the previous ten years of revolutionary experiences. This reflection provided the material for the texts on The Communist International after Lenin. In his critique of the program of the CI, published in Constantinople in 1929, Trotsky condemned the abandonment of the slogan of the Socialist United States of Europe. He rejected any confusion between his theory of permanent revolution and Bukharin's theory of the permanent offensive. He again characterised fascism as a 'state of civil war' carried out by capitalism against the proletariat.

Immediately after the Congress, through an about turn which ran in parallel with the policy of liquidation of the kulaks and forced collectivisation in Soviet Union, the CI adopted an orientation of 'class against class'. This made social democracy the principal enemy and produced a fatal division in the German labour movement faced with the rise of the Nazism. In a booklet entitled The Third Period of Error of the Communist International, Trotsky denounced this disastrous course not as a relapse into revolutionary enthusiasm, explicable as youthful leftism, but as a senile and bureaucratic leftism subordinated to the interests of the Kremlin and the zigzags of its diplomacy. In his History of the Russian Revolution, he insisted on the serious study of indices of mass radicalisation (the evolution of trade-union power, electoral results, the strike rate) instead of abstractedly proclaiming the constant possibility of revolutionary action: "the activity of the masses can take very different forms according to conditions. At certain times, the masses can be completely absorbed by economic struggles and express very little interest in political questions. Alternatively, after having undergone several important reverses on the economic front, they can abruptly shift attention onto the political field." His Writings on Germany day-by-day advance proposals for united action to overcome the resistible rise of Nazism. They provide a brilliant example of concrete political thought adjusted to the changes in the economic situation. They were thunderbolts hurled at German Communist Party 'orthodoxy', which was wedded to the stupid prophecy according to which 'after Hitler, comes the turn of Thälmann [then Secretary-General of the German CP]'.

In 1938, the founding Program of the Fourth International (or Transitional Program) summarised the lessons of these experiences:

"In the process of their daily struggle the masses should be helped to find a bridge between their immediate demands and the program of the socialist revolution. This bridge must consist of a system of transitional demands, based on current conditions and the real consciousness of broad layers of the working class, and inexorably leading them towards the single conclusion: the conquest of power by the proletariat [...] The Fourth International does not reject the claims of the old minimum program insofar as they retain some vitality. It tirelessly defends workers' democratic rights and their social achievements. But it undertakes this daily work from the revolutionary point of view."

The program included demands for sliding scales of wages and hours, for workers' control of production (a school for the planned economy) and financial transparency, for "the expropriation of certain groups of capitalists", for the nationalisation of credit. It attached particular importance to democratic and national claims in the colonial and semi-colonial countries. This program did not constitute a ready-made model of society; rather it developed a way of understanding action in which the emancipation of the workers remained the task of workers themselves.

The Fourth International and the Transitional Program.
Michel Pablo

In Germany between 1928 and 1933 the decisive fight developed between the proletariat – organized in two big parties, the Socialist and the Communist – and fascism.* The International Left Opposition, conscious of the historic importance of this struggle, called for a militant policy of United Front between the two parties, from the ranks to the top, aimed toward the seizure of power. The Communist Party, on the contrary, following the Kremlin's directives, applied a sectarian policy that maintained the division in the workers' movement and aggravated its confusion about the danger Hitler represented and about the best means to fight it. Here we are right in the middle of the famous "Third Period".

The International Left Opposition, in a series of important documents that even today retain all their validity, clarified the question of the nature of fascism, the class character of the Social-Democracy, and the United Front. It used all its strength to arouse and spur healthy reactions in the German CP and the Third International, in order to avoid the disaster of a Hitler victory. The German CP, however, as well as the Third International and the Kremlin, remained completely deaf to these appeals.

Hitler's victory in 1933 sealed the fate not only of the German CP, which has never recovered from that wreck, but also of the entire Third International. *In the light of a crucial historical experience these organizations, incapable of any healthy reaction, showed themselves to be incurably bureaucratised.*

The International Left Opposition drew the conclusion that thenceforth it was necessary to work for the construction of new revolutionary Marxist parties and a new International. Thus began a new period in the pre-history of the Fourth International, running from 1933 to 1938, during which the movement for the formation of a new International, the Fourth International, was launched.

Certainly that period was not propitious for rallying great masses around the idea, the program, and the organization of a new

---

* This is part of a lecture on the history, policy, and goals of the Fourth International given at the ILP Summer School in 1958. It was first published as *The 4th International: What it is, What it aims at.*

International. The consequences of the fascist victory in Germany were spreading through the whole workers' movement and the spectre of a new world war was being silhouetted on the horizon.

Furthermore, wherever the masses went over to the revolutionary offensive to block and crush fascism, as in Spain from 1934 to 1939 and in France from 1936 to 1938, the Socialist and Communist leaderships, collaborating with the bourgeois parties in "Popular Fronts," led the movements to failure and defeat. In a general way the 1933-1938 period accentuated the general decline of the international revolutionary movement and witnessed accumulated defeats.

Why then did the International Left Opposition persist in its propaganda and organization of a new International?

In one sense precisely because this evolution of the international workers' movement demonstrated the complete and irremediable bankruptcy of the traditional leaderships and consequently the imperious need for a new leadership. Now for such a goal, once its necessity has been historically proved, a start has to be made. It was necessary to begin seriously to prepare the future, by organizing in a single world party all revolutionary Marxists who were convinced of the correctness of the program that the International Left Opposition had been capable of forging, not artificially, but in the fire of the class struggle, both in the USSR and in the entire world.

It was beginning with the moment when we became sure, by the repeated proof of historic events, of the bankruptcy of the old leaderships, and had ourselves hammered out a complete program, distinct from any other international current in the workers' movement, that we formed a new International.

We are convinced, furthermore, that this program which unites us in one international organization is indeed the program of revolutionary Marxism in our time, basically different from the political behavior of both the Socialists and of the Communist Parties that are lieges of the Kremlin. As for the argument that broad masses were not yet following us, we did not consider it sufficient to postpone the proclamation of what was already a factual reality: our existence as a revolutionary Marxist international organization.

In order to make the masses come to us, we must show them a quite distinct banner, must set them an example, and not wait for the as-it-were spontaneous genesis of new leadership.

Naturally we have no illusions about our possibilities of guiding the action of the class as long as our mass base continues to be as limited as it is. We are today still only the *embryo* of the mass International of tomorrow. It was this reasoning which was also at the origin of the decision taken in September 1938 to proclaim – in spite of everything, at a quite culminating moment of imperialist and Stalinist reaction, and already on the eve of the Second World War – the birth of the Fourth International.

The main political document issued by the Founding Congress of the Fourth International was that called *The Transitional Program*, mainly worked out by Leon Trotsky himself. This program bore clear evidence to the fact that the Fourth International as an organization had arisen from within the living international workers' movement, and that it had the full intention of integrating itself further therein, and not of being either a sect or a general propaganda group. Indeed the *Transitional Program* is resolutely aimed at revolutionary action by the masses on the path to goal of winning power.

The *Transitional Program* aimed at extending a bridge between the objective conditions of capitalism ripe for socialism, and the retarded political consciousness of the masses, influenced by the traditional Socialist and Communist leaderships.

The *Transitional Program* contains a whole series of dialectically interconnected slogans which – starting out from the most immediate economic and political demands of the masses – have as their goal lifting the fight up to the level of the struggle for power, for the Workers' and Peasants' Government, the final stage before the Dictatorship of the Proletariat.

These slogans, far from being arbitrary and "intellectualist", are in fact the result of a thorough analysis of the objective conditions of capitalism in which the day-by-day struggle of the proletariat takes place. They furthermore, take into account the real experience of the international workers' movement in our time, and even – in their form – of the workers' mentality.

The conception of the *Transitional Program* is profoundly revolutionary and dialectical, which fundamentally distinguishes it from the programs of the Socialist or Communist Parties. These parties have a maximum general program which supposedly aims at the establishment of a proletarian power and a socialist society, and also a minimum program which insists upon elementary economic and political demands and reforms within the framework of the capitalist regime. But between these two programs there exists *no bridge*, no link connecting one with the other – the minimum with the maximum – through a chain of dialectically interconnected transitional demands.

In reality both the Socialist and the Communist Parties have *in practice* relegated their *maximum* program to the Greek kalends and recall it only on "great occasions" in order to draw the masses demagogically to their parties. *In practice* they apply only the minimum program within the framework of the capitalist regime. And we know why.

For in reality the Socialist Parties, while still having a working-class base, are led by apparatuses at the service of the regime of bourgeois democracy; while the Communist Parties are led by bureaucratic apparatuses at the service of the Kremlin, i.e., of the political leadership of the Soviet bureaucracy which is the dominant social stratum in the USSR. For this reason the Communist Parties are interested, not above all in promoting the socialist revolution in their respective countries, but in bringing their weight to bear on their national bourgeoisies so that they will apply a foreign policy favorable to the interest of the foreign policy of the Kremlin.

The *Transitional Program*, on the contrary, which reflects the thought and experience of an authentic revolutionary movement, aims really at aiding the highest possible revolutionary activity of the class, while starting out from its most elementary demands.

I must say that in 1938 several of the slogans of the *Transitional Program*, such as the sliding scale of wages to fight inflation, the sliding scale of hours to fight unemployment, workers' control, factory committees, nationalizations under labor control, militias, etc., seemed far from the mentality of the masses. But since these slogans correspond in spite of everything to the objective conditions of capitalism, the masses, educated by their own experience, did not fail, at one moment or another in their struggles, to make them their own. Twenty years later, the *Transitional Program* still has, to a very large extent, a surprising timeliness and youthfulness. This is particularly true of the spirit animating its conception, for it is the only one to guide a vanguard really decided to mobilize the masses for a fight not for *reforms*, but for *revolution* against the capitalist power and regime. It takes a Transitional Program aimed in the same way as that of 1938 effectively to promote such a struggle.

The Death Agony of Capitalism and the Tasks of the Fourth International- The Transitional Program.

Fourth International

The Objective Prerequisites for a Socialist Revolution

The world political situation as a whole is chiefly characterized by a historical crisis of the leadership of the proletariat.[*]

The economic prerequisite for the proletarian revolution has already in general achieved the highest point of fruition that can be reached under capitalism. Mankind's productive forces stagnate. Already new inventions and improvements fail to raise the level of material wealth. Conjunctural crises under the conditions of the social crisis of the whole capitalist system inflict ever heavier deprivations and sufferings upon the masses. Growing unemployment, in its turn, deepens the financial crisis of the state and undermines the unstable monetary systems. Democratic regimes, as well as fascist, stagger on from one bankruptcy to another.

The bourgeoisie itself sees no way out. In countries where it has already been forced to stake its last upon the card of fascism, it now toboggans with closed eyes toward an economic and military catastrophe. In the historically privileged countries, i.e., in those where the bourgeoisie can still for a certain period permit itself the luxury of democracy at the expense of national accumulations (Great Britain, France, United States, etc.), all of capital's traditional parties are in a state of perplexity bordering on a paralysis of will.

The "New Deal," despite its first period of pretentious resoluteness, represents but a special form of political perplexity, possible only in a country where the bourgeoisie succeeded in accumulating incalculable wealth. The present crisis, far from having run its full

---

[*] This resolution has become better known as *The Transitional Program* since its adoption by the founding congress of the Fourth International in 1938. When originally published, in the May-June 1938 edition of *Bulletin of the Opposition*, it was subtitled *The Mobilization of the Masses around Transitional Demands to Prepare the Conquest of Power*.

course, has already succeeded in showing that "New Deal" politics, like Popular Front politics in France, opens no new exit from the economic blind alley.

International relations present no better picture. Under the increasing tension of capitalist disintegration, imperialist antagonisms reach an impasse at the height of which separate clashes and bloody local disturbances (Ethiopia, Spain, the Far East, Central Europe) must inevitably coalesce into a conflagration of world dimensions. The bourgeoisie, of course, is aware of the mortal danger to its domination represented by a new war. But that class is now immeasurably less capable of averting war than on the eve of 1914.

All talk to the effect that historical conditions have not yet "ripened" for socialism is the product of ignorance or conscious deception. The objective prerequisites for the proletarian revolution have not only "ripened"; they have begun to get somewhat rotten. Without a socialist revolution, in the next historical period at that, a catastrophe threatens the whole culture of mankind. The turn is now to the proletariat, i.e., chiefly to its revolutionary vanguard. The historical crisis of mankind is reduced to the crisis of the revolutionary leadership.

The Proletariat and its Leadership

The economy, the state, the politics of the bourgeoisie and its international relations are completely blighted by a social crisis, characteristic of a prerevolutionary state of society. The chief obstacle in the path of transforming the prerevolutionary into a revolutionary state is the opportunist character of proletarian leadership: its petty bourgeois cowardice before the big bourgeoisie and its perfidious connection with it even in its death agony.

In all countries the proletariat is racked by a deep disquiet. The multimillioned masses again and again enter the road of revolution. But each time they are blocked by their own conservative bureaucratic machines.

The Spanish proletariat has made a series of heroic attempts since April 1931 to take power in its hands and guide the fate of society. However, its own parties (Social Democrats, Stalinists, Anarchists, POUMists) – each in its own way acted as a brake and thus prepared Franco's triumphs.

In France, the great wave of "sit down" strikes, particularly during June 1936, revealed the wholehearted readiness of the proletariat to overthrow the capitalist system. However, the leading organizations

(Socialists, Stalinists, Syndicalists) under the label of the Popular Front succeeded in canalizing and damming, at least temporarily, the revolutionary stream.

The unprecedented wave of sit down strikes and the amazingly rapid growth of industrial unionism in the United States (the CIO) is the most indisputable expression of the instinctive striving of the American workers to raise themselves to the level of the tasks imposed on them by history. But here too, the leading political organizations, including the newly created CIO, do everything possible to keep in check and paralyze the revolutionary pressure of the masses.

The definite passing over of the Comintern to the side of bourgeois order, its cynically counterrevolutionary role throughout the world, particularly in Spain, France, the United States and other "democratic" countries, created exceptional supplementary difficulties for the world proletariat. Under the banner of the October Revolution, the conciliatory politics practiced by the "People's Front" doom the working class to impotence and clear the road for fascism.

"People's Fronts" on the one hand – fascism on the other: these are the last political resources of imperialism in the struggle against the proletarian revolution. From the historical point of view, however, both these resources are stopgaps. The decay of capitalism continues under the sign of the Phrygian cap in France as under the sign of the swastika in Germany. Nothing short of the overthrow of the bourgeoisie can open a road out.

The orientation of the masses is determined first by the objective conditions of decaying capitalism, and second, by the treacherous politics of the old workers' organizations. Of these factors, the first, of course, is the decisive one: the laws of history are stronger than the bureaucratic apparatus. No matter how the methods of the social betrayers differ – from the "social" legislation of Blum to the judicial frame-ups of Stalin – they will never succeed in breaking the revolutionary will of the proletariat. As time goes on, their desperate efforts to hold back the wheel of history will demonstrate more clearly to the masses that the crisis of the proletarian leadership, having become the crisis in mankind's culture, can be resolved only by the Fourth International.

The Minimum Program and the Transitional Program

The strategic task of the next period – prerevolutionary period of agitation, propaganda and organization – consists in overcoming the contradiction between the maturity of the objective revolutionary conditions and the immaturity of the proletariat and its vanguard (the confusion and disappointment of the older generation, the inexperience of the younger generation . It is necessary to help the masses in the process of the daily struggle to find the bridge between present demand and the socialist program of the revolution. This bridge should include a system of *transitional demands*, stemming from today's conditions and from today's consciousness of wide layers of the working class and unalterably leading to one final conclusion: the conquest of power by the proletariat.

Classical Social Democracy, functioning in an epoch of progressive capitalism, divided its program into two parts independent of each other: the *minimum program* which limited itself to reforms within the framework of bourgeois society, and the *maximum program* which promised substitution of socialism for capitalism in the indefinite future. Between the minimum and the maximum program no bridge existed. And indeed Social Democracy has no need of such a bridge, since the word *socialism* is used only for holiday speechifying. The Comintern has set out to follow the path of Social Democracy in an epoch of decaying capitalism: when, in general, there can be no discussion of systematic social reforms and the raising of he masses' living standards; when every serious demand of the proletariat and even every serious demand of the petty bourgeoisie inevitably reaches beyond the limits of capitalist property relations and of the bourgeois state.

The strategic task of the Fourth International lies not in reforming capitalism but in its overthrow. Its political aim is the conquest of power by the proletariat for the purpose of expropriating the bourgeoisie. However, the achievement of this strategic task is unthinkable without the most considered attention to all, even small and partial, questions of tactics. All sections of the proletariat, all its layers, occupations and groups should be drawn into the revolutionary movement. The present epoch is distinguished not for the fact that it frees the revolutionary party from day-to-day work but because it permits this work to be carried on indissolubly with the actual tasks of the revolution.

The Fourth International does not discard the program of the old "minimal" demands to the degree to which these have preserved at least part of their vital forcefulness. Indefatigably, it defends the democratic rights and social conquests of the workers. But it carries on this day-to-day work within the framework of the correct actual, that is, revolutionary perspective. Insofar as the old, partial, "minimal" demands of the masses clash with the destructive and degrading tendencies of decadent capitalism – and this occurs at each step – the Fourth International advances a system of *transitional demands*, the essence of which is contained in the fact that ever more openly and decisively they will be directed against the very bases of the bourgeois regime. The old "minimal program" is superseded by the *transitional program*, the task of which lies in systematic mobilization of the masses for the proletarian revolution.

Sliding Scale of Wages and Sliding Scale of Hours

Under the conditions of disintegrating capitalism, the masses continue to live the meagerized life of the oppressed, threatened now more than at any other time with the danger of being cast into the pit of pauperism. They must defend their mouthful of bread, if they cannot increase or better it. There is neither the need nor the opportunity to enumerate here those separate, partial demands which time and again arise on the basis of concrete circumstances – national, local, trade union. But two basic economic afflictions, in which is summarized the increasing absurdity of the capitalist system, that is, *unemployment* and *high prices*, demand generalized slogans and methods of struggle.

The Fourth International declares uncompromising war on the politics of the capitalists which, to a considerable degree, like the politics of their agents, the reformists, aims to place the whole burden of militarism, the crisis, the disorganization of the monetary system and all other scourges stemming from capitalism's death agony upon the backs of the toilers. The Fourth International demands *employment* and *decent living conditions* for all.

Neither monetary inflation nor stabilization can serve as slogans for the proletariat because these are but two ends of the same stick. Against a bounding rise in prices, which with the approach of war will assume an ever more unbridled character, one can fight only under the slogan of a *sliding scale of wages*. This means that collective agreements should assure an automatic rise in wages in relation to the increase in price of consumer goods.

Under the menace of its own disintegration, the proletariat cannot permit the transformation of an increasing section of the workers into chronically unemployed paupers, living off the slops of a crumbling society. The *right to employment* is the only serious right left to the worker in a society based upon exploitation. This right today is left to the worker in a society based upon exploitation. This right today is being shorn from him at every step. Against unemployment, "structural" as well as "conjunctural," the time is ripe to advance along with the slogan of public works, the slogan of a *sliding scale of working hours*. Trade unions and other mass organizations should bind the workers and the unemployed together in the solidarity of mutual responsibility. On this basis all the work on hand would then be divided among all existing workers in accordance with how the extent of the working week is defined. The average wage of every worker remains the same as it was under the old working week. Wages, under a strictly guaranteed *minimum*, would follow the movement of prices. It is impossible to accept any other program for the present catastrophic period.

Property owners and their lawyers will prove the "unrealizability" of these demands. Smaller, especially ruined capitalists, in addition will refer to their account ledgers. The workers categorically denounce such conclusions and references. The question is not one of a "normal" collision between opposing material interests. The question is one of guarding the proletariat from decay, demoralization and ruin. The question is one of life or death of the only creative and progressive class, and by that token of the future of mankind. If capitalism is incapable of satisfying the demands inevitably arising from the calamities generated by itself, then let it perish. "Realizability" or "unrealizability" is in the given instance a question of the relationship of forces, which can be decided only by the struggle. By means of this struggle, no matter what immediate practical successes may be, the workers will best come to understand the necessity of liquidating capitalist slavery.

Trade Unions in the Transitional Epoch

In the struggle for partial and transitional demands, the workers now more than ever before need mass organizations, principally trade unions. The powerful growth of trade unionism in France and the United States is the best refutation of the preachments of those ultra-left doctrinaires who have been teaching that trade unions have "outlived their usefulness."

The Bolshevik-Leninist stands in the front-line trenches of all kinds of struggles, even when they involve only the most modest material interests or democratic rights of the working class. He takes active part in mass trade unions for the purpose of strengthening them and raising their spirit of militancy. He fights uncompromisingly against any attempt to subordinate the unions to the bourgeois state and bind the proletariat to "compulsory arbitration" and every other form of police guardianship – not only fascist but also "democratic." Only on the basis of such work within the trade unions is successful struggle possible against the reformists, including those of the Stalinist bureaucracy. Sectarian attempts to build or preserve small "revolutionary" unions, as a second edition of the party, signify in actuality the renouncing of the struggle for leadership of the working class. It is necessary to establish this firm rule: self-isolation of the capitulationist variety from mass trade unions, which is tantamount to a betrayal of the revolution, is incompatible with membership in the Fourth International.

At the same time, the Fourth International resolutely rejects and condemns trade union fetishism, equally characteristic of trade unionists and syndicalists.

a.   Trade unions do not offer, and in line with their task, composition and manner of recruiting membership, cannot offer a finished revolutionary program; in consequence, they cannot replace the *party*. The building of national revolutionary parties as sections of the Fourth International is the central task of the transitional epoch.

b.   Trade unions, even the most powerful, embrace no more than 20 to 25 percent of the working class, and at that, predominantly the more skilled and better paid layers. The more oppressed majority of the working class is drawn only episodically into the struggle, during a period of exceptional upsurges in the labor movement. During such moments it is necessary to create organizations *ad hoc*, embracing the whole fighting mass: strike committees, factory committees, and finally, soviets.

c.   As organizations expressive of the top layers of the proletariat, trade unions, as witnessed by all past historical experience, including the fresh experience of the anarcho-syndicalist unions in Spain, developed powerful tendencies toward compromise with the bourgeois-democratic regime. In periods of acute class struggle, the leading bodies of the trade unions aim to become masters of the mass movement in order to render it harmless. This is already occurring during the period of simple strikes, especially in the case of the mass sit-down strikes which shake the principle of bourgeois property. In time of war or revolution, when the bourgeoisie is plunged into exceptional difficulties, trade union leaders usually become bourgeois ministers.

Therefore, the sections of the Fourth International should always strive not only to renew the top leadership of the trade unions, boldly and resolutely in critical moments advancing new militant leaders in place of routine functionaries and careerists, but also to create in all possible instances independent militant organizations corresponding more closely to the tasks of mass struggle against bourgeois society; and, if necessary, not flinching even in the face of a direct break with the conservative apparatus of the trade unions. If it be criminal to turn one's back on mass organizations for the sake of fostering sectarian factions, it is no less so passively to tolerate subordination of the revolutionary mass movement to the control of openly reactionary or disguised conservative ("progressive") bureaucratic cliques. Trade unions are not ends in themselves; they are but means along the road to proletarian revolution.

Factory Committees

During a transitional epoch, the workers' movement does not have a systematic and well-balanced, but a feverish and explosive character. Slogans as well as organizational forms should be subordinated to the indices of the movement. On guard against routine handling of a situation as against a plague, the leadership should respond sensitively to the initiative of the masses.

Sit-down strikes, the latest expression of this kind of initiative, go beyond the limits of "normal" capitalist procedure. Independently of the demands of the strikers, the temporary seizure of factories deals a blow to the idol, capitalist property. Every sit-down strike poses in a practical manner the question of who is boss of the factory: the capitalist or the workers?

If the sit-down strike raises this question episodically, the *factory committee* gives it organized expression. Elected by all the factory employees, the factory committee immediately creates a counterweight to the will of the administration.

To the reformist criticism of bosses of the so-called "economic royalist" type like Ford in contradistinction to "good," "democratic" exploiters, we counterpose the slogan of factory committees as centers of struggle against both the first and the second.

Trade union bureaucrats will, as a general rule, resist the creation of factory committees, just as they resist every bold step along the road of mobilizing the masses.

However, the wider the sweep of the movement, the easier will it be to break this resistance. Where the closed shop has already been instituted in "peaceful" times, the committee will formally coincide with the usual organ of the trade union, but will renew its personnel and widen its functions. The prime significance of the committee, however, lies in the fact that it becomes the militant staff for such working class layers, as the trade union is usually incapable of moving to action. It is precisely from these more oppressed layers that the most self-sacrificing battalions of the revolution will come.

From the moment that the committee makes its appearance, a factual dual power is established in the factory. By its very essence it represents the transitional state, because it includes in itself two irreconcilable regimes: the capitalist and the proletarian. The fundamental significance of factory committees is precisely contained in the fact that they open the doors, if not to a direct revolutionary, then to a pre-revolutionary period – between the bourgeois and the proletarian regimes. That the propagation of the factory committee idea is neither premature nor artificial is amply attested to by the waves of sit-down strikes spreading through several countries. New waves of this type will be inevitable in the immediate future. It is necessary to begin a campaign in favor of factory committees in time in order not to be caught unawares.

"Business Secrets" and Workers' Control of Industry

Liberal capitalism, based upon competition and free trade, has completely receded into the past. Its successor, monopolistic capitalism not only does not mitigate the anarchy of the market, but on the contrary imparts to it a particularly convulsive character. The necessity of "controlling" economy, of placing state "guidance" over industry and of "planning" is today recognized – at least in words – by almost all current bourgeois and petty bourgeois tendencies, from fascist to Social Democratic. With the fascists, it is manly a question of "planned" plundering of the people for military purposes. The Social Democrats prepare to drain the ocean of anarchy with spoonfuls of bureaucratic "planning." Engineers and professors write articles about "technocracy." In their cowardly experiments in "regulation," democratic governments run head-on into the invincible sabotage of big capital.

The actual relationship existing between the exploiters and the democratic "controllers" is best characterized by the fact that the gentlemen "reformers" stop short in pious trepidation before the threshold of the trusts and their business "secrets." Here the principle of "non-interference" with business dominates. The accounts kept between the individual capitalist and society remain the secret of the capitalist: they are not the concern of society. The motivation offered for the principle of business "secrets" is ostensibly, as in the epoch of liberal capitalism, that of free competition." In reality, the trusts keep no secrets from one another. The business secrets of the present epoch are part of a persistent plot of monopoly capitalism against the interests of society. Projects for limiting the autocracy of "economic royalists" will continue to be pathetic farces as long as private owners of the social means of production can hide from producers and consumers the machinations of exploitation, robbery and fraud. The abolition of "business secrets" is the first step toward actual control of industry.

Workers no less than capitalists have the right to know the "secrets" of the factory, of the trust, of the whole branch of industry, of the national economy as a whole. First and foremost, banks, heavy industry and centralized transport should be placed under an observation glass.

The immediate tasks of workers' control should be to explain the debits and credits of society, beginning with individual business undertakings; to determine the actual share of the national income appropriated by individual capitalists and by the exploiters as a whole; to expose the behind-the-scenes deals and swindles of banks and trusts; finally, to reveal to all members of society that unconscionable squandering of human labor which is the result of capitalist anarchy and the naked pursuit of profits.

No office holder of the bourgeois state is in a position to carry out this work, no matter with how great authority one would wish to endow him. All the world was witness to the impotence of President Roosevelt and Premier Blum against the plottings of the "60" or "200 Families" of their respective nations. To break the resistance of the exploiters, the mass pressure of the proletariat is necessary. Only factory committees can bring about real control of production, calling in – as consultants but not as "technocrats" – specialists sincerely devoted to the people: accountants, statisticians, engineers, scientists, etc.

The struggle against unemployment is not to be considered without the calling for a broad and bold organization of *public works*. But public works can have a continuous and progressive significance for society, as for the unemployed themselves, only when they are made part of a general plan worked out to cover a considerable number of years. Within the framework of this plan, the workers would demand resumption, as public utilities, of work in private businesses closed as a result of the crisis. Workers' control in such case: would be replaced by direct workers' management.

The working out of even the most elementary economic plan – from the point of view of the exploited, not the exploiters – is impossible without workers' control, that is, without the penetration of the workers' eye into all open and concealed springs of capitalist economy. Committees representing individual business enterprises should meet at conference to choose corresponding committees of trusts, whole branches of industry, economic regions and finally, of national industry as a whole. Thus, workers' control becomes a *school for planned economy*. On the basis of the experience of control, the proletariat will prepare itself for direct management of nationalized industry when the hour for that eventuality strikes.

To those capitalists, mainly of the lower and middle strata, who of their own accord sometimes offer to throw open their books to the workers – usually to demonstrate the necessity of lowering wages – the workers answer that they are not interested in the bookkeeping of individual bankrupts or semi-bankrupts but in the account ledgers of all exploiters as a whole. The workers cannot and do not wish to accommodate the level of their living conditions to the exigencies of individual capitalists, themselves victims of their own regime. The task is one of reorganizing the whole system of production and distribution on a more dignified and workable basis if the abolition of business secrets be a necessary condition to workers' control, then control is the first step along the road to the socialist guidance of economy.

Expropriation of Separate Groups of Capitalists

The socialist program of expropriation, i.e., of political overthrow of the bourgeoisie and liquidation of its economic domination, should in no case during the present transitional period hinder us from advancing, when the occasion warrants, the demand for the expropriation of several key branches of industry vital for national existence or of the most parasitic group of the bourgeoisie.

Thus, in answer to the pathetic jeremiads of the gentlemen democrats anent the dictatorship of the "60 Families" of the United States or the "200 Families" of France, we counterpose the demand for the expropriation of those 60 or 200 feudalistic capitalist overlords.

In precisely the same way, we demand the expropriation of the corporations holding monopolies on war industries, railroads, the most important sources of raw materials, etc.

The difference between these demands and the muddleheaded reformist slogan of "nationalization" lies in the following: (1) we reject indemnification; (2) we warn the masses against demagogues of the People's Front who, giving lip service to nationalization, remain in reality agents of capital; (3) we call upon the masses to rely only upon their own revolutionary strength; (4) we link up the question of expropriation with that of seizure of power by the workers and farmers.

The necessity of advancing the slogan of expropriation in the course of daily *agitation* in partial form, and not only in our propaganda in its more comprehensive aspects, is dictated by the fact that different branches of industry are on different levels of development, occupy a different place in the life of society, and pass through different stages of the class struggle. Only a general revolutionary upsurge of the proletariat can place the complete expropriation of the bourgeoisie on the order of the day. The task of transitional demands is to prepare the proletariat to solve this problem.

Expropriation of the Private Banks and State-ization of the Credit System

Imperialism means the domination of *finance capital*. Side by side with the trusts and syndicates, and very frequently rising above them, the banks concentrate in their hands the actual command over the economy. In their structure the banks express in a concentrated form the entire structure of modern capital: they combine tendencies of *monopoly* with tendencies of *anarchy*. They organize the miracles of technology, giant enterprises, mighty trusts; and they also organize high prices, crises and unemployment. It is impossible to take a single serious step in the struggle against monopolistic despotism and capitalistic anarchy – which supplement one another in their work of destruction – if the commanding posts of banks are left in the hands of predatory capitalists. In order to create a unified system of investments and credits, along a rational plan corresponding to the interests of the entire people, it is necessary to merge all the banks into a single national institution. Only the expropriation of the private banks and the concentration of the entire credit system in the hands of the state will provide the latter with the necessary actual, i.e., material resources – and not merely paper and bureaucratic resources – for economic planning.

The expropriation of the banks in no case implies the expropriation of bank deposits. On the contrary, the single *state bank* will be able to create much more favorable conditions for the small depositors than could the private banks. In the same way, only the state bank can establish for farmers, tradesmen and small merchants conditions of favorable, that is, cheap credit. Even more important, however, is the circumstance that the entire economy – first and foremost large-scale industry and transport directed by a single financial staff, will serve the vital interests of the workers and all other toilers.

However, the *state-ization of the banks* will produce these favorable results only if the state power itself passes completely from the hands of the exploiters into the hands of the toilers.

The Picket Line, Defence Guards/Workers' Militia and the Arming of the Proletariat

Sit-down strikes are a serious warning from the masses addressed not only to the bourgeoisie but also to the organizations of the workers, including the Fourth International. In 1919-20, the Italian workers seized factories on their own initiative, thus signaling the news to their "leaders" of the coming of the social revolution. The "leaders" paid no heed to the signal. The victory of fascism was the result.

Sit down strikes do not yet mean the seizure of factories in the Italian manner, but they are a decisive step toward such seizures. The present crisis can sharpen the class struggle to an extreme point and bring nearer the moment of denouement. But that does not mean that a revolutionary situation comes on at one strokc. Actually, its approach is signalized by a continuous series of convulsions. One of these is the wave of sit-down strikes. The problem of the sections of the Fourth International is to help the proletarian vanguard understand the general character and tempo of our epoch and to fructify in time the struggle of the masses with ever more resolute and organizational measures.

The sharpening of the proletariat's struggle means the sharpening of the methods of counterattack on the part of capital. New waves of sit down strikes can call forth and undoubtedly will call forth resolute countermeasures on the part of the bourgeoisie. Preparatory work is already being done by the confidential staffs of big trusts. Woe to the revolutionary organizations, woe to the proletariat if it is again caught unawares!

The bourgeoisie is nowhere satisfied with the official police and army. In the United States even during "peaceful" times the bourgeoisie maintains militarized battalions of scabs and privately armed thugs in factories. To this must now be added the various groups of American Nazis. The French bourgeoisie at the first approach of danger mobilized semi-legal and illegal fascist detachments, including such as are in the army. No sooner does the pressure of the English workers once again become stronger than immediately the fascist bands are doubled, trebled, increased tenfold to come out in bloody march against the workers. The bourgeoisie keeps itself most accurately informed about the fact that in the present epoch the class struggle irresistibly tends to transform itself into civil war. The examples of Italy, Germany, Austria, Spain and other countries taught considerably more to the magnates and lackeys of capital than to the official leaders of the proletariat.

The politicians of the Second and Third Internationals as well as the bureaucrats of the trade unions, consciously close their eyes to the bourgeoisie's private army; otherwise they could not preserve their alliance with it for even twenty-four hours. The reformists systematically implant in the minds of the workers the notion that the sacredness of democracy is best guaranteed when the bourgeoisie is armed to the teeth and the workers are unarmed.

The duty of the Fourth International is to put an end to such slavish polices once and for all. The petty bourgeois democrats – including Social Democrats, Stalinists and Anarchists – yell louder about the struggle against fascism the more cravenly they capitulate to it in actuality. Only armed workers' detachments, who feel the support of tens of millions of toilers behind them, can successfully prevail against the fascist bands. The struggle against fascism does not start in the liberal editorial office but in the factory – and ends in the street. Scabs and private gunmen in factory plants are the basic nuclei of the fascist army. *Strike pickets* are the basic nuclei of the proletarian army. This is our point of departure. In connection with every strike and street demonstration, it is imperative to propagate the necessity of creating *workers' groups for self-defense*. It is necessary to write this slogan into the program of the revolutionary wing of the trade unions. It is imperative wherever possible, beginning with the youth groups, to organize groups for self-defense, to drill and acquaint them with the use of arms.

A new upsurge of the mass movement should serve not only to increase the number of these units but also to unite them according to neighborhoods, cities, regions. It is necessary to give organized expression to the valid hatred of the workers toward scabs and bands of gangsters and fascists. It is necessary to advance the slogan of a *workers' militia* as the one serious guarantee for the inviolability of workers' organizations, meetings and press.

Only with the help of such systematic, persistent, indefatigable, courageous agitational and organizational work always on the basis of the experience of the masses themselves, is it possible to root out from their consciousness the traditions of submissiveness and passivity; to train detachments of heroic fighters capable of setting an example to all toilers; to inflict a series of tactical defeats upon the armed thugs of counterrevolution; to raise the self-confidence of the exploited and oppressed; to compromise Fascism in the eyes of the petty bourgeoisie and pave the road for the conquest of power by the proletariat.

Engels defined the state as "bodies of armed men." *The arming of the proletariat* is an imperative concomitant element to its struggle for liberation. When the proletariat wills it, it will find the road and the means to arming. In this field, also, else leadership falls naturally to the sections of the Fourth International.

The Alliance of the Workers and Farmers

The brother-in-arms and counterpart of the worker in the country is the agricultural laborer. They are two parts of one and the same class. Their interests are inseparable. The industrial workers' program of transitional demands, with changes here and there, is likewise the program of the agricultural proletariat.

The peasants (farmers) represent another class: they are the petty bourgeoisie of the village. The petty bourgeoisie is made up of various layers, from the semi-proletarian to the exploiter elements. In accordance with this, the political task of the industrial proletariat is to carry the class struggle into the country. Only thus will he be able to draw a dividing line between his allies and his enemies.

The peculiarities of national development of each country find their queerest expression in the status of farmers and, to some extent, of the urban petty bourgeoisie (artisans and shopkeepers). These classes, no matter how numerically strong they may be, essentially are representative survivals of pre-capitalist forms of production. The sections of the Fourth International should work out with all possible concreteness a program of transitional demands concerning the peasants (farmers) and urban petty bourgeoisie, in conformity with the conditions of each country. The advanced workers should learn to give clear and concrete answers to the questions put by their future allies.

While the farmer remains an "independent" petty producer he is in need of cheap credit, of agricultural machines and fertilizer at prices he can afford to pay, favorable conditions of transport, and conscientious organization of the market for his agricultural products. But the banks, the trusts, the merchants rob the farmer from every side. Only the farmers themselves with the help of the workers can curb this robbery. *Committees elected by small farmers* should make their appearance on the national scene and jointly with the workers' committees and committees of bank employees take into their hands control of transport, credit, and mercantile operations affecting agriculture.

By falsely citing the "excessive" demands of the workers the big bourgeoisie skillfully transforms the question of *commodity prices* into a wedge to be driven between the workers and farmers and between the workers and the petty bourgeoisie of the cities. The peasant, artisan, small merchant, unlike the industrial worker, office and civil service employee, cannot demand a wage increase corresponding to the increase in prices. The official struggle of the government with high prices is only a deception of the masses. But the farmers, artisans, merchants, in their capacity of consumers, can step into the politics of price-fixing shoulder to shoulder with the workers. To the capitalist's lamentations about costs of production, of transport and trade, the consumers answer: "Show us your books; we demand control over the fixing of prices." The organs of this control should be the *committees on prices*, made up of delegates from the factories, trade unions, cooperatives, farmers' organizations, the "little man" of the city, housewives, etc. By this means the workers will be able to prove to the farmers that the real reason for high prices is not high wages but the exorbitant profits of the capitalists and the overhead expenses of capitalist anarchy.

The program for the *nationalization of the land and collectivization of agriculture* should be so drawn that from its very basis it should exclude the possibility of expropriation of small farmers and their compulsory collectivization. The farmer will remain owner of his plot of land as long as he himself believes it possible or necessary. In order to rehabilitate the program of socialism in the eyes of the farmer, it is necessary to expose mercilessly the Stalinist methods of collectivization, which are dictated not by the interests of the farmers or workers but by the interests of the bureaucracy.

The expropriation of the expropriators likewise does not signify forcible confiscation of the property of artisans and shopkeepers. On the contrary, workers' control of banks and trusts – even more, the nationalization of these concerns, can create for the urban petty bourgeoisie incomparably more favorable conditions of credit purchase, and sale than is possible under the unchecked domination of the monopolies. Dependence upon private capital will be replaced by dependence upon the state, which will be the more attentive to the needs of its small co-workers and agents the more firmly the toilers themselves keep the state in their own hands .

The practical participation of the exploited farmers in the control of different fields of economy will allow them to decide for themselves whether or not it would be profitable for them to go over to collective working of the land – at what date and on what scale. Industrial workers should consider themselves duty-bound to show farmers every cooperation in traveling this road: through the trade unions, factory committees, and, above all, through a workers' and farmers' government.

The alliance proposed by the proletariat – not to the "middle classes in general but to the exploited layers of the urban and rural petty bourgeoisie, against all exploiters, including those of the "middle classes" – can be based not on compulsion but only on free consent, which should be consolidated in a special "contract." This "contract" is the program of transitional demands voluntarily accepted by both sides.

The Struggle Against Imperialism and War

The whole world outlook, and consequently also the inner political life of individual countries, is overcast by the threat of world war. Already the imminent catastrophe sends violent ripples of apprehension through the very broadest masses of mankind.

The Second International repeats its infamous politics of 1914 with all the greater assurance since today it is the Comintern which plays first fiddle in chauvinism. As quickly as the danger of war assumed concrete outline the Stalinists, outstripping the bourgeois and petty bourgeois pacifists by far, became blatant haranguers for so-called "national defense." The revolutionary struggle against war thus rests fully on the shoulders of the Fourth International.

The Bolshevik-Leninist policy regarding this question, formulated in the thesis of the International Secretariat (*War and the Fourth International*, 1934), preserves all of its force today.

In the next period a revolutionary party will depend for success primarily on its policy on the question of war. A correct policy is composed of two elements: an uncompromising attitude on imperialism and its wars, and the ability to base one's program on the experience of the masses themselves.

The bourgeoisie and its agents use the war question, more than any other, to deceive the people by means of abstractions, general formulas, lame phraseology: "neutrality," "collective defense," "arming for the defense of peace," "struggle against fascism," and so on. All such formulas reduce themselves in the end to the fact that the war question, i.e., the fate of the people, is left in the hands of the imperialists, their governing staffs, their diplomacy, their generals, with all their intrigues and plots against the people.

The Fourth International rejects with abhorrence all such abstractions which play the same role in the democratic camp as in the fascist: "honor," "blood," "race." But abhorrence is not enough. It is imperative to help the masses discern, by means of verifying criteria, slogans and demands, the concrete essence of fraudulent abstractions.

"*Disarmament?*" – But the entire question revolves around who will disarm whom. The only disarmament which can avert or end war is the disarmament of the bourgeoisie by the workers. But to disarm the bourgeoisie, the workers must arm themselves.

"*Neutrality?*" – But the proletariat is nothing like neutral in the war between Japan and China, or a war between Germany and the USSR. "Then what is meant Is the defense of China and the USSR?" Of course! But not by the imperialists who will strangle both China and the USSR.

"*Defense of the Fatherland?*" – But by this abstraction, the bourgeoisie understands the defense of its profits and plunder. We stand ready to defend the fatherland from foreign capitalists, if we first bind our own (capitalists) hand and foot and hinder them from attacking foreign fatherlands; if the workers and the farmers of our country become its real masters, if the wealth of the country be transferred from the hands of a tiny minority to the hands of the people; if the army becomes a weapon of the exploited instead of the exploiters.

It is necessary to interpret these fundamental ideas by breaking them up into more concrete and partial ones, dependent upon the course of events and the orientation of thought of the masses. In addition, it is necessary to differentiate strictly between the pacifism of the diplomat, professor, journalist, and the pacifism of the carpenter, agricultural worker, and the charwoman. In one case, pacifism is a screen for imperialism; in the other, it is the confused expression of distrust in imperialism. When the small farmer or worker speaks about the defense of the fatherland, he means defense of his home, his family and other similar families from invasion, bombs and poison gas. The capitalist and his journalist understand by the defense of the fatherland the seizure of colonies and markets, the predatory increase of the "national" share of world income. Bourgeois pacifism and patriotism are shot through with deceit. In the pacifism and even patriotism of the oppressed, there are elements which reflect on the one hand a hatred of destructive war, and on the other a clinging to what they believe to be their own good – elements which we must know how to seize upon in order to draw the requisite conclusions.

Using these considerations as its point of departure, the Fourth International supports every, even if insufficient, demand, if it can draw the masses to a certain extent into active politics, awaken their criticism and strengthen their control over the machinations of the bourgeoisie.

From this point of view, our American section, for example, entirely supports the proposal for establishing a referendum on the question of declaring war. No democratic reform, it is understood, can by itself prevent the rulers from provoking war when they wish it. It is necessary to give frank warning of this. But notwithstanding the illusions of the masses in regard to the proposed referendum, their support of it reflects the distrust felt by workers and farmers for bourgeois government and Congress. Without supporting and without sparing illusions, it is necessary to support with all possible strength the progressive distrust of the exploited toward the exploiters. The more widespread the movement for the referendum becomes, the sooner will the bourgeois pacifists move away from it; the more completely will the betrayers of the Comintern be compromised; the more acute will distrust of the imperialists become.

From this viewpoint, it is necessary to advance the demand: electoral rights for men and women beginning with age of 18. Those who will be called upon to die for the fatherland tomorrow should have the right to vote today. The struggle against war must first of all begin with the *revolutionary mobilization of the youth*.

Light must be shed upon the problem of war from all angles, hinging upon the side from which it will confront the masses at a given moment.

War is a gigantic commercial enterprise, especially for the war industry. The "60 Families" are therefore first-line patriots and the chief provocateurs of war. *Workers' control of war industries* is the first step in the struggle against the "manufacturers" of war.

To the slogan of the reformists: *a tax on military profit*, we counterpose the slogans: *confiscation of military profit* and *expropriation of the traffickers in war industries*. Where military industry is "nationalized," as in France, the slogan of *workers' control* preserves its full strength. The proletariat has as little confidence in the government of the bourgeoisie as in an individual capitalist

Not one man and not one penny for the bourgeois government!

Not an armaments program but a program of useful public works!

Complete independence of workers' organizations from military-police control!

Once and for all we must tear from the hands of the greedy and merciless imperialist clique, scheming behind the backs of the people, the disposition of the people's fate. In accordance with this, we demand:

- Complete abolition of secret diplomacy;
- all treaties and agreements to be made accessible to all workers and farmers;
- Military training and arming of workers and farmers under direct control of workers' and farmers' committees;
- Creation of military schools for the training of commanders among the toilers, chosen by workers' organizations;
- Substitution for the standing army of a *people's militia*, indissolubly linked up with factories, mines, farms, etc.

Imperialist war is the continuation and sharpening of the predatory politics of the bourgeoisie. The struggle of the proletariat against war is the continuation and sharpening of its class struggle. The beginning of war alters the situation and partially the means of struggle between the classes, but not the aim and basic course. The imperialist bourgeoisie dominates the world. In its basic character the approaching war will therefore be an imperialist war. The fundamental content of the politics of the international proletariat will consequently be a struggle against imperialism and its war. In this struggle the basic principle is: "the chief enemy is in *your own* country" or "the defeat of *your own* (imperialist) government is the lesser evil."

But not all countries of the world are imperialist countries. On the contrary, the majority are victims of imperialism. Some of the colonial or semi colonial countries will undoubtedly attempt to utilize the war in order to east off the yoke of slavery. Their war will be not imperialist but liberating. It will be the duty of the international proletariat to aid the oppressed countries in their war against oppressors. The same duty applies in regard to aiding the USSR, or whatever other workers' government might arise before the war or during the war. The defeat of *every* imperialist government in the struggle with the workers' state or with a colonial country is the lesser evil.

The workers of imperialist countries, however, cannot help an anti-imperialist country through their own government, no matter what might be the diplomatic and military relations between the two countries at a given moment. If the governments find themselves in a temporary and, by the very essence of the matter, unreliable alliance, then the proletariat of the imperialist country continues to remain in class opposition to its own government and supports the non-imperialist "ally" through its *own* methods, i.e., through the methods of the international class struggle (agitation not only against their perfidious allies, but also in favor of a workers' state in a colonial country; boycott, strikes, in one case; rejection of boycott and strikes in another case, etc.)

In supporting the colonial country or the USSR in a war, the proletariat does not in the slightest degree solidarize either with the bourgeois government of the colonial country or with the Thermidorian bureaucracy of the USSR. On the contrary, it maintains full political independence from the one as from the other. Giving aid in a just and progressive war, the revolutionary proletariat wins the sympathy of the workers in the colonies and in the USSR, strengthens there the authority and influence of the Fourth International, and increases its ability to help overthrow the bourgeois government in the colonial country, the reactionary bureaucracy in the USSR.

At the beginning of the war the sections of the Fourth International will inevitably feel themselves isolated: every war takes the national masses unawares and impels them to the side of the government apparatus. The internationalists will have to swim against the stream. However, the devastation and misery brought about by the new war, which in the first months will far outstrip the bloody horrors of 1914-18 will quickly prove sobering. The discontents of the masses and their revolt will grow by leaps and bounds. The sections of the Fourth International will be found at the head of the revolutionary tide. The program of transitional demands will gain burning actuality. The problem of the conquest of power by the proletariat will loom in full stature.

Before exhausting or drowning mankind in blood, capitalism befouls the world atmosphere with the poisonous vapors of national and race hatred. *Anti-Semitism* today is one of the most malignant convulsions of capitalism's death agony.

An uncompromising disclosure of the roots of race prejudice and all forms and shades of national arrogance and chauvinism, particularly anti-Semitism, should become part of the daily work of all sections of the Fourth International, as the most important part of the struggle against imperialism and war. Our basic slogan remains: Workers of the World Unite!

Workers' and Farmers' Government

This formula, "workers' and farmers' government," first appeared in the agitation of the Bolsheviks in 1917 and was definitely accepted after the October Revolution. In the final instance it represented nothing more than the popular designation for the already established dictatorship of the proletariat. The significance of this designation comes mainly from that it underscored the idea of an *alliance between the proletariat and the peasantry* upon which the Soviet power rests.

When the Comintern of the epigones tried to revive the formula buried by history of the "democratic dictatorship of the proletariat and peasantry," it gave to the formula of the "workers' and peasants' government" a completely different, purely "democratic," i.e., bourgeois content, *counterposing* it to the dictatorship of the proletariat. The Bolshevik-Leninists resolutely rejected the slogan of the "workers' and peasants' government" in the bourgeois-democratic version. They affirmed then and affirm now that. when the party of the proletariat refuses to step beyond bourgeois democratic limits, its alliance with the peasantry is simply turned into a support for capital, as was the ease with the Mensheviks and the Social Revolutionaries in 1917, with the Chinese Communist Party in 1925-27, and as is now the ease with the "People's Front" in Spain, France and other countries.

From April to September 1917, the Bolsheviks demanded that the SRs and Mensheviks break with the liberal bourgeoisie and take power into their own hands. Under this provision the Bolshevik Party promised the Mensheviks and the SRs, as the petty bourgeois representatives of the worker and peasants, its revolutionary aid against the bourgeoisie categorically refusing, however, either to enter into the government of the Mensheviks and SRs or to carry political responsibility for it. If the Mensheviks and SRs had actually broke with the Cadets (liberals) and with foreign imperialism, then the "workers' and peasants' government" created by them could only have hastened and facilitated the establishment of the dictatorship of the proletariat. But it was exactly because of this that the leadership of petty bourgeois democracy resisted with all possible strength the establishment of its own government. The experience of Russia demonstrated, and the experience of Spain and France once again confirms, that even under very favorable conditions the parties of petty bourgeois democracy (SRs, Social Democrats, Stalinists, Anarchists) are incapable of creating a government of workers and peasants, that is, a government independent of the bourgeoisie.

Nevertheless, the demand of the Bolsheviks, addressed to the Mensheviks and the SRs: "Break with the bourgeoisie, take the power into your own hands!" had for the masses tremendous educational significance. The obstinate unwillingness of the Mensheviks and SRs to take power, so dramatically exposed during the July Days, definitely doomed them before mass opinion and prepared the victory of the Bolsheviks.

The central task of the Fourth International consists in freeing the proletariat from the old leadership, whose conservatism is in complete contradiction to the catastrophic eruptions of disintegrating capitalism and represents the chief obstacle to historical progress. The chief accusation which the Fourth International advances against the traditional organizations of the proletariat is the fact that they do not wish to tear themselves away from the political semi-corpse of the bourgeoisie. Under these conditions the demand, systematically addressed to the old leadership: "Break with the bourgeoisie, take the power!" is an extremely important weapon for exposing the treacherous character of the parties and organizations of the Second, Third and Amsterdam Internationals. The slogan, "workers' and farmers' government," is thus acceptable to us only in the sense that it had in 1917 with the Bolsheviks, i.e., as an anti-bourgeois and anti-capitalist slogan. but in no case in that "democratic" sense which later the epigones gave it, transforming it from a bridge to Socialist revolution into the chief barrier upon its path.

Of all parties and organizations which base themselves on the workers and peasants and speak in their name, we demand that they break politically from the bourgeoisie and enter upon the road of struggle for the workers' and farmers' government. On this road we promise them full support against capitalist reaction. At the same time, we indefatigably develop agitation around those transitional demands which should in our opinion form the program of the "workers' and farmers' government."

Is the creation of such a government by the traditional workers' organizations possible? Past experience shows, as has already been stated, that this is, to say the least, highly improbable. However, one cannot categorically deny in advance the theoretical possibility that, under the influence of completely exceptional circumstances (war, defeat, financial crash, mass revolutionary pressure, etc.), the petty bourgeois parties, including the Stalinists, may go further than they wish along the road to a break with the bourgeoisie. In any case one thing is not to be doubted: even if this highly improbable variant somewhere at some time becomes a reality and the "workers' and farmers' government" in the above-mentioned sense is established in fact, it would represent merely a short episode on the road to the actual dictatorship of the proletariat.

However, there is no need to indulge in guesswork. The agitation around the slogan of a workers'-farmers' government preserves under all conditions a tremendous educational value. And not accidentally. This generalized slogan proceeds entirely along the line of the political development of our epoch (the bankruptcy and decomposition of the old bourgeois parties, the downfall of democracy, the growth of fascism, the accelerated drive of the workers toward more active and aggressive politics). Each of the transitional demands should, therefore, lead to one and the same political conclusion: the workers need to break with all traditional parties of the bourgeoisie in order, jointly with the farmers, to establish their own power.

It is impossible in advance to foresee what will be the concrete stages of the revolutionary mobilization of the masses. The sections of the Fourth International should critically orient themselves at each new stage and advance such slogans as will aid the striving of the workers for independent politics, deepen the class struggle of these politics, destroy reformist and pacifist illusions, strengthen the connection of the vanguard with the masses, and prepare the revolutionary conquest of power.

Soviets

Factory committees, as already stated, are elements of dual power inside the factory. Consequently, their existence is possible only under conditions of increasing pressure by the masses. This is likewise true of special mass groupings for the struggle *against war*, of the *committees on prices*, and all other new centers of the movement, the very appearance of which bears witness to the fact that the class struggle has overflowed the limits of the traditional organizations of the proletariat.

These new organs and centers, however, will soon begin to feel their lack of cohesion and their insufficiency. Not one of the transitional demands can be fully met under the conditions of preserving the bourgeois regime. At the same time, the deepening of the social crisis will increase not only the sufferings of the masses but also their impatience, persistence and pressure. Ever new layers of the oppressed will raise their heads and come forward with their demands. Millions of toil-worn "little men," to whom the reformist leaders never gave a thought, will begin to pound insistently on the doors of the workers' organizations. The unemployed will join the movement. The agricultural workers, the ruined and semi-ruined farmers, the oppressed of the cities, the women workers, housewives, proletarianized layers of the intelligentsia – all of these will seek unity and leadership.

How are the different demands and forms of struggle to be harmonized, even if only within the limits of one city? History has already answered this question: through *soviets*. These will unite the representatives of all the fighting groups. For this purpose, no one has yet proposed a different form of organization; indeed, it would hardly be possible to think up a better one. Soviets are not limited to an *a priori* party program. They throw open their doors to all the exploited. Through these doors pass representatives of all strata, drawn into the general current of the struggle. The organization, broadening out together with the movement, is renewed again and again in its womb. All political currents of the proletariat can struggle for leadership of the soviets on the basis of the widest democracy. The slogan of *soviets*, therefore, crowns the program of transitional demands.

Soviets can arise only at the time when the mass movement enters into an openly revolutionary stage. From the first moment of their appearance, the soviets, acting as a pivot around which millions of toilers are united in their struggle against the exploiters, become competitors and opponents of local authorities and then of the central government. If the factory committee creates a dual power in the factory, then the soviets initiate a period of dual power in the country.

Dual power in its turn is the culminating point of the transitional period. Two regimes, the bourgeois and the proletarian, are irreconcilably opposed to each other. Conflict between them is inevitable. The fate of society depends on the outcome. Should the revolution be defeated, the fascist dictatorship of the bourgeoisie will follow. In the case of victory, the power of the soviets, that is, the dictatorship of the proletariat and the socialist reconstruction of society will arise.

Backward Countries and the Program of Transitional Demands

Colonial and semi-colonial countries are backward countries by their very essence. But backward countries are part of a world dominated by imperialism. Their development, therefore, has a *combined* character: the most primitive economic forms are combined with the last word in capitalist technique and culture. In like manner are defined the political strivings of the proletariat of backward countries: the struggle for the most elementary achievements of national independence and bourgeois democracy is combined with the socialist struggle against world imperialism. Democratic slogans, transitional demands and the problems of the socialist revolution are not divided into separate historical epochs in this struggle, but stem directly from one another. The Chinese proletariat had barely begun to organize trade unions before it had to provide for soviets. In this sense, the present program is completely applicable to colonial and semi-colonial countries, at least to those where the proletariat has become capable of carrying on independent politics.

The central task of the colonial and semi-colonial countries is the *agrarian revolution*, i.e., liquidation of feudal heritages, and *national independence*, i.e., the overthrow of the imperialist yoke. Both tasks are closely linked with each other.

It is impossible merely to reject the democratic program; it is imperative that in the struggle the masses outgrow it. The slogan for a National (or Constituent) Assembly preserves its full force for such countries as China or India. This slogan must be indissolubly tied up with the problem of national liberation and agrarian reform. As a primary step, the workers must be armed with this democratic program. Only they will be able to summon and unite the farmers. On the basis of the revolutionary democratic program, it is necessary to oppose the workers to the "national" bourgeoisie. Then, at a certain stage in the mobilization of the masses under the slogans of revolutionary democracy, soviets can and should arise. Their historical role in each given period, particularly their relation to the National Assembly, will be determined by the political level of the proletariat, the bond between them and the peasantry, and the character of the proletarian party policies. Sooner or later, the soviets should overthrow bourgeois democracy. Only they are capable of bringing the democratic revolution to a conclusion and likewise opening an era of socialist revolution.

The relative weight of the individual democratic and transitional demands in the proletariat's struggle, their mutual ties and their order of presentation, is determined by the peculiarities and specific conditions of each backward country and to a considerable extent by the *degree* of its backwardness. Nevertheless, the general trend of revolutionary development in all backward countries can be determined by the formula of the permanent revolution in the sense definitely imparted to it by the three revolutions in Russia (1905, February 1917, October 1917).

The Comintern has provided backward countries with a classic example of how it is possible to ruin a powerful and promising revolution. During the stormy mass upsurge in China in 1925-27, the Comintern failed to advance the slogan for a National Assembly, and at the same time forbade the creation of soviets. (The bourgeois party, the Kuomintang, was to replace, according to Stalin's plan, both the National Assembly and soviets.) After the masses had been smashed by the Kuomintang, the Comintern organized a caricature of a soviet in Canton. Following the inevitable collapse of the Canton uprising, the Comintern took the road of guerrilla warfare a peasant soviets with complete passivity on the part of the industrial proletariat. Landing thus in a blind alley, the Comintern took advantage of the Sino-Japanese War to liquidate "Soviet China" with a stroke of the pen, subordinating not only the peasant "Red Army" but also the so-called "Communist" Party to the identical Kuomintang, i.e., the bourgeoisie.

Having betrayed the international proletarian revolution for the sake of friendship with the "democratic" slavemasters, the Comintern could not help betraying simultaneously also the struggle for liberation of the colonial masses, and, indeed, with even greater cynicism than did the Second International before it. One of the tasks of People's Front and "national defense" politics is to turn hundreds of millions of the colonial population into cannon fodder for "democratic" imperialism. The banner on which is emblazoned the struggle for the liberation of the colonial and semi-colonial peoples, i.e., a good half of mankind, has definitely passed into the hands of the Fourth International.

The Program of Transitional Demands in Fascist Countries

It is a far cry today from the time when the strategists of the Comintern announced the victory of Hitler as being merely a step toward the victory of Thaelmann. Thaelmann has been in Hitler's prisons now for more than five years. Mussolini has held Italy enchained by fascism for more than sixteen years. Throughout this time, the parties of the Second and Third Internationals have been impotent, not only to conduct a mass movement, but even to create a serious illegal organization, even to some extent comparable to the Russian revolutionary parties during the epoch of Tsarism.

Not the least reason exists for explaining these failures by reference to the power of fascist ideology. (Essentially, Mussolini never advanced any sort of ideology.) Hitler's "ideology" never seriously gripped the workers. Those layers of the population which at one time were intoxicated with fascism i.e., chiefly the middle classes, have had enough time in which to sober up. The fact that a somewhat perceptible opposition is limited to Protestant and Catholic church circles is not explained by the might of the semi-delirious and semi-charlatan theories of "race" and "blood," but by the terrific collapse of the ideologies of democracy, Social Democracy and the Comintern.

After the massacre of the Paris Commune, black reaction reigned for nearly eight years. After the defeat of the 1905 Russian revolution, the toiling masses remained in a stupor for almost as long a period. But in both instances the phenomenon was only one of physical defeat, conditioned by the relationship of forces. In Russia, in addition, it concerned an almost virgin proletariat. The Bolshevik faction had at that time not celebrated even its third birthday. It is completely otherwise in Germany where the leadership came from powerful parties one of which had existed for seventy years, the other almost fifteen. Both these parties, with millions of voters behind them, were morally paralyzed before the battle and capitulated without a battle. History has recorded no parallel catastrophe. The German proletariat was not smashed by the enemy in battle. It was crushed by the cowardice, baseness, perfidy of its own parties. Small wonder then that it has lost faith in everything in which it had been accustomed to believe for almost three generations. Hitler's victory in turn strengthened Mussolini.

The protracted failure of revolutionary work in Spain or Germany is but the reward for the criminal politics of the Social Democracy and the Comintern. Illegal work needs not only the sympathy of the masses but the conscious enthusiasm of its advanced strata. But can enthusiasm possibly be expected for historically bankrupt organizations? The majority of those who come forth as emigre leaders are either demoralized to the very marrow of their bones, agents of the Kremlin and the GPU, or Social Democratic ex-ministers, who dream that the workers by some sort of miracle will return them to their lost posts. Is it possible to imagine even for a minute these gentlemen in the role of future leaders of the "anti-fascist" revolution?

And events on the world arena – the smashing of the Austrian workers, the defeat of the Spanish Revolution, the degeneration of the Soviet state – could not give aid to a revolutionary upsurge in Italy and Germany. Since for political information the German and Italian workers depend in great measure upon the radio, it is possible to say with assurance that the Moscow radio station, combining Thermidorian lies with stupidity and insolence, has become the most powerful factor in the demoralization of the workers in the totalitarian states. In this respect as in others, Stalin acts merely as Goebbels' assistant.

At the same time, the class antagonisms which brought about the victory of fascism, continuing their work under fascism too, are gradually undermining it. The masses are more dissatisfied than ever. Hundreds and thousands of self-sacrificing workers, in spite of everything, continue to carry on revolutionary mole-work. A new generation, which has nor directly experienced the shattering of old traditions and high hopes, has come to the fore. Irresistibly, the molecular preparation of the proletarian revolution proceeds beneath the heavy totalitarian tombstone. But, for concealed energy to flare into open revolt, it is necessary that the vanguard of the proletariat find new perspectives, a new program and a new unblemished banner.

Herein lies the chief handicap. It is extremely difficult for workers in fascist countries to make a choice of a new program. A program is verified by experience. And it is precisely experience in mass movements which is lacking in countries of totalitarian despotism. It is very likely that a genuine proletarian success in one of the "democratic" countries will be necessary to give impetus to the revolutionary movement on fascist territory. A similar effect is possible by means of a financial or military catastrophe. At present, it is imperative that primarily propagandistic, preparatory work be carried on which will yield large-scale results only in the future. One thing can be stated with conviction even at this point: once it breaks through, the revolutionary wave in fascist countries will immediately be a grandiose sweep and under no circumstances will stop short at the experiment of resuscitating some sort of Weimar corpse.

It is from this point onward that an uncompromising divergence begins between the Fourth International and the old parties, which outlive their bankruptcy. The emigre "People's Front" is the most malignant and perfidious variety of all possible People's Fronts. Essentially, it signifies the impotent longing for coalition with a nonexistent liberal bourgeoisie. Had it met with success, it would simply have prepared a series of new defeats of the Spanish type for the proletariat. A merciless exposure of the theory and practice of the "People's Front" is therefore the first condition for a revolutionary struggle against fascism.

Of course, this does not mean that the Fourth International rejects democratic slogans as a means of mobilizing the masses against fascism. On the contrary, such slogans at certain moments can play a serious role. But the formulae of democracy (freedom of press, the right to unionize, etc.) mean for us only incidental or episodic slogans in the independent movement of the proletariat and not a democratic noose fastened to the neck of the proletariat by the bourgeoisie's agents (Spain!). As soon as the movement assumes something of a mass character, the democratic slogans will be intertwined with the transitional ones; factory committees, it may be supposed, will appear before the old routinists rush from their chancelleries to organize trade unions; soviets will cover Germany before a new Constituent Assembly will gather in Weimar. The same applies to Italy and the rest of the totalitarian and semi-totalitarian countries.

Fascism plunged these countries into political barbarism. But it did not change their social structure. Fascism is a tool in the hands of finance capital and not of feudal landowners. A revolutionary program should base itself on the dialectics of the class struggle, obligatory also to fascist countries, and not on the psychology of terrified bankrupts. The Fourth International rejects with disgust the ways of political masquerade which impelled the Stalinists, the former heroes of the "Third Period," to appear in turn behind the masks of Catholics, Protestants, Jews, German nationalists, liberals – only in order to hide their own unattractive face. The Fourth International always and everywhere appears under its own banner. It proposes its own program openly to the proletariat in fascist countries. The advanced workers of all the world are already firmly convinced that the overthrow of Mussolini, Hitler and their agents and imitators will occur only under the leadership of the Fourth International.

The USSR and Problems of the Transitional Epoch

The Soviet Union emerged from the October Revolution as a workers' state. State ownership of the means of production, a necessary prerequisite to socialist development, opened up the possibility of rapid growth of the productive forces. But the apparatus of the workers' state underwent a complete degeneration at the same time: it was transformed from a weapon of the working class into a weapon of bureaucratic violence against the working class and more and more a weapon for the sabotage of the country's economy. The bureaucratization of a backward and isolated workers' state and the transformation of the bureaucracy into an all-powerful privileged caste constitute the most convincing refutation – not only theoretically, but this time, practically – of the theory of socialism in one country.

The USSR thus embodies terrific contradictions. But it still remains a *degenerated workers' state*. Such is the social diagnosis. The political prognosis has an alternative character: either the bureaucracy, becoming ever more the organ of the world bourgeoisie in the workers' state, will overthrow the new forms of property and plunge the country back to capitalism; or the working class will crush the bureaucracy and open the way to socialism.

To the sections of the Fourth International, the Moscow Trials came not as a surprise and not as a result of the personal madness of the Kremlin dictator, but as the legitimate offspring of the Thermidor. They grew out of the unbearable conflicts within the Soviet bureaucracy itself, which in turn mirror the contradictions between the bureaucracy and the people, as well as the deepening antagonisms among the "people" themselves. The bloody "fantastic" nature of the trials gives the measure of the intensity of the contradictions and by the same token predicts the approach of the denouement.

The public utterances of former foreign representatives of the Kremlin, who refused to return to Moscow, irrefutably confirm in their own way that all shades of political thought are to be found among the bureaucracy: from genuine Bolshevism (Ignace Reiss) to complete fascism (F. Butenko). The revolutionary elements within the bureaucracy, only a small minority, reflect, passively it is true, the socialist interests of the proletariat. The fascist, counterrevolutionary elements, growing uninterruptedly, express with even greater consistency the interests of world imperialism. These candidates for the role of compradors consider, not without reason, that the new ruling layer can insure their positions of privilege only through rejection of nationalization, collectivization and monopoly of foreign trade in the name of the assimilation of "Western civilization." i.e., capitalism. Between these two poles, there are intermediate, diffused Menshevik-SR-liberal tendencies which gravitate toward bourgeois democracy.

Within the very ranks of that so-called "classless" society, there unquestionably exist groupings exactly similar to those in the bureaucracy, only less sharply expressed and in inverse proportions: conscious capitalist tendencies distinguish mainly the prosperous part of the collective farms *(kolkhozi)* and are characteristic of only a small minority of the population. But this layer provides itself with a wide base for petty bourgeois tendencies of accumulating personal wealth at the expense of general poverty, and are consciously encouraged by the bureaucracy.

Atop this system of mounting antagonisms, trespassing ever more on the social equilibrium, the Thermidorian oligarchy, today reduced mainly to Stalin's Bonapartist clique, hangs on by terroristic methods. The latest judicial frame-ups were aimed as a blow *against the left*. This is true also of the mopping up of the leaders of the Right Opposition, because the Right group of the old Bolshevik Party, seen from the view point of the bureaucracy's interests and tendencies, represented a *left* danger. The fact that the Bonapartist clique, likewise in fear of its own right allies of the type of Butenko, is forced in the interests of self-preservation to execute the generation of Old Bolsheviks almost to a man, offers indisputable testimony of the vitality of revolutionary traditions among the masses as well as of their growing discontent.

Petty bourgeois democrats of the West, having but yesterday assayed the Moscow Trials as unalloyed gold, today repeat insistently that there is "neither Trotskyism nor Trotskyists within the USSR." They fail to explain, however, why all the purges are conducted under the banner of a struggle with precisely this danger. If we are to examine "Trotskyism" as a finished program, and, even more to the point, as an organization, then unquestionably "Trotskyism" is extremely weak in the USSR. However, its indestructible force stems from the fact that it expresses not only revolutionary tradition, but also today's actual opposition of the Russian working class. The social hatred stored up by the workers against the bureaucracy – this is precisely what from the viewpoint of the Kremlin clique constitutes "Trotskyism." It fears with a deathly and thoroughly well-grounded fear the bond between the deep but inarticulate indignation of the workers and the organization of the Fourth International.

The extermination of the generation of Old Bolsheviks and of the revolutionary representatives of the middle and young generations has acted to disrupt the political equilibrium still more in favor of the right, bourgeois wing of the bureaucracy and of its allies throughout the land. From them, i.e., from the right, we can expect ever more determined attempts in the next period to revise the socialist character of the USSR and bring it closer in pattern to "Western civilization" in its fascist form.

From this perspective, impelling concreteness is imparted to the question of the "defense of the USSR." If tomorrow the bourgeois-fascist grouping, the "faction of Butenko," so to speak, should attempt the conquest of power, the "faction of Reiss" inevitably would align itself on the opposite side of the barricades. Although it would find itself temporarily the ally of Stalin, it would nevertheless defend not the Bonapartist clique but the social base of the USSR, i.e., the property wrenched away from the capitalists and transformed into state property. Should the "faction of Butenko" prove to be in alliance with Hitler, then the "faction of Reiss" would defend the USSR from military intervention, inside the country as well as on the world arena. Any other course would be a betrayal.

Although it is thus impermissible to deny in advance the possibility, in strictly defined instances, of a "united front" with the Thermidorian section of the bureaucracy against open attack by capitalist counterrevolution, the chief political task in the USSR still remains the *overthrow of this same Thermidorian bureaucracy*. Each day added to its domination helps rot the foundations of the socialist elements of economy and increases the chances for capitalist restoration. It is in precisely this direction that the Comintern moves as the agent and accomplice of the Stalinist clique in strangling the Spanish Revolution and demoralizing the international proletariat.

As in fascist countries, the chief strength of the bureaucracy lies not in itself but in the disillusionment of the masses, in their lack of a new perspective. As in fascist countries, from which Stalin's *political* apparatus does not differ, save in more unbridled savagery, only preparatory propagandistic work is possible today in the USSR. As in fascist countries, the impetus to the Soviet workers' revolutionary upsurge will probably be given by events outside the country. The struggle against the Comintern on the world arena is the most important part today of the struggle against the Stalinist dictatorship. There are many signs that the Comintern's downfall, because it does not have a *direct* base in the GPU, will precede the downfall of the Bonapartist clique and the Thermidorian bureaucracy as a whole.

A fresh upsurge of the revolution in the USSR will undoubtedly begin under the banner of the struggle against *social inequality and political oppression*. Down with the privileges of the bureaucracy! Down with Stakhanovism! Down with the Soviet aristocracy and its ranks and orders! Greater equality of wages for all forms of labor!

The struggle for the freedom of the trade unions and the factory committees, for the right of assembly and freedom of the press, will unfold in the struggle for the regeneration and development of *Soviet democracy*.

The bureaucracy replaced the soviets as class organs with the fiction of universal electoral rights – in the style of Hitler-Goebbels. It is necessary to return to the soviets not only their free democratic form but also their class content. As once the bourgeoisie and kulaks were not permitted to enter the soviets, so now *it is necessary to drive the bureaucracy and the new aristocracy out of the soviets*. In the soviets there is room only for representatives of the workers, rank-and-file collective farmers peasants and Red Army men.

Democratization of the soviets is impossible without legalization of *soviet parties*. The workers and peasants themselves by their own free vote will indicate what parties they recognize as soviet parties.

A revision of *planned economy* from top to bottom in the interests of producers and consumers! Factory committees should be returned the right to control production. A democratically organized consumers' cooperative should control the quality and price of products.

Reorganization of the *collective farms* in accordance with the will and in the interests of the workers there engaged!

The reactionary *international policy* of the bureaucracy should be replaced by the policy of proletarian internationalism. The complete diplomatic correspondence of the Kremlin to be published. *Down with secret diplomacy!*

All political trials, staged by the Thermidorian bureaucracy, to be reviewed in the light of complete publicity and controversial openness and integrity. Only the victorious revolutionary uprising of the oppressed masses can revive the Soviet regime and guarantee its further development toward socialism. There is but one party capable of leading the Soviet masses to insurrection – the party of the Fourth International!

Down with the bureaucratic gang of Cain-Stalin!
Long live Soviet democracy!
Long live the international socialist revolution!

Against Opportunism and Unprincipled Revisionism

The politics of Leon Blum's party in France demonstrate anew that reformists are incapable of learning anything from even the most tragic lessons of history. French Social Democracy slavishly copies the politics of German Social Democracy and goes to meet the same end. Within a few decades the Second International intertwined itself with the bourgeois democratic regime, became, in fact, a part of it, and is rotting away together with it.

The Third International has taken to the road of reformism at a time when the crisis of capitalism definitely placed the proletarian revolution on the order of the day. The Comintern's policy in Spain and China today – the policy of cringing before the "democratic" and "national" bourgeoisie – demonstrates that the Comintern is likewise incapable of learning anything further or of changing. The bureaucracy which became a reactionary force in the USSR cannot play a revolutionary role on the world arena.

Anarcho-syndicalism in general has passed through the same kind of evolution. In France the syndicalist bureaucracy of Leon Jouhaux has long since become a bourgeois agency in the working class. In Spain, anarcho-syndicalism shook off its ostensible revolutionism and became the fifth wheel in the chariot of bourgeois democracy.

Intermediate centrist organizations centered about the London Bureau represent merely "left" appendages of Social Democracy or of the Comintern. They have displayed a complete inability to make head or tail of the political situation and draw revolutionary conclusions from it. Their highest point was the Spanish POUM, which under revolutionary conditions proved completely incapable of following a revolutionary line.

The tragic defeats suffered by the world proletariat over a long period of years doomed the official organizations to yet greater conservatism and simultaneously sent disillusioned petty bourgeois "revolutionists" in pursuit of "new ways." As always during epochs of reaction and decay, quacks and charlatans appear on all sides, desirous of revising the whole course of revolutionary thought. Instead of learning from the past, they "reject" it. Some discover the inconsistency of Marxism, others announce the downfall of Bolshevism. There are those who put responsibility upon revolutionary doctrine for the mistakes and crimes of those who betrayed it; others who curse the medicine because it does not guarantee an instantaneous and miraculous cure. The more daring promise to discover a panacea and, in anticipation, recommend the halting of the class struggle. A good many prophets of "new morals" are preparing to regenerate the labor movement with the help of ethical homeopathy. The majority of these apostles have succeeded in becoming themselves moral invalids before arriving on the field of battle. Thus, under the aspect of "new ways," old recipes, long since buried in the archives of pre-Marxian socialism, are offered to the proletariat.

The Fourth International declares uncompromising war on the bureaucracies of the Second, Third, Amsterdam and Anarcho-syndicalist Internationals, as on their centrist satellites; on reformism without reforms; democracy in alliance with the GPU; pacifism without peace; anarchism in the service of the bourgeoisie; on "revolutionists" who live in deathly fear of revolution. All of these organizations are not pledges for the future, but decayed survivals of the past. The epoch of wars and revolutions will raze them to the ground.

The Fourth International does not search after and does not invent panaceas. It takes its stand completely on Marxism as the only revolutionary doctrine that enables one to understand reality, unearth the cause behind the defeats and consciously prepare for victory. The Fourth International continues the tradition of Bolshevism which first showed the proletariat how to conquer power. The Fourth International sweeps away the quacks, charlatans and unsolicited teachers of morals. In a society based upon exploitation, the highest moral is that of the social revolution. All methods are good which raise the class consciousness of the workers, their trust in their own forces, their readiness for self-sacrifice in the struggle. The impermissible methods are those which implant fear and submissiveness in the oppressed before their oppressors, which crush the spirit of protest and indignation or substitute for the will of the masses – the will of the leaders; for conviction – compulsion; for an analysis of reality – demagogy and frame-up. That is why Social Democracy, prostituting Marxism, and Stalinism – the antithesis of Bolshevism – are both mortal enemies of the proletarian revolution and its morals.

To face reality squarely; not to seek the line of least resistance; to call things by their right names; to speak the truth to the masses, no matter how bitter it may be; not to fear obstacles; to be true in little things as in big ones; to base one's program on the logic of the class struggle; to be bold when the hour for action arrives – these are the rules of the Fourth International. It has shown that it could swim against the stream. The approaching historical wave will raise it on its crest.

Against Sectarianism

Under the influence of the betrayal by the historical organizations of the proletariat, certain sectarian moods and groupings of various kinds arise or are regenerated at the periphery of the Fourth International. At their base lies a refusal to struggle for partial and transitional demands, i.e., for the elementary interests and needs of the working masses, as they are today. Preparing for the revolution means to the sectarians, convincing themselves of the superiority of socialism. They propose turning their backs on the "old" trade unions, i.e., to tens of millions of organized workers – as if the masses could somehow live outside of the conditions of the actual class struggle!

They remain indifferent to the inner struggle within reformist organizations – as if one could win the masses without intervening in their daily strife! They refuse to draw a distinction between the bourgeois democracy and fascism – as if the masses could help but feel the difference on every hand!

Sectarians are capable of differentiating between but two colors: red and black. So as not to tempt themselves, they simplify reality. They refuse to draw a distinction between the fighting camps in Spain for the reason that both camps have a bourgeois character. For the same reason they consider it necessary to preserve "neutrality" in the war between Japan and China. They deny the principled difference between the USSR and the imperialist countries, and because of the reactionary policies of the Soviet bureaucracy they reject defense of the new forms of property, created by the October Revolution, against the onslaughts of imperialism. Incapable of finding access to the masses, they therefore zealously accuse the masses of inability to raise themselves to revolutionary ideas.

These sterile politicians generally have no need of a bridge in the form of transitional demands because they do not intend to cross over to the other shore. They simply dawdle in one place, satisfying themselves with a repetition of the same meager abstractions. Political events are for them an occasion for comment but not for action. Since sectarians as in genera every kind of blunderer and miracle-man, are toppled by reality at each step, they live in a state of perpetual exasperation, complaining about the "regime" and the "methods" and ceaselessly wallowing in small intrigues. In their own circles they customarily carry on a regime of despotism. The political prostration of sectarianism serves to complement, shadow-like, the prostration of opportunism, revealing no revolutionary vistas. In practical politics, sectarians unite with opportunists, particularly with centrists, every time in the struggle against Marxism.

Most of the sectarian groups and cliques, nourished on accidental crumbs from the table of the Fourth International lead an "independent" organizational existence, with great pretensions but without the least chance for success. Bolshevik-Leninists, without waste of time, calmly leave these groups to their own fate. However, sectarian tendencies are to be found also in our own ranks and display a ruinous influence on the work of the individual sections. It is impossible to make any further compromise with them even for a single day. A correct policy regarding trade unions is a basic condition for adherence to the Fourth International. He who does not seek and does not find the road to the masses is not a fighter but a dead weight to the party. A program is formulated not for the editorial board or for the leaders of discussion clubs, but for the revolutionary action of millions. The cleansing of the ranks of the Fourth International of sectarianism and incurable sectarians is a primary condition for revolutionary success.

Open the Road to the Woman Worker! Open the Road to the Youth!

The defeat of the Spanish Revolution engineered by its "leaders," the shameful bankruptcy of the People's Front in France, and the exposure of the Moscow juridical swindles – these three facts in their aggregate deal an irreparable blow to the Comintern and, incidentally, grave wounds to its allies: the Social Democrats and Anarcho-syndicalists. This does not mean, of course, that the members of these organizations will immediately turn to the Fourth International. The older generation, having suffered terrible defeats, will leave the movement in significant numbers. In addition, the Fourth International is certainly not striving to become an asylum for revolutionary invalids, disillusioned bureaucrats and careerists. On the contrary, against a possible influx into our party of petty bourgeois elements, now reigning in the apparatus of the old organizations, strict preventive measures are necessary: a prolonged probationary period for those candidates who are not workers, especially former party bureaucrats: prevention from holding any responsible post for the first three years, etc. There is not and there will not be any place for careerism, the ulcer of the old internationals, in the Fourth International. Only those who wish to live for the movement, and not at the expense of the movement, will find access to us. The revolutionary workers should feel themselves to be the masters. The doors of our organization are wide open to them.

Of course, even among the workers who had at one time risen to the first ranks, there are not a few tired and disillusioned ones. They will remain, at least for the next period as bystanders. When a program or an organization wears out the generation which carried it on its shoulders wears out with it. The movement is revitalized by the youth who are free of responsibility for the past. The Fourth International pays particular attention to the young generation of the proletariat. All of its policies strive to inspire the youth with belief in its own strength and in the future. Only the fresh enthusiasm and aggressive spirit of the youth can guarantee the preliminary successes in the struggle; only these successes can return the best elements of the older generation to the road of revolution. Thus it was thus it will be.

Opportunist organizations by their very nature concentrate their chief attention on the top layers of the working class and therefore ignore both the youth and the women workers. The decay of capitalism, however, deals its heaviest blows to the woman as a wage earner and as a housewife. The sections of the Fourth International should seek bases of support among the most exploited layers of the working class; consequently, among the women workers. Here they will find inexhaustible stores of devotion, selflessness and readiness to sacrifice.

> ***Down with the bureaucracy and careerism!***
> ***Open the road to the youth!***
> ***Turn to the woman worker!***

These slogans are emblazoned on the banner of the Fourth International.

Under the Banner of the Fourth International!

Skeptics ask: But has the moment for the creation of the Fourth International yet arrived? It is impossible, they say, to create an International "artificially"; it can arise only out of great events, etc., etc. All of these objections merely show that skeptics are no good for the building of a new International. They are good for scarcely anything at all.

The Fourth International has already arisen out of great events: the greatest defeats of the proletariat in history. The cause for these defeats is to be found in the degeneration and perfidy of the old leadership. The class struggle does not tolerate an interruption. The Third International, following the Second, is dead for purposes of revolution. Long live the Fourth International!

But has the time yet arrived to proclaim its creation? ... the skeptics are not quieted down. The Fourth International, we answer, has no need of being "proclaimed." It exists and it fights. It is weak? Yes, its ranks are not numerous because it is still young. They are as yet chiefly cadres. But these cadres are pledges for the future. Outside these cadres there does not exist a single revolutionary current on this planet really meriting the name. If our international be still weak in numbers, it is strong in doctrine, program, tradition, in the incomparable tempering of its cadres. Who does not perceive this today, let him in the meantime stand aside. Tomorrow it will become more evident.

The Fourth International, already today, is deservedly hated by the Stalinists, Social Democrats, bourgeois liberals and fascists. There is not and there cannot be a place for it in any of the People's Fronts. It uncompromisingly gives battle to all political groupings tied to the apron-strings of the bourgeoisie. Its task – the abolition of capitalism's domination. Its aim – socialism. Its method – the proletarian revolution.

Without inner democracy – no revolutionary education. Without discipline – no revolutionary action. The inner structure of the Fourth International is based on the principles of *democratic centralism*: full freedom in discussion, complete unity in action.

The present crisis in human culture is the crisis in the proletarian leadership. The advanced workers, united in the Fourth International, show their class the way out of the crisis. They offer a program based on international experience in the struggle of the proletariat and of all the oppressed of the world for liberation. They offer a spotless banner.

Workers – men and women – of all countries, place yourselves under the banner of the Fourth International. It is the banner of your approaching victory!

Discussions with Leon Trotsky on the Transitional Program.

Trotsky: The significance of the program is the significance of the party. The party is the vanguard of the class. The party is formed by selection from the most conscious, most advanced, most devoted elements and the party can play an important historical political role not in direct relation to its numerical strength. It can be a small party and play a great part. For example, in the first Russian Revolution of 1905, the Bolshevik fraction had not more than 10,000 members, the Mensheviks 10,000 to 12,000; that is the maximum. At that time they belonged to the same party, so that the party as a whole had not more than 20,000 to 22,000 workers. The party guided the Soviets throughout the whole country thanks to correct policy and to cohesion. It can be objected that the difference between the Russians and the Americans, or any other old capitalist country, was that the Russian proletariat was a totally fresh, virgin proletariat without any tradition of trade unions, conservative reformism. It was a young fresh virgin working class which needed direction and looked for this direction and in spite of the fact that the party as a whole had not more than 20,000 workers this party guided 23,000,000 workers in the fight.*

Now, what is the party? In what does the cohesion consist? This cohesion is a common understanding of the events, of the tasks, and this common understanding - that is the program of the party. Just as modern workers more than the barbarian cannot work without tools so in the party the program is the instrument. Without the program every worker must improvise his tool, find improvised tools, and one contradicts another.

Only when we have the vanguard organized upon the basis of common conceptions then we can act.

One can say that we didn't have a program until this day. Yet we acted. But this program was formulated under different articles, different motions, etc. In this sense the draft program doesn't presage a new invention, it is not the writing of one man. It is the summation of

---

* This discussion on June 7, 1938 appeared in *Fourth International*, New York, Vol.7 No.2 (Whole No.63), February 1946.

collective work up until today. But such a summation is absolutely necessary in order to give to the comrades an idea of the situation, a common understanding. Petty bourgeois anarchists and intellectuals are afraid to subscribe to giving a party common ideas, a common attitude. In opposition they wish moral programs. But for us this program is the result of common experience. It is not imposed upon anybody for whoever joins the party does so voluntarily.

I believe it is important in this connection to underline what we mean by freedom in contradiction to necessity. It is very often a petty bourgeois conception that we should have a free individuality. It is only a fiction, an error. We are not free. We have no free will in the sense of metaphysical philosophy. When I wish to drink a glass of beer I act as a free man but I don't invent the need for beer. That comes from my body. I am only the executor. But insofar as I understand the needs of my body and can satisfy them consciously then I have the sensation of freedom, freedom through understanding the necessity. Here the correct understanding of the necessity of my body is the only real freedom given to animals in any question and man is an animal. The same holds true for the class. The program for the class cannot fall from heaven. We can arrive only at an understanding of the necessity. In one case it was my body in the other it is the necessity of society. The program is the articulation of the necessity, that we learned to understand, and since the necessity is the same for all members of the class, we can reach a common understanding of the tasks and the understanding of this necessity is the program.

We can go further and say that the discipline of our party must be very severe because we are a revolutionary party against a tremendous bloc of enemies conscious of their interests and now we are attacked not only by the bourgeoisie but by the Stalinists, the most venomous of the bourgeois agents. Absolute discipline is necessary but it must come from common understanding. If it is imposed from without it is a yoke. If it comes from understanding it is an expression of personality, but otherwise it is a yoke. Then discipline is an expression of my free individuality. It is not opposition between personal will and the party because I entered of my free will. The program too is on this basis and this program can be upon a sure political and moral basis only if we understand it very well.

Why Draft Program Is Not Complete

The draft program is not a complete program. We can say that in this draft program there are things which are lacking and there are things which by their nature don't belong to the program. Things which don't belong to the program are the comments. This program contains not only slogans but also comments and polemics against the adversaries. But it is not a complete program. A complete program should have a theoretical expression of the modern capitalist society in its imperialist stage. The reasons of the crisis, the growth of unemployed, and so on and in this draft this analysis is briefly summarized only in the first chapter because we have written about these things in articles, books, and so on. We will write more and better. But for practical purposes what is said here is enough because we are all of the same opinion. The beginning of the program is not complete. The first chapter is only a hint and not a complete expression. Also the end of the program is not complete because we don't speak here about the social revolution, about the seizure of power by insurrection, the transformation of capitalist society into the dictatorship, the dictatorship into the socialist society. This brings the reader only to the doorstep. It is a program for action from today until the beginning of the socialist revolution. And from the practical point of view what is now the most important is how can we guide the different strata of the proletariat in the direction of the social revolution. I have heard that now the New York comrades are beginning to organize circles with the purpose of not only studying and criticizing the draft program but also elaborating the ways and means in order to present the program to the masses and I believe that it is the best method which our party can utilize.

The program is only the first approximation. It is too general in the sense in which it is presented to the international conference in the next period. It expresses the general tendency of development in the whole world. We have here a short chapter devoted to the semi-colonial and colonial countries. We have here a chapter devoted to the fascist countries, a chapter on the Soviet Union and so on. It is clear that the general characteristics of the world situation are common because they are all under the pressure of the imperialist economy, but every country has its peculiar conditions and real live politics must begin with these peculiar conditions in each country and even in each part of the country. That is why a very serious approach to the program is the first duty of every comrade in the United States.

There are two dangers in the elaboration of the program. The first is to remain on general abstract lines and to repeat the general slogan without real connection with the trade unions in the locality. That is the direction of sectarian abstraction. The other danger is the contrary, to adapt too much to the local conditions, to the specific conditions, to lose the general revolutionary line. I believe that in the United States the second danger is the more immediate. I remember it most especially in the matter of militarization, armed pickets, etc. Some comrades were afraid that it is not real for the workers, etc.

In the last few days I read a French book written by an Italian worker about the rise of Fascism in Italy. The writer is opportunistic. He was a Socialist, but it is not his conclusions which are interesting but the facts which he presents. He gives the picture of the Italian proletariat in 1920-1921 especially. It was a powerful organization. They had 160 socialist parliamentary deputies. They had more than one-third of the communities in their hands, the most important sections of Italy were in the hands of the socialists, the center of the power of the workers. No capitalist could hire or fire without union consent and this applied to agricultural workers as well as industrial. It seemed to be 49 percent of the dictatorship of the proletariat, but the reaction of the small bourgeoisie, the demobilized officers was terrible against this situation. Then the author tells how they organized small bands under the guidance of officers and sent them in buses in every direction. In cities of 10,000 in the hands of the Socialists thirty organized men came into the town, burned up the municipality, burned the houses, shot the leaders, imposed on them the conditions of working for capitalists, then they went elsewhere and repeated the same in hundreds and hundreds of towns, one after the other. With terrible terror and these systematic acts the totally destroyed the trade unions and thus became bosses of Italy. They were a tiny minority.

Methods of the Fascists

The workers declared a general strike. The Fascists sent their buses and destroyed every local strike and with a small organized minority wiped out the workers' organizations. After this came elections and the workers under the terror elected the same number of deputies. They protested in parliament until it was dissolved. That is the difference between formal and actual power. All the deputies were sure that they would have power, yet this tremendous movement with its spirit of sacrifice was smashed, crushed, abolished by some 10,000 fascists well-organized with a spirit of sacrifice and good military leaders.

In the United States it might be different but the fundamental tasks are the same. I read about the tactics of Hague [The Major of Jersey

City, New Jersey, in the United States, who functioned, more or less, as a Fascist]. It is a rehearsal of a Fascist overthrow. He represents small bosses who became infuriated because the crisis deepened. He has his gang which is absolutely unconstitutional. This is very, very contagious. With the deepening of the crisis it will spread all over the country and Roosevelt who is a very good democrat will say, "Perhaps it is the only solution."

It was the same in Italy. They had a minister who invited the Socialists. The Socialists refused. He admitted the Fascists. He thought he could balance them against the Socialists, but they smashed the minister too. Now I think the example of New Jersey is very important. We should utilize everything, but this especially. I will propose a special series of articles on how the Fascists became victorious. We can become victorious the same way but we must have a small armed body with the support of the big body of workers. We must have the best discipline, organized workers, defense committees, otherwise we will be crushed and I believe that our comrades in the United States don't realize the importance of this question. A Fascist wave can spread in two or three years and the best workers' leaders will he lynched in the worst possible way like the Negroes in the South. I believe that the terror in the United States will be the most terrible of all. That is why we must begin very modestly that is with defense groups but it should be launched immediately.

Question: How do we go about launching the defense groups practically?

Trotsky: It is very simple. Do you have a picket line in a strike? When the strike is over we say we must defend our union by making this picket line permanent.

Question: Does the party itself create the defense group with its own members?

Trotsky: The slogans of the party must be placed in quarters where we have sympathizers and workers who will defend us. But a party cannot create an independent defense organization. The task is to create such a body in the trade unions. We must have these groups of comrades with very good discipline, with good cautious leaders not easily provoked because such groups can be provoked easily. The main task for the next year would be to avoid conflicts and bloody clashes. We must reduce them to a minimum with a minority organization during strikes, during peaceful times. In order to prevent fascist meetings it is a question of the relationship of forces. We alone are not strong, but we propose a united front.

Hitler explains his success in his book. The Social Democracy was extremely powerful. To a meeting of the Social Democracy he sent a band with Rudolf Hess. He says that at the end of the meeting his thirty boys evicted all the workers and they were incapable of opposing them. Then he knew he would be victorious. The workers were only organized to pay dues. No preparation at all for other tasks. Now we must do what Hitler did except in reverse. Send 40 to 50 men to dissolve the meeting. This has tremendous importance. The workers become steeled, fighting elements. They become trumpets. The petty bourgeoisie think these are serious people. Such a success! This has tremendous importance as so much of the populace is blind, backward, oppressed, they can be aroused only by success. We can only arouse the vanguard but this vanguard must then arouse the others. That is why I repeat it is a very important question. In Minneapolis where we have very skilled powerful comrades we can begin and show the entire country.

I believe that it would be useful to discuss a little this part of the draft which is not sufficiently developed in our text. It is the general theoretical part. In the last discussion I remarked that the theoretical part of the program as a general analysis of society is not given completely in this draft but is replaced by some short hints. On the other side it does not contain the parts dealing with the revolution, the dictatorship of the proletariat, and the construction of society after the revolution: Only the transition period is covered. We have repeated many times that the scientific character of our activity consists in the fact that we adapt our program not to political conjunctures or the thought or mood of the masses as this mood is today, but we adapt our program to the objective situation as it is represented by the economic class structure of society. The mentality can be backward; then the political task of the party is to bring the mentality into harmony with the objective facts, to make the workers understand the objective task. But we cannot adapt the program to the backward mentality of the workers, the mentality, the mood is a secondary factor – the prime factor is the objective situation. That is why we have heard these criticisms or these appreciations that some parts of the program do not conform to the situation.

Our Program Must Fit Objective Situation

Everywhere I ask what should we do? Make our program fit the objective situation or the mentality of the workers? And I believe that this question must be put before every comrade who says that this program is not fit for the American situation. This program is a scientific program. It is based on an objective analysis of the objective situation. It cannot be understood by the workers as a whole. It would be very good if the vanguard would understand it in the next period and that they would then turn and say to the workers, "You must cave yourselves from fascism."

What do we understand by objective situation? Here we must analyze the objective conditions for a social revolution. These conditions are given in the works of Marx-Engels and remain in their essence unchanged today. First, Marx one time said that no one society leaves its place until it totally exhausts its possibilities. What does this signify? That we cannot eliminate a society by subjective will, that we cannot organize an insurrection like the Blanquists. What do "possibilities" signify? That a "society cannot leave?" So long as society is capable of developing the productive forces and making the nation richer it remains strong, stable. That was the condition with slave society, with feudal, and with capitalist society. Here we come to a very interesting point which I analyzed previously in my introduction to the Communist *Manifesto*. Marx and Engels waited for a revolution during their lifetime. Especially in the years 1848-1850 did they expect a social revolution. Why? They said that the capitalist system based on private profit had become a brake upon the development of the productive forces. Was this correct? Yes and no. It was correct in the sense that if the workers had been capable of meeting the needs of the nineteenth century and seizing power, the development of the productive forces would have been more rapid and the nation richer. But given that the workers were not capable, the capitalist system remained with its crisis, etc. Yet the general line ascended. The last war (1914-1918) was a result of the fact that the world market became too narrow for the development of the productive forces and each nation tried to repulse all the others and to seize the world market for its own purposes. They could not succeed and now we see that capitalist society enters into a new stage. Many say it was a result of the war, but the war was a result of the fact that the society exhausted its possibilities. The war was only an expression of its inability to further expand. We have after the war the historic crisis becoming deeper and deeper. Capitalist development everywhere was prosperity and crisis but the summation of the crises and prosperity was an ascendancy. Beginning with the war we see the cycles of crisis and prosperity forming a declining line. It signifies now that this society exhausted totally its inner possibilities and must be replaced by a new society or the old society will go into barbarism just as the civilization of Greece and Rome because they had exhausted their possibilities and no class could replace them.

Three Requisites for New Society

That is the question now and especially in the United States. The first requisite now for a new society is that the productive forces must be sufficiently developed in order to give birth to a higher. Are the productive forces sufficiently developed for this? Yes, they were developed sufficiently in the nineteenth century – not as well as now but sufficiently. Now especially in the United States it would be very easy for a good statistician to prove that if the American productive forces were unleased that even now today they could be doubled or tripled. I believe that our comrades should make such statistical survey.

The second condition – there must be a new progressive class which is sufficiently numerous and economically influential in order to impose its will upon society. This class is the proletariat. It must be the majority of the nation or must have the possibility to lead the majority. In England the working class is the absolute majority. In Russia it was a minority but it had the possibility to lead the poor peasants. In the United States it is at least half of the population but it has the possibility to lead the farmers.

The third condition is the subjective factor. This class must understand its position in society and have its own organizations. That is the condition which is now lacking from the historic point of view. Socially it is not only possible but an absolute necessity in the sense that it is either socialism or barbarism. That is the historical alternative.

We mentioned in the discussion that Mr. Hague is not some stupid old man who imagines some medieval system exists in his town. He is an advance scout of the American capitalist class.

Jack London wrote a book, *The Iron Heel*. I recommend it now. It was written in 1907. At that time it seemed a terrible dream but now it is absolute reality. He gives the development of the class struggle in the United States with the capitalist class retaining power through terrible repressions. It is the picture of Fascism. The ideology he gives even corresponds with Hitler. It is very interesting.

In Newark, the Mayor begins to imitate Hague and they are all inspired by Hague and by the big bosses. It is absolutely certain that Roosevelt will observe that now in the crisis he can do nothing with democratic means. He is not a fascist as the Stalinists claimed in 1932. But his initiative will be paralyzed. What can he do? The workers are dissatisfied. The big bosses are dissatisfied. He can only maneuver until the end of his term and then say goodbye. A third term for Roosevelt is absolutely excluded.

The imitation of the Newark mayor has tremendous importance. In two or three years you can have a powerful fascist movement of American character. What is Hague? He has nothing to do with Mussolini or Hitler, but he is an American fascist. Why is he aroused? Because the society can no longer be run by democratic means.

It would of course be impermissible to fall into hysteria.

The danger of the working class being out-run by events is indisputable, but we can combat this danger only by energetic systematic development of our own activity under adequate revolutionary slogans and not by fantastic efforts to spring over our own heads.

Democracy is only the rule of big bosses. We must understand well what Lundberg showed in his book, that 60 families govern the United States. But how? By democratic means up until today. They are a small minority surrounded by middle classes, the petty bourgeoisie, workers. They must have the possibility of interesting the middle classes in this society. They must not be desperate. The same holds true for the worker. At least for the higher strata. If they are opposed they can break the revolutionary possibilities of the lower strata and this is the only way of working democracy.

"Democratic" Regime Possible Only for Rich Nations

The democratic regime is the most aristocratic way of ruling. It is possible only to a rich nation. Every British democrat has 9 or 10 slaves working in the colonies. The antique Greek society was a slave democracy. The same in a certain sense can be said of British democracy, Holland, France, Belgium. The United States has no direct colonies but they have Latin America and the whole world is a sort of colony for the United States, not to speak about appropriating the richest continent and developing without a feudal tradition. It is a historically privileged nation but the privileged capitalist nations differ from the most "pariah" capitalist nations only from the point of view of delay. Italy, the poorest of the great capitalist nations first became fascist. Germany became second because Germany has no colonies or rich subsidiary countries and on this poor base exhausted all the possibilities and the workers could not replace the bourgeoisie. Now it is the turn of the United States even before Great Britain or France. The duty of our party is to seize every American worker and shake him ten times so he will understand what the situation is in the

United States. That it is not a conjunctural crisis but a social crisis. Our party can play a very great role. What is difficult for a young party in a very thick atmosphere of previous traditions, hypocrisy, is to launch a revolutionary slogan. "It is fantastic," "not adequate in America," but it is possible that this will change by the time you launch the revolutionary slogans of our program. Somebody will laugh. But revolutionary courage is not only to be shot but to support the laughter of stupid people who are in the majority. But when one of them is beaten by Hague's gang he will think it is good to have a defense committee and his ironic attitude will change.

Question: *Isn't the ideology of the workers a part of the objective factors?*

Trotsky: For us as a small minority this whole thing is objective including the mood of the workers. But we must analyze and classify those elements of the objective situation which can be changed by our paper and those which cannot be changed. That is why we say that the program is adapted to the fundamental stable elements of the objective situation and the task is to adapt the mentality of the masses to those objective factors. To adapt the mentality is a pedagogical task. We must be patient, etc. The crisis of society is given as the base of our activity. The mentality is the political arena of our activity. We must change it. We must give a scientific explanation of society, and clearly explain it to the masses. That is the difference between Marxism and reformism.

The reformists have a good smell for what the audience wants as Norman Thomas – he gives them that. But that is not serious revolutionary activity. We must have the courage to be unpopular, to say "you are fools," "you are stupid," "they betray you," and every once in a while with a scandal launch our ideas with passion. It is necessary to shake the worker from time to time, to explain, and then shake him again – that all belongs to the art of propaganda. But it must be scientific, not bent to the moods of the masses. We are the most realistic people because we reckon with facts which cannot be changed by the eloquence of Norman Thomas. If we win immediate success we swim with the current of the masses and that current is the revolution.

Question: *Sometimes I think that our own leaders don't feel these problems.*

Trotsky: Possibly it is two things. One is to understand, the other feel it with muscles, fibers. It is necessary now to be penetrated by this understanding that we must change our politics. It is a question not only for the masses, but for the party. It is a question not only for the party but also for the leaders. We had some discussions, some differences. It is impossible to come to the position at the same time. There are always frictions. They are inevitable and even necessary. It was the reason for this program, to provoke this discussion.

Question: *How much time should we allow for this discussion among the leaders?*

Trotsky: It is very difficult to say. It will depend on many factors. We cannot allow too of a great deal of time. We must now accomplish this new orientation. It is new and old. It is based on all past activity but now it opens a new chapter. In spite of errors, frictions, and fights, now a new chapter opens and we must mobilize all our forces upon it in more energetic attitude. What is important, when the program is definitely established, is to know the slogans very well and to maneuver them skillfully so that in every part of the country everyone uses the same slogans at the same time. 3,000 can make the impression of 15,000 or 50,000.

Question: *Comrades may agree abstractly to this program but do we have experienced comrades to carry out slogans in the masses? They agree abstractly but what can I do with the backward workers in my union?*

Trotsky: Our party is a party of the American working class. You must remember – that a powerful proletarian movement not to speak of a powerful proletarian revolution has not occurred in the United States. In 1917 we didn't have the possibility to win without 1905. My generation was very young. During 12 years we had a very good chance to understand our defeats and correct them and to win. But even then we lost again to the new bureaucrats. That is why we cannot see whether our party will directly lead the American working class to victory. It is possible that the American workers, who are patriotic, whose standard of living is high will have rebellions, strikes. On one side Hague, the other Lewis. That can last for a long period, years and years, and during this time our people will steel themselves, become more sure of themselves, and the workers will say, "They are the only people capable of seeing the path." Only war produces war heroes. For the beginning we have excellent elements, very good men, seriously educated, a good staff, and not a small staff. In this more general sense I am totally optimistic. Then I believe that the change in the mentality of the American workers will come at a very speedy rhythm. What to do? Everybody is disquieted, looking for something new. It is very favorable for revolutionary propaganda.

We must remember not only the aristocratic elements but the poorest elements. The cultivated American workers have a plus and a minus such as English sports. It is very good but also a device to demoralize the workers. All the revolutionary energy was expended in sports. It was cultivated by the British, the most intelligent of the capitalist nations. Sports should be in the hands of the trade unions as a part of the revolutionary education. But you have a good part of the youth and women who are not rich enough for these things. We must have tentacles to penetrate everywhere into the deepest strata.

Question: *I think the party has made a great advance since the last convention.*

Trotsky: A very important turn has been accomplished. Now it is necessary to give this weapon a concentrated action. General dispersed agitation doesn't penetrate into the minds of the uneducated. But if you repeat the same slogans, adapting them to the situation, then repetition which is the mother of teaching will act likewise in politics. Very often it happens not only with the intellectual but with a worker that he believes that everybody understands what he has learned. It is necessary to repeat with insistence, to repeat every day and everywhere. That is the task of the draft program – to issue a homogeneous impression.

A Revolutionary Tool for Modern Times:
A Transitional Program.
Steve Bloom

Many who would call themselves Marxists have probably never heard of it. It is one of the least utilized tools in the arsenal of revolutionaries. Yet the transitional program is, at the same time, one of the most important acquisitions of the Marxist movement in this century.*

What is the transitional program? In its most narrow sense the term refers to a specific document – the original title of which was *The Death Agony of Capitalism and the Tasks of the Fourth International*. It was drafted by Leon Trotsky during his last exile in Mexico and was adopted as the founding program of the FI in 1938. But the concept of a transitional program has a broader meaning as well. That specific document was, in fact, the codification of decades of experience by revolutionary Marxists around the world.

The term "transitional program" also refers to a general method of approaching the class struggle – a method which was first utilized by Marx and Engels in drafting the *Communist Manifesto*, was applied by the Bolsheviks during the course of the Russian revolution and afterward through the early years of the Comintern, and was finally codified at the founding conference of the Fourth International. Since 1938, the parties of the Fourth International have sought to continue applying the general methodology of the transitional program in approaching new developments in the class struggle.

Key Problem

The reason the transitional program is so important is that it addresses the most difficult problem that revolutionaries face in the epoch of transition from capitalism to socialism: How to develop the consciousness of the masses, who are imbued with bourgeois values and assumptions, i.e., who take the current socio-economic system as inevitable in their lives. How do we help to develop their consciousness beyond this, to an understanding of the necessity and possibility of socialist revolution?

---

* This article is based on a talk given by the author in Cleveland Ohio, on August 16, 1985. It was published as Fourth International Tendency pamphlet in February, 1988

Surprisingly, this key problem is rarely considered by those who would like to see the overthrow of capitalism. Most who call themselves revolutionaries act as if the consciousness of the workers and their allies will develop spontaneously, or automatically, and that when this happens the "genuine" Marxists will, as a matter of course, gain their rightful place at the head of the insurrection. Such a view is completely schematic, but its prevalence accounts for the lack of attention paid in most "revolutionary" circles to the problem of a transitional approach.

The transitional method begins with the immediate needs and concerns of the masses, the most obvious and pressing problems, yet does this in a way that helps to show that they are connected to, and a result of, much more fundamental difficulties – the basic structural problems and contradictions that are inherent in the capitalist economic system. Through this process overall class consciousness can be advanced and the idea of the socialist revolution becomes a natural outgrowth of day-to-day struggles.

The *Death Agony of Capitalism* document followed this approach. It contained both a conjunctural analysis of the immediate situation faced by the workers movement internationally in 1938 – with its economic depression, the imminent threat of world war, and fascist dictatorships in a number of developed countries – as well as a set of specific demands and slogans that addressed this situation. Considering the big changes which have taken place in the world between 1938 and today it is remarkable to what extent many of the demands and slogans of this resolution maintain their relevance. Of course much of the conjunctural analysis is now of primarily historical interest, and some of the medium term prognoses were simply wrong. (For example, the war did not lead to socialist revolutions led by mass Fourth Internationalist parties.)

If we look critically at any document from the history of the Marxist movement – and that is the only way to look from the *Communist Manifesto* to the present day, we will discover this same reality. Some parts will be outdated; some parts have turned out to be wrong; while others remain strikingly fresh and alive. The *Death Agony of Capitalism and the Tasks of the Fourth International* took up the world in 1938; we must take it up almost fifty years later.

But the fact that so much of this resolution does maintain its vitality despite the changes in the world since 1938 shows that the demands and slogans of the transitional program really do capture something about the essence of the crisis of capitalism – a crisis which has the same fundamental elements today even though many of the specific symptoms are different. These are not demands dreamed up as a result of divine inspiration, but reflect the real experiences of the class struggle.

Not a rigid text

At the same time, the transitional program cannot be viewed as some rigid set of slogans fixed and determined in 1938 and valid for all times and places. The importance of a particular aspect of the system's crisis may come to the fore at one moment, only to recede in importance later on, or be superseded by some other aspect at a different time. In different parts of the world, a variety of questions and issues are likely to be of primary urgency.

In addition, the contradictions of the capitalist system emerge unevenly. New aspects of reality constantly reveal themselves. The movements of Blacks and other oppressed nationalities in the United States, of youth and women around the world, have all become much more pressing since 1938. The revolutionary movement has had to address itself to these and other new developments.

That's how new slogans and ideas become part of the transitional program. In fact, the Socialist Workers Party in the United States adopted *A Transitional Program for Black Liberation* in 1969, and in the same year the Fourth International adopted a resolution titled *A Strategy for Revolutionary Youth*. These attempted to codify the specific lessons of these struggles and explain how they could contribute to our overall goal of a socialist revolution. (Both of these documents are published as appendices to the third edition of the book, *The Transitional Program for Socialist Revolution*, by Leon Trotsky, 1977, Pathfinder Press. The same book contains the text of *The Death Agony of Capitalism and the Tasks of the Fourth International*, and related material.)

The development of such documents by our movement today would be far more difficult without the dramatic effect which the original codification of the transitional approach in 1938 had on our methodology. This was one of Trotsky's last great contributions before his death. Although a transitional method was inherent in Marxism from its inception, and the Comintern even had a brief discussion of the concept of transitional demands in 1922, it was not something about which revolutionists had been truly conscious. Through the process of drafting the *Death Agony of Capitalism* resolution and the discussions about the program which led up to it, Trotsky helped those who came after him apply a transitional approach in a more systematic, and therefore more effective, manner.

Three kinds of demands

There are three different kinds of demands that make up the transitional program: immediate demands; democratic demands; and transitional demands. Each of them has an important place, and understanding their different but interconnected roles is essential to understanding the transitional program itself.

Immediate demands are those that flow from, and can be formulated spontaneously as a result of, the day-to-day experiences of the masses. Trade union demands for higher wages, or defense of workers rights on the job, are a good example.

Democratic demands reflect the continued fight for basic liberties formally won in this country as a result of the 1776 War of Independence and the Civil War – our two bourgeois democratic revolutions. These are things such as free speech and the right to political organization (which are supposedly guaranteed by the Bill of Rights but which, as we know, we must continually fight to maintain); and the equality of all citizens regardless of race, or nationality (which is again legally recognized but honored more in the breach), or sex (which is not yet even legally recognized in this country).

Finally we have transitional demands proper. These are the slogans which lead directly toward the idea of workers control and a socialist reorganization of society: "Organize a labor party which can run the government in the interests of working people, not the rich!" "Open the books of the corporations which claim they cannot afford to pay decent wages!" "Reduce the workweek with no loss of pay to provide more jobs!" "Organize a massive public-works program to build roads, hospitals, schools and also provide jobs!" "Let the bosses, not the workers, pay for the crisis – raise wages to keep up with the cost of living!" "Nationalize companies that claim they can't continue to operate profitably and turn control of them over to the workers!"

All of these ideas can be presented in a way that seems eminently reasonable to people based on their experiences within the present system. But in reality they require socialism for their *full* implementation. I stress the words full implementation, because there is a common misconception about transitional slogans – that it is impossible for them to be won under capitalism. That isn't true. Struggles of the workers can win aspects of these demands – for example a reduction of the workweek or an escalator clause in a union contract. But the full implementation of a system whereby the necessary social labor is shared equally among all those who need a job and everyone gets her or his fair share of the collective economic product will require a socialist transformation of the economy.

Interrelationship of demands

While it is transitional demands in particular which are the unique contribution of the revolutionary Marxist movement, the transitional method is not reducible to transitional demands alone. What is key is the interaction and interrelationship between the three types of slogans. This, too, is a unique understanding of revolutionary Marxism.

Unlike reformists, we don't see the struggle for immediate and democratic demands as ends in themselves. This doesn't mean that they are unimportant in their own right; they are. But this is not their only or even their primary importance. Revolutionaries try to use struggles for immediate and democratic demands to advance the consciousness and organization of the masses as one part of the broader struggle for socialism. This also differs from the attitude of ultraleft currents, which tend to disdain any struggles which aren't radical enough for their taste.

One good illustration of the interaction of the three kinds of demands which comes from the *Death Agony of Capitalism* document itself is the way it treats the trade union movement and the economic struggles of the working class. It presents a series of ideas, which start from the simple strengthening and defense of the unions and their struggles.

From there it discusses the obvious need to broaden out such struggles in order to gain more power, and of the need for factory committees to wry out a particular battle in a more militant and all-encompassing fashion. From a discussion of the difficulties that will arise in the course of the activity of the factory committee we move on to the need to open the books – to provide that committee with the knowledge it needs to help suggest solutions to the problems faced by the workers it represents.

When the capitalists continue to insist that they cannot apply such solutions and still make a profit, the transitional program raises the idea of expropriation of the capitalists, so the workers – who don't have to worry about profits – can solve the problems themselves. This leads in turn to the need for armed self-defense by the workers so they can protect themselves against the inevitable attacks of the capitalists who will resist such expropriations. The final conclusion is the need for the workers to take over the government, as this will be the final support of the capitalists against the armed workers. We proceed logically from a simple defense of workers rights on the job – i.e., immediate demands - to the conquest of state power.

Method of struggle

A related aspect of the transitional program, which distinguishes a revolutionary Marxist understanding, is our approach to the: methods of struggle that are used even in the fight for immediate and democratic demands. We insist on those methods that educate the masses, that teach them to rely on themselves and on *themselves* alone to resolve their problems.

This is why we are particularly insistent on the question of mass action, of militant pickets and street demonstrations as the best way to make the power of the workers and their allies felt – both by the ruling class and by the masses themselves. This is directly counterposed to the strategy advocated by many in the radical movement who believe that the way to win reforms is by getting Congress to pass some particular piece of legislation. Such forces may organize demonstrations, but it is always and only as an adjunct to their lobbying and legislative efforts.

Our view is the opposite. We aren't opposed to parliamentary initiatives *per se*; getting specific legislation adopted can be of crucial importance at times. But we don't see this as the main vehicle for social change. Legislative initiatives are useful primarily when they serve as an aid to the self-organization of the masses. The fight for the Equal Rights Amendment is a good example. Ratification of the ERA by the state legislatures would have been a big victory. But ratification of the amendment would not have guaranteed equal rights for women, any more than adoption of the Fifteenth Amendment guaranteed equal rights to ex-slaves.

What could begin to win equality for women would be the kind of massive mobilization of women themselves, along with the workers movement and others in this country, that remain necessary to win the ERA – just as it was the mobilization of the Black masses that finally won an end to Jim Crow segregation in the South. This is the main reason why the NOW leadership's pro-Democratic Party, "respectable" campaign for the ERA was such a disaster, It was not just because that campaign failed to gain ratification of the amendment, but primarily because it failed to mobilize the movement that can truly win a measure of equality – whether or not the ERA is formally adopted.

The difference between these two approaches may seem like a subtle one, but understanding it is crucial to understanding the transitional approach. No basic political question has ever been decided by parliamentary means – only by the clash of social forces. One clear illustration of this is the conflict over slavery in this country in the middle of the last century. The "democratic process" expressed itself on this issue through the election of Lincoln as president. The Southern slaveowners knew full well what that election meant, and launched a bloody civil war – the most brutal sort of mass action – to test the real relationship of forces. And it took a victory by the North in the war to actually bring about an end to slavery. The Southern ruling class wasn't willing to accede to any sort of parliamentary process. The same reality holds true for the U.S. ruling class today.

That's why revolutionary Marxists, applying the transitional program, *insist* on methods which don't simply appeal to the good will or morality of this country's rulers. We must understand that any concessions we might win will be forced from them. Our task is to organize struggles which help the workers to understand this as well.

Relevance for today

The relevance of the transitional program for our situation today can be seen if we look at some of the specific pressing problems faced by working people in the U.S. Let's take the question of the trade union movement and the workers fightback. It's easy to see that workers are under attack and that the unions are in crisis. The elementary solution to this is also fairly obvious: a good dose of class solidarity.

But how do we forge this solidarity? This is where the role of conscious revolutionists and other class-struggle militants in the unions comes in. We can find demands in the transitional program which correspond to the present level of consciousness of the workers and begin to raise them in a systematic way. We have already discussed the most important of these: a labor party; escalator clause; shorter workweek with no cut in pay; open the books; organize the unorganized. All of these can be explained in reasonable terms. They may seem outlandish or impractical to many at first, but steady propaganda and education can win ever broader layers to the fight for these goals.

And through that fight we can see how the transitional dynamic will be unleashed. Every working person understands the need for a job at a decent wage. But this idea, perceived as an elementary right, comes squarely into conflict with the basic laws of bourgeois economics – which dictate that capitalism cannot provide a steady job at a living wage for all of its working class. The struggle around this issue begins to break down the illusions of the masses in the benevolence of the bourgeois system – illusions which provide the primary prop by which the bourgeoisie remains in power. This, in turn, leads to a further radicalization and a readiness to fight for more radical demands.

It is important to note here another aspect of the transitional method. We do not approach the masses all at once with the entire program and demand that they accept it completely. We propose only a struggle around those items on which support from large numbers can be mobilized. We pick and choose battles which correspond to the actual consciousness and conditions, and the fight for these leads to more radical conclusions.

We follow a similar method in another area with striking relevance for this country at the present time, the demand: "Let the people vote on war!" Another way of saying the same thing would be, "Let the majority of the population decide on questions of war and peace!" This was a vital issue in 1938 when the *Death Agony* document was drafted, with preparations being made by the imperialist ruling classes for World War II, and it remains so today with the campaign of the Reagan administration in Central America.

We don't ask people in this country to support socialist revolution in Central America (or to be consciously "anti-imperialist") before we will join with them to demand that this government cease its attempt to unilaterally overthrow the FSLN in Nicaragua, or to prop up dictatorial regimes in other Central American countries against the will of the peoples of those countries. We simply ask that they agree with us that every country in Latin America be given the right to determine its own form of government for itself, without interference from the United States – a basic democratic demand.

What happened during the Vietnam war helps make the dynamic of this type of development clear. The campaign we waged in this country against that war was capsulized in the simple slogan "Bring the Troops Home Now!" which was eventually shortened to "Out Now!" This meant two things: first, let the people of Vietnam decide for themselves what kind of government they want without interference from U.S. troops; and second, let the majority of the population of the United States, which doesn't want the war to continue, have the final say over whether or not it does.

The campaign around these elementary democratic ideas were instrumental in the radicalization of an entire generation in the U.S. The massive movement that arose exposed the hypocrisy and cynicism of the U.S. ruling class – its role as the defender of the rich and privileged – far more effectively than revolutionists could ever have done had we been limited to abstract propaganda on the same subject. The experiences of millions in that movement was a giant class struggle school. The danger that the masses might learn their lesson in that school too well was one of the major factors which prompted the decision of the U.S. rulers to disengage from the war, even at the expense of a "Communist takeover" of Indochina.

Today we are faced with a similar challenge and opportunity regarding U.S. policy in Central America, and in South Africa as well. Once again, the basic democratic right of oppressed peoples to self-determination must be stressed in an effort to mobilize the most massive protests against the policies of our own government.

An international program

Vietnam, Central America, and South Africa also point out another aspect of the transitional program – its deep and thoroughgoing internationalism. It is not a program for any specific country, but for the entire world – even though individual aspects of it are aimed at specific regions of the globe. This internationalist perspective is also unique to revolutionary Marxists.

Our fight for the third American revolution is part of a worldwide struggle for socialism. We must be concerned with and help think through every aspect of that worldwide struggle, and understand the relationship between our battles here and those in every other country. In addition to the questions of Central America and South Africa, which are on everyone's mind today, events over the last few years in other countries, like the rise of Solidarnosc in Poland and the British coal miners' strike, have deeply affected the class struggle in the United States. The solidarity, or lack of it, by workers here also affects the outcome of these and similar battles.

The transitional program takes up the problems of the revolution in the advanced capitalist countries, of the political revolution against the Stalinist bureaucracies which have usurped power in the deformed and degenerated workers' states, and of the colonial revolution against imperialist domination. All of these battles, taken together, constitute our worldwide struggle for socialism.

Reformists and sectarians

It should now be obvious why the transitional program is an essential tool for those who want to make a revolution in today's world. And it should not be hard to understand, as a corollary, why revolutionary Marxists are the only ones who have concerned themselves with the development of such a program – both in the sense of a specific document and set of demands, and in the sense of an overall method.

The transitional program has frequently been likened to a bridge between the capitalist present and the socialist future, or between the present consciousness of the working masses and their future revolutionary consciousness. Neither reformists nor sectarians have any need for such a bridge.

Reformists are firmly planted in the present. They don't need a transition to the future because they have no intention of ever going there.

Sectarians, on the other hand, are already – at least in their own minds-living in a period of mass revolutionary consciousness. All that's needed, they seem to think, is for someone with sufficient authority to come along and issue a call to action. That's why they spend much of their time decrying the fact that the present leadership of whatever movement they happen to be interested in hasn't yet issued the demand for a socialist revolution. They seem to think that this would solve the problem.

It is also instructive to look at a specific group of sectarians who do tend to identify with what they call the *Transitional Program*. In fact, they tend to shout long and loud about it. These groups are descended from and try to identify with the Trotskyist current in the working class movement, but they have nothing in common with the methods of Trotsky or the transitional program.

For them the *Transitional Program* is a specific set of ideas written down on paper in 1938. They reject thinking of it as a method with which to approach the class struggle. They refuse to recognize any idea that was not incorporated into the 1938 resolution, and when they look for slogans or ideas within that resolution to apply to the present day, they tend to pick the most extreme possible demands, or ask the workers to swallow the whole thing at one gulp.

**PART 3
UNITED FRONT vs.
POPULAR FRONT**

For Committees of Action, Not the People's Front!
Leon Trotsky

"The People's Front" represents the coalition of the proletariat with the imperialist bourgeoisie, in the shape of the Radical Party and smaller tripe of the same sort. The coalition extends both to the parliamentary and the extra-parliamentary spheres. In both spheres the Radical Party, preserving for itself complete freedom of action, coarsely imposes restrictions upon the freedom of action of the proletariat.*

The Radical Party itself is undergoing decay. Each new election gives added proof of the passage of supporters away from it to the right and to the left. On the other hand, the Socialist and Communist Parties, because of the absence of a genuinely revolutionary party – are growing stronger. The general trend of the toiling masses, including the petty bourgeoisie, is quite clearly to the left. The orientation of the leaders of the workers' parties is no less self evident: *to the right.* At the time when the masses by their votes and their struggle seek to cast off the party of the Radicals, the leaders of the United Front, on the contrary, seek to save it. After obtaining the confidence of the masses of workers on the basis of a "socialist" program, the leaders of the workers' parties then proceeded to concede voluntarily a lion's share of this confidence to the Radicals, in whom the masses of workers have absolutely no confidence.

"The People's Front" in its present guise, shamelessly tramples not only upon workers' democracy but also upon formal, i.e. bourgeois democracy. The majority of the Radical voters do not participate in the struggle of the toilers and consequently in the People's Front. Yet the Radical Party occupies in this front not only an equal but a privileged position; the workers parties are compelled to restrict their activity to the program of the Radical Party. This idea is most outspokenly advanced by the cynics of *l'Humanité*. The latest elections in the Senate have illuminated with special clarity the *privileged* position of the Radicals in the People's Front. The leaders of the Communist Party boasted openly of the fact that they renounced in favour of non-proletarian parties several mandates which justly belonged to the workers. This merely means that the

---

* Written on November 26, 1935, this article appeared in the *New Militant* on December 14th.

united front re-established in part the property qualification in favour of the bourgeoisie.

The "Front", as it is conceived, is an organization for a direct and immediate struggle. When struggle is in question, every worker is worth ten bourgeois, even those adhering to the united front. From the standpoint of the revolutionary fighting strength of the Front, the electoral privileges should have been given not to radical bourgeois but to workers. But in essence, privileges are uncalled for here. Is the People's Front intended for defence of "democracy"? Then let it begin by applying it to its own ranks. This means: *the leadership of the People's Front must be the direct and immediate reflection of the will of the struggling masses.*

How? Very simply: through elections. The proletariat does not deny anyone the right to struggle side by side with it against Fascism, the Bonapartist régime of Laval, the war plot of the imperialists, and all other forms of oppression and violence. The sole demand that class-conscious workers put to their actual or potential allies is that they struggle *in action*. Every group of the population really participating in the struggle at a given stage, and ready to submit to common discipline, must have the equal right to exert influence on the leadership of the People's Front.

Each two hundred, five hundred or thousand citizens adhering in a given city, district, factory, barrack and village to the People's Front, in time of fighting actions, elect their representative to the local committee of action. All the participants in the struggle are bound by its discipline.

The last Congress of the Communist International in its resolution on the Dimitrov report expressed itself in favour of elected Committees of Action as the mass support for the People's Front. This is perhaps the only progressive idea in the entire resolution. But precisely for this reason the Stalinists do nothing to realize it. They dare not do so for fear of breaking off collaboration with the bourgeoisie.

To be sure, in the election of Committees not only workers will be able to participate but also civil service employees, functionaries, war veterans, artisans, small merchants, and small peasants. Thus the Committees of Action are in closest harmony with the tasks of the struggle of the proletariat for influence over the petty bourgeoisie. But they complicate to the extreme the collaboration between the workers' bureaucracy and the bourgeoisie. In the meantime the People's Front in its present form is nothing else than the organization of class collaboration between the political exploiters of the proletariat (the reformists and the Stalinists) and the political exploiters of the petty bourgeoisie (the Radicals). Real mass elections of the Committees of Action would automatically eject the bourgeois middlemen (the Radicals) from the ranks of the People's Front and thus blow to smithereens the criminal policy dictated by Moscow.

However it would be a mistake to think that it is possible at a set day and hour to call the proletarian and petty-bourgeois masses to elect Committees of Action on the basis of a given statute. Such an approach would be purely bureaucratic and consequently barren. The workers will be able to elect a Committee of Action only in those cases when they themselves participate in some sort of action and feel the need for revolutionary leadership. In question here is not the *formal democratic* representation of *all* and *any* masses but the revolutionary representation of the *struggling* masses. The Committee of Action is an apparatus of struggle. There is no sense in guessing beforehand precisely what strata of the toilers will be attracted to the creation of Committees of Action: the lines of demarcation in the struggling masses will be established during the struggle itself.

The greatest danger in France lies in the fact that the revolutionary energy of the masses will be dissipated in spurts, in isolated explosions like Toulon, Brest and Limoges, and give way to apathy. Only conscious traitors or hopeless muddle-heads are capable of thinking that in the present situation it is possible to hold the masses immobilized up to the moment when they will be blessed from above by the government of the People's Front. Strikes, protests, street clashes, direct uprisings are absolutely inevitable in the present situation. The task of the proletarian party consists not in checking and paralysing these movements but in unifying them and investing them with the greatest possible force.

The reformists and Stalinists fear, above all, to frighten the Radicals. The apparatus of the united front quite consciously plays the role of disorganizer in relation to sporadic movements of the masses. And the "lefts" of the Marceau Pivert type serve to shield this apparatus from the indignation of the masses. The situation can be saved only by aiding the struggling masses to create a new apparatus, in the process of the struggle itself, which meets the requirements of the moment. The Committees of Action are intended for this very purpose. During the struggle in Toulon and Brest, the workers would have created without any hesitation a local fighting organization had they been called upon to do so. On the very next day after the bloody assault in Limoges, the workers and a considerable section of the petty bourgeoisie would have indubitably revealed their readiness to create an elected committee to investigate the bloody events and to prevent them in the future. During the movement in the barracks, in the summer of this year, against Rabiot (the extension of the term of military service), the soldiers, without much ado, would have elected battalion, regimental and garrison committees of action had such a road been suggested to them. Similar situations arise and will continue to arise at every step. In most cases on a local but, often, also on a national scale. The task is not to miss a single situation of this kind. The first condition for this is a clear understanding of the import of the Committee of Action *as the only means of breaking the anti-revolutionary opposition of party and trade-union apparatus.*

Does this mean to say that the Committees of Action are substitutes for party and trade-union organizations? It would be stupid to pose the question in this manner. The masses enter into the struggle with all their ideas, traditions, groupings and organizations. The parties continue to exist and to struggle. During elections to the Committees of Action each party will naturally seek to elect its own adherents. The Committees of Action will arrive at decisions through a majority (given complete freedom of party and factional groupings). In relation to parties, the Committees of Action may be called the *revolutionary parliament*: the parties are not excluded but on the contrary they are necessarily presupposed; at the same time they are tested in action and the masses learn to free themselves from the influence of rotten parties.

Does this mean, then, that the Committees of Action are simply – *soviets*? Under certain conditions the Committees of Action can transform themselves into soviets. However, it would be incorrect to call the Committees of Action by this name. Today, in 1935, the popular masses have become accustomed to associate with the word soviets the conception of power already conquered; but France today is still considerably removed from this. The Russian soviets during their initial stages were not at all what they subsequently became and in those days they were often called by the modest name of workers' or strike committees. Committees of Action at their present stage have as their task to unite in a defensive struggle the toiling masses of France and thus imbue these masses with the consciousness of their own power for the coming offensive. Whether matters will reach genuine soviets depends on whether the present critical situation in France will unfold to the ultimate revolutionary conclusions. This of course depends not only upon the will of the revolutionary vanguard but also upon a number of objective conditions; in any case the mass movement, that has today run up against the barrier of the People's Front, will be unable to move forward without the Committees of Action.

Such tasks as the creation of *workers' militia, the arming of the workers*, the preparation of a *general strike*, will remain on paper if the struggling masses themselves, through their authoritative organs, do not occupy themselves with these tasks. Only Committees of Action born in the struggle can assure a real militia numbering fighters not by the thousand but the tens of thousands. Only Committees of Action embracing the most important centres of the country will be able to choose the moment for transition to more decisive methods of struggle, the leadership of which will be rightly theirs.

* * *

From the propositions sketched above there flows a number of conclusions for the political activity of the proletarian revolutionists in France. The cardinal conclusion touches upon the so-called "revolutionary (?) left". This grouping is characterized by a complete lack of understanding of the laws that govern the movement of the revolutionary masses. No matter how much the centrists babble about the "masses" they always orient themselves upon the reformist apparatus. Repeating this or that revolutionary slogan, Marceau Pivert subordinates it to the abstract principle of "organizational unity" which in action turns out to be unity with the patriots against the revolutionists. At the time when it is a life and death question for the masses to *smash* the opposition of the united social-patriotic apparatuses as an absolute "good" which stands above the interests of revolutionary struggle.

Committees of Action will be built only by those who understand, to the end, the necessity of *freeing the masses from the treacherous leadership of the social-patriots*. Yet Pivert clutches at Zyromsky, who clutches at Blum, who in turn, together with Thorez, clutches at Herriot, who clutches at Laval. Pivert enters into the system of the People's Front (not for nothing did he vote for the shameful resolution of Blum at the last National Council meeting!) and the People's Front enters as a wing into the Bonapartist régime of Laval. The downfall of the Bonapartist régime is inevitable. Should the leadership of the People's Front (Herriot-Blum-Cachin-Thorez-Zyromsky-Pivert) succeed in remaining on its feet in the course of the entire approaching and decisive period, then the Bonapartist régime will inevitably give way to Fascism. The condition for the victory of the proletariat is the *liquidation of the present leadership*. The slogan of "unity" becomes under these conditions not only a stupidity but a crime. *No unity with the agents of French imperialism and of the League of nations*. To their perfidious leadership it is necessary to counterpose revolutionary Committees of Action. It is possible to build these committees only by mercilessly exposing the anti-revolutionary policies of the so-called "revolutionary left" with Marceau Pivert at the head. There is of course no room in our ranks for illusions and doubts on this score.

The People's Front: The New Betrayal.
James Burnham

I. Origin and Theory of the Peoples' Front

THE slogans of the Peoples' Front were first advanced by the Communist International and its sections. They began to appear toward the end of 1933; moved forward slowly for some while; and received official sanction and theoretical expression at the Seventh Congress of the Communist International held during the summer of 1935. From then on they spread out at a headlong pace, and now present themselves as the key question of proletarian strategy throughout the world.[*]

For some time these policies and slogans met with frantic resistance from those outside of the ranks of the Comintern and its sympathizers. This resistance, however, was largely based on a misunderstanding. Reformists and social-patriots could not at first convince themselves of the Comintern's "sincerity." They thought still in terms of the preceding strategy of the Comintern, the strategy of the so-called "Third Period." Their minds were filled with memories of "social-fascism," "united front from below," and dual "red unions." But the resistance was steadily overcome. The Comintern no longer even mentioned social fascism; the united front from below went into the discard; the red unions were liquidated.

And, one after another, the reformist parties went over to the slogans of the Peoples' Front. In France the Peoples' Front was formally established; soon afterwards, in Spain. Throughout the world it made headway in giant strides. Soon liberals and progressives" began to come over, in addition to the reformists and social-patriots. In this country, for example, *The Nation* and *The New Republic*, the leading liberal periodicals, became wholehearted Peoples' Fronters. By now, within the labor movement, and among the social groups sympathetic to the labor movement, only one firm opposition to the Peoples' Front remains the opposition, namely, of the revolutionary socialists.

---

[*] These are the first two chapters of *The People's Front: The New Betrayal*, by James Burnham, Pioneer Publishers, New York, 1937.

The Peoples' Front movement began under certain special international conditions, and it is necessary to review these, at least briefly.

First: The series of defeats of the working class, following the post-war revolutionary wave, had reached a climax in the triumph of Hitler. Hitler came to power without a blow struck against him by either of the great mass working-class parties of Germany Fascism seemed irresistibly on the ascendant.

Second: The threat of the new imperialist war, enhanced by the victory of Hitler, was growing ever more menacing.

Third: Within the Soviet Union itself, where the Peoples' Front has its origin, great changes have been taking place during these years since 1933. The First Five Year Plan, with its forced and ruthlessly carried through collectivization of the peasantry, and its almost exclusive emphasis on the building up of heavy industry, gave way to the Second Five Year Plan. Among the important characteristics of the new Plan, we find more emphasis on "consumers goods" as against heavy industry; conciliation of the peasantry; the introduction of Stakhanovism, with its stimulus to increased differentiation of wages and salaries, leading to the rise of a labor aristocracy economically far removed from the mass of the workers; abolition of the special economic and social privileges of the urban proletariat All of these and a multitude of other similar changes are most strikingly summed up in the New Constitution, adopted in November, 1936, which puts the legal finish to the Soviet foundation of political power in favor of a plebiscite form of parliamentarism.

Fourth: During these years the "Litvinov period" of Soviet diplomacy reached its climax. The Soviet Union entered the League of Nations; and its series of treaties and alliances found culmination in the signing of the Franco-Soviet Pact of military assistance.

As I shall show later on, these four major features of the recent past provide a background necessary to any understanding of the policy of the Peoples' Front.

The most authoritative statements on the theory and justification of the Peoples' Front are contained in the speeches of Dimitroff, new Secretary of the Comintern, to the Seventh Congress; and in a short book, *The Work of the Seventh Congress*, written by the Comintern theoretician, Manuilsky. I shall, therefore, base my presentation of the theory of the Peoples' Front on these works.

We begin, then, with an alleged "analysis" of the nature of the present historical period. In this period, according to these new oracles of the

Stalinist Delphi, "the main danger is Fascism"—from whence the Peoples' Front is ordinarily known as the "anti-fascist" Peoples' Front. The Seventh Congress, Manuilsky remarks on page 16, "turned its fire mainly against fascism." But, it seems, there are many varieties of fascism, "good" and "bad" fascisms. And much the worst kind of fascism is German fascism, Nazism. Dimitroff explains: "The most reactionary variety of fascism is the *German type* of fascism... . German fascism is acting as *the spearhead of international counter-revolution, as the chief incendiary of imperialist war, as the initiator of a crusade against the Soviet Union, the great fatherland of the toilers of the whole world."* (The italics are all Dimitroff's.)

Now fascism, we are told, threatens not only the working class, but also the peasantry, the middle classes generally, and even certain sections of the bourgeoisie, especially the "small business man." Indeed, fascism in actuality is nothing else than a plot or conspiracy on the party of a small and vicious clique among the ruling class ("the two hundred families," as the clique is known in France, from the fact that two hundred large stockholders guide the destiny of the Bank of France). Let us hear again from Dimitroff: "... fascism in power is *the open terrorist dictatorship of the most reactionary, most chauvinistic and most imperialist elements of finance capital. ...* Fascism acts in the interests of the extreme imperialists... . It is in the interests of the most reactionary circles of the bourgeoisie that fascism intercepts the disappointed masses as they leave the old bourgeois parties." Manuilsky repeats virtually the same words, though adding a psychological adjective of his own: "... fascism is the open and cynical form of the dictatorship of the most reactionary, most chauvinist, most imperialist [this matter of "degrees" of imperialism is a most subtle point] elements of finance capital."

It is, moreover, fascism that makes war. Manuilsky: "The growing menace of world imperialist war is causing all class, national and state forces to separate into two camps: *the camp of war and the camp of peace* . The *center of the forces* which are operating to bring about war, to accelerate its outbreak, is *fascism."* This idea has been repeated and reinforced until it is now a Stalinist commonplace.

From these various premises, it follows, according to the Comintern logic, that the struggle for the proletarian dictatorship and for socialism is in the present period definitely removed from the agenda. "The situation is different today," writes Manuilsky. "Today, the proletariat in most capitalist countries are not confronted with the alternative of bourgeois democracy or proletarian democracy; they are confronted with the alternative of bourgeois democracy or fascism." Dimitroff amplifies: "Our attitude towards bourgeois democracy is not the same under all conditions. For instance, at the time of the October Revolution, the Russian Bolsheviks engaged in a life-and-death .struggle against all political parties which opposed the establishment of the proletarian dictatorship under the slogan of the defense of bourgeois democracy. The Bolsheviks fought these parties because the banner of bourgeois democracy had at that time become the standard around which all counter-revolutionary forces mobilized to challenge the victory of the proletariat. The situation is quite different in the capitalist countries at present. Now the fascist counter-revolution is attacking bourgeois democracy in an effort to establish a most barbaric regime of exploitation and suppression of the toiling masses. Now the toiling masses in a number of capitalist countries are faced with the necessity of making a *definite* choice, and of making it today, not between proletarian dictatorship and bourgeois democracy, but between bourgeois democracy and fascism."

This, then, is the theoretical foundation which provides the justification for the policy and tactics of the Peoples' Front. And, in point of fact, the Peoples' Front does follow legitimately enough from this foundation. There is only one difficulty: the foundation itself is entirely false.

By their definition of the nature of the present historical period, our Comintern scholars have already implied the proper strategy for the proletariat. The task of the proletariat is, quite flatly, to defend bourgeois democracy. And, in accomplishing this task, the proletariat must aim to ally itself with all other social groups which are threatened by the encroachments of fascism. These include, we have seen, the peasants, the middle classes generally, and likewise the non-fascist or rather "anti-fascist" sections of the bourgeoisie. All of these social groups, from proletariat to "anti-fascist bourgeoisie," can, it is claimed, unite in a common program for the defense of bourgeois democracy against fascism. "We must," Dimitroff advises, "strive everywhere for a broad anti-fascist people's front of struggle against fascism."

This, then, is what the Peoples' Front is, as defined and advocated by its most authoritative sponsors: the broad union of these various social classes and groups on the basis of a common program for the defense of bourgeois democracy against fascism.

It is the avowed aim of such a Peoples' Front not merely to carry on the day-by-day struggle and agitation; but, when conditions are favorable, to accept governmental power. "If we Communists are asked," says Dimitroff, "whether we advocate the united front [and, as is shown by the next sentence, the Peoples' Front] *only* in the struggle for partial demands, or whether we are prepared to share the responsibility even when it will be a question of forming a *government* on the basis of the united front then we say with a full sense of our responsibility: Yes, we recognize that a situation may arise in which the formation of a *government of the proletarian united front*, or of the *anti-fascist people's front*, will become not only possible but necessary in the interests of the proletariat. And in that case we shall declare for the formation of such a government without the slightest hesitation."

What is such a Peoples' Front movement and such a Peoples' Front government able to accomplish? Our teachers will once again provide the answers.

(1) The Peoples' Front can win the middle classes to the side of the proletariat, can win even the actual organizations and parties of the non-proletarian groups. Dimitroff: "In the mobilization of the toiling masses for the struggle against fascism, the formation of a *broad people's anti-fascist front on the basis of the proletarian united front* is a particularly important task. The success of the entire struggle of the proletariat is closely connected with the establishment of a fighting alliance between the proletariat on the one hand and the toiling peasantry and the basic mass of the urban petty bourgeoisie constituting a majority in the population of even industrially developed countries, on the other (...). In forming the anti-fascist people's front, a correct approach to those organizations and parties to which a considerable number of the toiling peasantry and the mass of the urban petty bourgeoisie belong is of great importance. In the capitalist countries the majority of these parties and organizations, political as well as economic, are still under the influence of the bourgeoisie and follow it. The social composition of these parties and organizations is heterogeneous.

This makes it our duty to *approach* these organizations in *different ways*, taking into consideration that not infrequently the bulk of the membership does not know anything about the real political character of its leadership. Under certain conditions, we can and must bend our efforts to the task of drawing these parties and organizations or certain sections of them to the side of the anti-fascist people's front, despite their bourgeois leadership. Such, for instance, is today the situation in France with the Radical Party..."

(2) The Peoples' Front can prevent war (the claims, we see, are by no means modest). Dimitroff: "The extent to which this world-wide front is realized and put into action will determine whether the fascist and other imperialist war incendiaries will be able in the near future to

kindle a new imperialist war, or whether their fiendish hands will be hacked off by the ax of a powerful anti-war front." Or Manuilsky: "We now have greater opportunities for waging a successful struggle against imperialist wars than we had on the eve of 1914... . Today, relying on the U.S.S.R., taking advantage of the antagonism among the capitalist states, the world proletariat has the opportunity of creating a broad people's anti-war front, which should not only include other classes, but also weak nations and peoples whose independence is menaced by war."

(3) The Peoples' Front can stop fascism. Dimitroff: "Will the movement of the united proletarian front and the anti-fascist people's front at the particular stage be in a position only to suppress or overthrow fascism [Note: This is the *minimum* claim which Dimitroff makes for it.—J. B.], without directly proceeding to abolish the dictatorship of the bourgeoisie?" Or Manuilsky: "By its experience [in setting up the Peoples' Front], the French proletariat enriched the whole of the world working class movement and demonstrated to it that *timely* action against fascism (unlike what happened in Austria and Spain) can avert heavy sacrifices and the bitterness of defeat." Or from our own Earl Browder, in his pamphlet, *The Peoples' Front in America* : "There is a tremendous need for the united front of progressives [i.e., the Peoples' Front] which can awake the country to the danger of fascism, and organize the country to defeat this danger."

(4) Lastly, the Peoples' Front government can provide a transitional step to the proletarian dictatorship. Manuilsky sums up what he pretends to be the differences between the "old-fashioned" type of Social-Democratic coalition government and the new-fashioned Peoples' Front government, as follows: "One government [the Social-Democratic coalition] paved the way for the fascist dictatorship; the other government [of the Peoples' Front] must pave the way for the victory of the working class."

* * *

Here, then, in summary, is the ideological structure through which the Soviet bureaucracy and the Communist International throughout the world attempt to deceive and betray the masses in the present historical crisis.

II. Analysis of the Theory of the Peoples' Front

IT would be a great mistake to imagine that the Peoples' Front is a new policy. It is, it is true, a new *slogan*; but, in actual content, it is simply an old policy in a new disguise, an old strategy dressed up for the new, occasion.

The words of its defenders make entirely clear what the real content of the policy of the Peoples' Front is, and it is, therefore, not necessary to give elaborate external proof The Peoples' Front is merely a rewording of the theories and practices of class collaboration and coalition government, as these have been advocated by reformists since the beginning of the modern labor movement Class collaboration is what the Peoples' Front specifically proposes: the union of organizations and parties representing various classes and sections of classes on the basis of a common program to defend bourgeois democracy A Peoples' Front government means, as defined by Dimitroff and Manuilsky, the assumption of governmental responsibility in a capitalist state by the coalition of these organizations and parties.

It is not profitable to argue about words. There are many honest supporters of the Peoples' Front who will dislike and try to reject the realization that it is identical with class collaboration and coalition government. This is because they have previously been trained in an attitude of hostility toward class collaboration and coalition government as betrayals of Marxism Indeed, this training is one of the reasons why the Comintern nvented the new phrase, "Peoples' Front," thereby hoping to make the policy acceptable to those who would have been suspicious of the old phrases. However, if we examine the actual content, there can be no dispute. The Peoples' Front proposes, quite openly and explicitly, the collaboration of classes and a coalition form of government. Naturally it does so in the name of the proletariat, on the alleged grounds that this strategy will under present conditions best serve the interests of the proletariat. But reformism has always tried to justify itself on such grounds—otherwise the proletariat would not be influenced by it.

A striking indication of the fundamental identity between the Peoples' Front and the traditional policies of class collaboration and coalition government is provided by the ease with which reformists and liberals in every country (who have always stood for these latter policies and stand for them today) have gone over to the slogans of the Peoples' Front. They have done so because they have recognized that in the Peoples' Front, Stalinism—for its own reasons—has gone over to their own policies, that is, to reformism. And, of course, they welcome this; though they are still shy of the Comintern, fearing that Stalin offers his reformist gifts only for the chance to swallow them up.

It is necessary to make a sharp distinction between the Peoples' Front and the United Front. The Stalinist spokesmen are anxious to lump the two together, and to claim that the Peoples' Front is nothing more than the logical extension of the United Front "to a higher plane." Similarly, they attempt to confuse the workers by trying to make it appear that revolutionary socialists, in their consistent Opposition to the Peoples' Front, are attacking the United Front. Nothing could be further from the truth.

Revolutionary socialists have consistently stood for, and fought for, the united front, and continue to do so. Indeed, during the years of Hitler's rise to power, one of the chief criticisms leveled against the Comintern by the revolutionary Marxists was that by failing to adopt a united front tactic in Germany, the Comintern guaranteed the victory of Hitler. For this criticism, at that time, the Comintern branded the Marxists as capitulators to the Social-Democracy, and as social-fascists. The most elaborate defense ever made of the united front is to be found in the pamphlets written about Germany during that time by Trotsky.

The united front, however, has nothing at all in common with the Peoples' Front. The united front Consists in an agreement reached between two or more parties and organizations, which have *different programs*, for joint action on specific issues. In this agreement there is absolutely no question of a common political program. Each organization retains intact its entire program; retains the right to put it forward; retains the right to criticize the other organizations in the united front agreement, either in general, or for failure to carry out properly the united front agreement. Thus, in the united front each organization guards its full independence; while at the same time the widest possible unity can be achieved for carrying through some action accepted as desirable by all of the constituent organizations of the united front.

The united front is possible because various organizations differing in complete program or in final social aim may nevertheless all be in favor of some specific action or set of actions For example, united fronts are readily possible on such issues as defense cases, support of a strike, resistance to attack on civil liberties and other democratic rights, breaking of injunctions, holding of demonstrations, etc. At more advanced stages of social crisis, they must be formed on such issues as the building of a workers' militia, defense against fascist gangs, the founding of workers' and peasants' and soldiers' committees The united front on such issues is in fact not merely possible but indispensable for successful struggle Through it the widest possible forces are organized, and at the same time the masses are given a chance to compare in action the worth and dependability of the ideas and methods of the various organizations and parties which strive for their allegiance.

Revolutionary socialists do not merely accept the united front passively. They are the most active and the only consistent advocates of the united front; whereas reformists always resist the united front and must be forced into it—just as the Stalinists now, in basing their policy on the reformist Peoples' Front, resist and fight a united front of action. How could it be otherwise? The ideas and principles of the revolutionary Marxists represent the historical interests of the proletariat. Consequently, any joint struggle by specific actions to the advantage of the proletariat will be welcomed by the Marxists, and the broader the basis, the better. At the same the Marxists are anxious to have an ever broader mass arena for the presentation of their own ideas and a demonstration of their own methods, confident that a true understanding of them will turn the masses away from the reformists toward the revolutionists.

The Peoples' Front, on the other hand, is not merely, not even primarily, an agreement for joint action on specific issues It first and foremost involves the acceptance by all members of the Peoples' Front of a *common program*. This difference is the key to the gulf which separates the Peoples' Front from the united front.

What program? We have already seen the answer. The program of the Peoples' Front is a program for the defense of bourgeois democracy: that is, for the defense of one form of capitalism

Whose program is this? It is obviously not the program of the proletariat. The program of the proletariat, accepted by revolutionists since the publication of the *Communist Manifesto*, can be summed up in two slogans: for workers' power and for socialism. Naturally the immediate tactic of the proletariat is not on all occasions the struggle for state power: that is possible only in a revolutionary crisis. But at all times and on all occasions the fundamental program remains the same—for the overthrow of capitalism, for workers' power and for socialism. This program expresses the basic class conflict in modern Society; records the Marxist understanding that the problems of society can be solved only by socialism, and that socialism can be achieved only through the conquest of power by the proletariat. The duty of the revolutionary party, the conscious vanguard of the proletariat, is to keep this full and fundamental program always to the fore and always uncompromised. In its program, the revolutionary party thus sums up the independence of the proletariat as a class, and asserts its independent historical destiny.

For the proletariat, through its parties, to give up its own independent program means to give up its independent functioning as a class. And this is precisely the meaning of the Peoples' Front. In the Peoples' Front the proletariat renounces its *class* independence, gives up its *class* aims—the *only* aims, as Marxism teaches, which can serve its interests. By accepting the program of the Peoples' Front, it thereby accepts the aims of another section of society; it accepts the aim of the defense of capitalism when all history demonstrates that the interests of the proletariat can be served only by the overthrow of capitalism. It subordinates itself to a middle-class version of how best and most comfortably to preserve the capitalist order. The Peoples' Front is thus thoroughly and irrevocably non-proletarian, anti-proletarian.

By its very nature, the Peoples' Front *must* be so. The establishment of the Peoples' Front, by definition, requires agreement on a common program between the working...class parties and non-working class parties. But the non-proletarian parties cannot agree to the proletarian program- the program of revolutionary socialism...without ceasing to be what they are, without becoming themselves revolutionary workers' parties. But if that should happen, then there would be no basis left for a Peoples' Front: there would be only revolutionary proletarian unity. Consequently, the Peoples' Front must *always* be an abandonment of the proletarian program, a subordination of the proletariat to non-proletarian social interests. In the Peoples' Front, it is the proletariat and the proletariat alone that loses. Earl Browder, in his report to his Central Committee on December 4th, 1936, summed up the whole matter: "We can organize and rouse them [the majority of the people"] provided we do not demand of them that they agree with our socialist program, but unite with them on the basis of their program *which we make also our own* ." [My italics.- J. B.]

The attempt of the Comintern apologists to find a theoretical foundation which will justify the Peoples' Front compels them to make a completely anti-Marxist analysis of the present historical situation. They must corrupt Marxism with respect to every single important issue: bourgeois democracy; fascism; war; the problem and task of the proletariat.

Let us summarize briefly the analysis which Marxists make of the present period, so that it may be compared with the Dimitroff-Manuilsky analysis outlined in the preceding chapter:

Marxism always approaches every social, political, and historical question from the point of view of the class struggle. The basic conflict in modern society—capitalist society—is, according to Marxism, the conflict and struggle between the bourgeoisie and the proletariat. This conflict must continue, and progressively deepen, until capitalism, on a world scale, is overthrown, and the bourgeoisie defeated, and liquidated as a class. Only the two basic classes of modern society—the bourgeoisie and the proletariat—are capable of independent historical action, and thus of formulating independent social and political programs. Reduced to simplest terms, the program of the bourgeoisie is the defense of the capitalist order; the program of the proletariat, its overthrow. The intermediary classes, however they may try to escape it, always in actuality support one side or another in the basic conflict.

In the light of these elementary first principles of Marxism, the Comintern division of the world into "war makers" and "peace lovers," its statement that the two great hostile camps are "democracy" and "fascism," its contention that the issue is "between democracy and fascism," are seen to have nothing in common with Marxism. Its propagation of a program for the defense of capitalist democracy represents merely the extension of one type of bourgeois ideology into the ranks of the working class.

Capitalism, Marxism teaches, went through a great progressive phase. It was the bourgeoisie, the builders of capitalist society, who broke through the fetters of feudal society, who developed modern science and technic, who completely revolutionized industry and communication, who laid the material basis for the adequate fulfillment of human needs. During its progressive phase, capitalism was marked by terrible and devastating conflicts, and by the periodic ravages of the business crises. But after each crisis, capitalism rose stronger than ever, and went to new heights.

Now, however, capitalism, in the advanced period of imperialism, has entered the phase of its general decline as a world system. It is strangling itself. The very factors which once made it a progressive force now act as a brake and obstacle to its further progress. The capitalist system can no longer handle the things which it has itself created. And, as a consequence the conflicts and crises redouble in intensity. After each periodic crisis, capitalism rises weaker, not stronger. Permanent unemployment insecurity hunger, mass discontent progressively grow. Great social upheavals multiply and increase in scope and intensity. Wars and revolutions, on an unprecedented scale, become the general rule instead of the exception, quieting down only long enough to prepare for new world-wide outbreaks.

In the face of this perspective, in the general decline of the capitalist order, the proletarian revolution on a world scale, the building of socialism, presents itself as the *only* solution. Nothing else whatever can alter the perspective, nothing else can halt the progressive degeneration if not the utter destruction of Civilization.

Bourgeois democracy, Marxism teaches further, is a form of capitalism, one of the political forms through which the dictatorship of the bourgeoisie over the proletariat is exercised. It is, in a sense, the "normal" form of bourgeois dictatorship during the progressive phase of capitalism. But Marxism is as unalterably opposed to *bourgeois* democracy as to any other form of capitalist rule; it is opposed because it is opposed in general to capitalism and to bourgeois rule, and aims at the overthrow of capitalism and the defeat of the bourgeoisie. During the decline of capitalism the bourgeoisie finds greater and greater difficulty in keeping the deepening social conflicts within the basic framework of democratic parliamentarism. Democracy becomes too awkward, too clumsy, slow, inefficient unreliable, as a mechanism for class rule. Consequently, manipulating middle-class discontent through a demagogic pseudo-radicalism, the bourgeoisie is compelled to resort to the iron strait-jacket of fascism to insure its continuance in power. Fascism, that is to say, is not a conspiracy or plot on the part of anybody. It is nothing accidental; nothing that results from any peculiar ill-will or viciousness. Fascism, or a fascist type of government, is, on the contrary, a wholly normal development: the normal (though not necessarily universal) mechanism for capitalist rule as the decline and disintegration of the capitalist order deepens, just as bourgeois democracy, parliamentarism, is the normal (though not necessarily universal) mechanism during the progressive phase of capitalism.

It may thus be seen that there is no basic *social* conflict between bourgeois democracy and fascism. If we examine social questions historically, as Marxism does, we find in a sense the contrary: fascism is the resultant of bourgeois democracy in the period of capitalist decline; bourgeois democracy is the precursor of and the preparation for fascism.

A similar analysis applies in the question of war. War, imperialist war, is caused by the basic conflicts of capitalist society, by the struggle to which every capitalist power is forced for cheap raw materials, additional markets, opportunities for the export of capital. These causes operate within democratic capitalist nations as fully as in fascist nations. Fascism, though it may be a stimulus to war, is not at all the cause of war; war and fascism are both the results of capitalism. War, or the approach of war, may, on the other hand, be an immediate stimulus to fascism: since a nation faced by war, or the prospect of war, may well require the totalitarian state in order to prosecute the war successfully.

It follows with full certainty that fascism and war can be defeated only by the overthrow of capitalism. The attempt of the Peoples' Front to preserve bourgeois democracy, any attempt to base a strategy on such a conception, is not merely helpless in the struggle against war and fascism. It makes both inevitable.

The Lessons of Spain: The Last Warning.
Leon Trotsky

Menshevism and Bolshevism in Spain

All general staffs are studying closely the military operations in Ethiopia, in Spain and in the Far East in preparation for the great future war. The battles of the Spanish proletariat heat lightening flashes of the coming world revolution, should be no less attentively studied by the revolutionary staffs. Under this condition and this condition alone will the coming events not take us unawares.*

Three ideologies fought – with unequal forces – in the so-called republican camp, namely, Menshevism, Bolshevism, and anarchism. As regards the bourgeois republican parties, they were without either independent ideas or independent political significance and were able to maintain themselves only by climbing on the backs of the reformists and Anarchists. Moreover, it is no exaggeration to say that the leaders of Spanish anarcho-syndicalism did everything to repudiate their doctrine and virtually reduce its significance to zero. Actually two doctrines in the so-called republican camp fought – Menshevism and Bolshevism.

According to the Socialists and Stalinists, i.e., the Mensheviks of the first and second instances, the Spanish revolution was called upon to solve only its "democratic" tasks, for which a united front with the "democratic" bourgeoisie was indispensable. From this point of view, any and all attempts of the proletariat to go beyond the limits of bourgeois democracy are not only premature but also fatal. Furthermore, on the agenda stands not the revolution but the struggle against insurgent Franco.

Fascism, however, is not feudal but bourgeois reaction. A successful fight against bourgeois reaction can be waged only with the forces and methods of the proletariat revolution. Menshevism, itself a branch of bourgeois thought, does not have and cannot have any inkling of these facts.

The Bolshevik point of view, clearly expressed only by the young section of the Fourth International, takes the theory of permanent revolution as its starting point, namely, that even purely democratic problems, like the liquidation of semi-feudal land ownership, cannot

---

* From the *Socialist Appeal*, New York, January 8th and 15th, 1938.

be solved without the conquest of power by the proletariat; but this in turn places the socialist revolution on the agenda. Moreover, during the very first stages of the revolution, the Spanish workers themselves posed in practice not merely democratic problems but also purely socialist ones. The demand not to transgress the bounds of bourgeois democracy signifies in practice not a defense of the democratic revolution but a repudiation of it. Only through an overturn in agrarian relations could the peasantry, the great mass of the population, have been transformed into a powerful bulwark against fascism. But the landowners are intimately bound up with the commercial, industrial, and banking bourgeoisie, and the bourgeois intelligentsia that depends on them. The party of the proletariat was thus faced with a choice between going with the peasant masses or with the liberal bourgeoisie. There could be only one reason to include the peasantry and the liberal bourgeoisie in the same coalition at the same time: to help the bourgeoisie deceive the peasantry and thus isolate the workers. The agrarian revolution could have been accomplished only against the bourgeoisie, and therefore only through the masses of the dictatorship of the proletariat. There is no third, intermediate regime.

From the standpoint of theory, the most astonishing thing about Stalin's Spanish policy is the utter disregard for the ABC of Leninism. After a delay of several decades – and what decades! – the Comintern has fully rehabilitated the doctrine of Menshevism. More than that, the Comintern has contrived to render this doctrine more "consistent" and by that token more absurd. In czarist Russia, on the threshold of 1905, the formula of "purely democratic revolution" had behind it, in any case, immeasurably more arguments than in 1937 in Spain. It is hardly astonishing that in modern Spain "the liberal labor policy" of Menshevism has been converted into the reactionary anti-labor policy of Stalinism. At the same time the doctrine of the Mensheviks, this caricature of Marxism, has been converted into a caricature of itself.

"Theory" of the Popular Front

It would be naive, however, to think that the politics of the Comintern in Spain stem from a theoretical "mistake". Stalinism is not guided by Marxist Theory, or for that matter any theory at all, but by the empirical interests of the Soviet bureaucracy. In their intimate circles, the Soviet cynics mock Dimitrov's "philosophy" of the Popular Front. But they have at their disposal for deceiving the masses large cadres of propagators of this holy formula, sincere ones and cheats, simpletons and charlatans. Louis Fischer, with his ignorance and smugness, with his provincial rationalism and congenital deafness to revolution, is the most repulsive representative of this unattractive brotherhood. "The union of progressive forces!" "The Triumph of the idea of the Popular Front!" "The assault of the Trotskyists on the unity of the anti-fascist ranks!"... Who will believe that the *Communist Manifesto* was written ninety years ago?

The theoreticians of the Popular Front do not essentially go beyond the first rule of arithmetic, that is, addition: "Communists" plus Socialists plus Anarchists plus liberals add up to a total which is greater than their respective isolated numbers. Such is all their wisdom. However, arithmetic alone does not suffice here. One needs as well at least mechanics. The law of the parallelogram of forces applies to politics as well. In such a parallelogram, we know that the resultant is shorter, the more component forces diverge from each other. When political allies tend to pull in opposite directions, the resultant prove equal to zero.

A bloc of divergent political groups of the working class is sometimes completely indispensable for the solution of common practical problems. In certain historical circumstances, such a bloc is capable of attracting the oppressed petty-bourgeois masses whose interests are close to the interests of the proletariat. The joint force of such a bloc can prove far stronger than the sum of the forces of each of its component parts. On the contrary, the political alliance between the proletariat and the bourgeoisie, whose interests on basic questions in the present epoch diverge at an angle of 180 degrees, as a general rule is capable only of paralyzing the revolutionary force of the proletariat.

Civil war, in which the force of naked coercion is hardly effective, demands of its participants the spirit of supreme self-abnegation. The workers and peasants can assure victory only if they wage a struggle for their own emancipation. Under these conditions, to subordinate the proletariat to the leadership of the bourgeoisie means beforehand to assure defeat in the civil war.

These simple truths are least of all the products of pure theoretical analysis. On the contrary, they represent the unassailable deduction from the entire experience if history, beginning at least with 1848. The modern history of bourgeois society is filled with all sorts of Popular Fronts, i.e. the most diverse political combinations for the deception of the toilers. The Spanish experience is only a new and tragic link in this chain of crimes and betrayals.

Alliance with the Bourgeoisie's Shadow

Politically most striking is the fact that the Spanish Popular Front lacked in reality even a parallelogram of forces. The bourgeoisie's place was occupied by its shadow. Through the medium of the Stalinists, Socialists, and Anarchists, the Spanish bourgeoisie subordinated the proletariat to itself without even bothering to participate in the Popular Front. The overwhelming majority of the exploiters of all political shades openly went over to the camp of Franco. Without any theory of "permanent revolution," the Spanish bourgeoisie understood from the outset that the revolutionary mass movement, no matter how it starts, is directed against private ownership of land and the means of production, and that it is utterly impossible to cope with this movement by democratic measures.

That is why only insignificant debris from the possessing classes remained in the republican camp: Messrs. Azaña, Companys, and the like – political attorneys of the bourgeoisie but not the bourgeoisie itself. Having staked everything on a military dictatorship, the possessing classes were able, at the same time, to make use of the political representatives of yesterday in order to paralyze, disorganize, and afterward strangle the socialist movement of the masses in "republican" territory.

Without in the slightest degree representing the Spanish bourgeoisie, the left republicans still less represented the workers and peasants. They represented no one but themselves. Thanks, however, to their allies – the Socialists, Stalinists, and Anarchists – these political phantoms played decisive role in the revolution. How? Very simply. By incarnating the principles of the "democratic revolution," that is, the inviolability of private property.

The Stalinists in the Popular Front

The reasons of the rise of the Spanish Popular Front and its inner mechanics are perfectly clear. The task of the retired leaders of the left bourgeoisie consisted in checking the revolution of the masses and the regaining for themselves the lost confidence of the exploiters: "Why do you need Franco if we, the republicans, can do the same thing?" The interests of Azaña and Companys fully coincided at this central point with the interests of Stalin, who needed gain the confidence of the French and British bourgeoisie by proving to them in action his ability to preserve "order" against "anarchy." Stalin needed Azaña and Companys as a cover before the workers: Stalin himself, of course, is for socialism, but one must take care not to repel the republican bourgeoisie! Azaña and Companys needed Stalin as an experienced executioner, with the authority of a revols time not at all thanks to high and mighty foreign patrons who supplied "this time not at all thanks to be dared to attack the workers.

The classic reformists of the Second International, long ago derailed by the course of the class struggle, began to feel a new tide of confidence, thanks to the support of Moscow. This support, incidentally, was not given to all reformists but only to those most reactionary. Caballero represented that face of the Socialist Party that was turned toward the workers' aristocracy. Negrin and Prieto always looked towards the bourgeoisie. Negrin won over Caballero with the help of Moscow. The left Socialists and Anarchists, the captives of the Popular Front, tried, it is true, to save whatever could be saved of democracy. But inasmuch as they did not dare to mobilize the masses against the gendarmes of the Popular Front, their efforts at the end were reduced to plaints and wails. The Stalinists were thus in alliance with the extreme right, avowedly bourgeois wing of the Socialist Party. They directed their repressions against the left – the POUM, the Anarchists, the "left" Socialists – in other words, against the centrist groupings who reflected, even in a most remote degree, the pressure of the revolutionary masses,

This political fact, very significant in itself, provides at the same time the measure of the degeneration of the Comintern in the last few years. I once defined Stalinism as bureaucratic centrism, and events brought a series of corroborations of the correctness of this definition. But it is obviously obsolete today. The interests of the Bonapartist bureaucracy can no longer be reconciled with centrist hesitation and vacillation. In search of reconciliation with the bourgeoisie, the Stalinist clique is capable of entering into alliances only with the most conservative groupings among the international labor aristocracy. This has acted to fix definitively the counterrevolutionary character of Stalinism on the international arena.

Counter-Revolutionary Superiorities of Stalinism

This brings us right up to the solution of the enigma of how and why the Communist Party of Spain, so insignificant numerically and with a leadership so poor in caliber, proved capable of gathering into its hands all reins of power, in the face of the incomparably more powerful organizations of the Socialists and Anarchists. The usual explanation that the Stalinists simply bartered Soviet weapons for power is far too superficial. In return for munitions, Moscow received Spanish gold. According to the laws of the capitalist market, this covers everything. How then did Stalin contrive to get power in the bargain?

The customary answer is that the Soviet government, having raised its authority in the eyes of the masses by furnishing military supplies, demanded as a condition of its "collaboration" drastic measures against revolutionists and thus removed dangerous opponents from its path. All this is quite indisputable but it is only one aspect of the matter, and the least important at that.

Despite the "authority" created by Soviet shipments, the Spanish Communist Party remained a small minority and met with ever-growing hatred on the part of the workers. On the other hand, it was not enough for Moscow to set conditions; Valencia had to accede to them. This is the heart of the matter. Not only Zamora, Companys, and Negrin, but also Caballero, during his incumbency as premier, were all more or less ready to accede to the demands of Moscow. Why? Because these gentlemen themselves wished to keep the revolution within bourgeois limits. They were deathly afraid of every revolutionary onslaught of the workers.

Stalin with his munitions and with his counterrevolutionary ultimatum was a savior for all these groups. He guaranteed them, so they hoped, military victory over Franco, and at the same time, he freed them from all responsibility for the course of the revolution. They hastened to put their Socialist and Anarchist masks into the closet in the hope of making use of them again after Moscow reestablished bourgeois democracy for them. As the finishing touch to their comfort, these gentlemen could henceforth, justify their betrayal to the workers by the necessity of a military agreement with Stalin. Stalin on his part justifies his counterrevolutionary politics by the necessity of maintaining an alliance with the republican bourgeoisie.

Only from this broader point of view can we get a clear picture of the angelic toleration which such champions of justice and freedom as Azaña, Negrin, Companys, Caballero, Garcia Oliver, and others showed towards the crimes of the GPU. If they had no other choice, as they affirm, it was not at all because they had no means of paying for airplanes and tanks other than with the heads of the revolutionists and the rights of the workers, but because their own "purely democratic", that is, anti-socialist, program could be realized by no other measures save terror. When the workers and peasants enter on the path of their revolution – when they seize factories and estates, drive out old owners, conquer power in the provinces – then the bourgeois counterrevolution – democratic, Stalinist, or fascist alike – has no other means of checking this movement except through bloody coercion, supplemented by lies and deceit. The superiority of the Stalinist clique on this road consisted in its ability to apply instantly measures that were beyond the capacity of Azaña, Companys, Negrin, and their left allies.

Stalin Confirms in His Own Way the Correctness of the Theory of Permanent Revolution

Two irreconcilable programs thus confronted each other on the territory of republican Spain. On the one hand, the program of saving at any cost private property from the proletariat, and saving as far as possible democracy from Franco; on the other hand, the program of abolishing private property through the conquest of power by the proletariat. The first program expressed the interest of capitalism through the medium of the labor aristocracy, the top petty-bourgeois circles, and especially the Soviet bureaucracy. The second program translated into the language of Marxism the tendencies of the revolutionary mass movement, not fully conscious but powerful. Unfortunately for the revolution, between the handful of Bolsheviks and the revolutionary proletariat stood counter-revolutionary wall of the Popular Front.

The policy of the Popular Front was, in its turn, not at all determined by the blackmail of Stalin as supplier of arms. There was, of course, no lack of blackmail. But the reason for the success of this blackmail was inherent in the inner conditions of the revolution itself. For six years, its social setting was the growing onslaught of the masses against the regime of semi-feudal and bourgeois property. The need of defending this property by the most extreme measures threw the bourgeoisie into Franco's arms. The republican government had promised the bourgeoisie to defend property by "democratic" measures, but revealed, especially in July 1936, its complete bankruptcy. When the situation on the property front became even more threatening than on the military front, the democrats of all colors, including the Anarchists, bowed before Stalin; and he found no other methods, in his own arsenal than the methods of Franco.

The hounding of "Trotskyists", POUMists, revolutionary Anarchists and left Socialists; the filthy slander; the false documents; the tortures in Stalinist prisons; the murders from ambush – without all this the bourgeois regime under the republican flag could not have lasted even two months. The GPU proved to be the master of the situation only because it defended the interests of the bourgeoisie against the proletariat more consistently than the others, i.e., with the greatest baseness and bloodthirstiness.

In the struggle against the socialist revolution, the "democratic" Kerensky at first sought support in the military dictatorship of

Kornilov and later tried to enter Petrograd in the baggage train of the monarchist general Krasnov. On the other hand, the Bolsheviks were compelled, in order to carry the democratic revolution through to the end, to overthrow the government of "democratic" charlatans and babblers. In the process they put an end thereby to every kind of attempt at military (or "fascist") dictatorship.

The Spanish revolution once again demonstrates that it is impossible to defend democracy against the methods of fascist reaction. And conversely, it is impossible to conduct a genuine struggle against fascism otherwise than through the methods of the proletarian revolution. Stalin waged war against "Trotskyism" (proletarian revolution), destroying democracy by the Bonapartist measures of the GPU. This refutes once again and once and for all the old Menshevik theory, adopted by the Comintern, in accordance with which the democratic and socialist revolutions are transformed into two independent historic chapters, separated from each other in point of time. The work of the Moscow executioners confirms in its own way the correctness of the theory of permanent revolution.

Role of the Anarchists

The Anarchists had no independent position of any kind in the Spanish revolution. All they did was waver between Bolshevism and Menshevism. More precisely, the Anarchist workers instinctively yearned to enter the Bolshevik road (July 19, 1936, and May days of 1937) while their leaders, on the contrary, with all their might drove the masses into the camp of the Popular Front, i.e., of the bourgeois regime.

The Anarchists revealed a fatal lack of understanding of the laws of the revolution and its tasks by seeking to limit themselves to their own trade unions, that is, to organizations permeated with the routine of peaceful times, and by ignoring what went on outside the framework of the trade unions, among the masses, among the political parties, and in the government apparatus. Had the Anarchists been revolutionists, they would first of all have called for the creation of soviets, which unite the representatives of all the toilers of city and country, including the most oppressed strata, who never joined the trade unions. The revolutionary workers would have naturally occupied the dominant position in these soviets. The Stalinists would have remained an insignificant minority. The proletariat would have convinced itself of its own invincible strength. The apparatus of the bourgeois state would have hung suspended in the air. One strong blow would have sufficed to pulverize this apparatus. The socialist revolution would have received a powerful impetus. The French proletariat would not for long permitted Leon Blum to blockade the proletariat revolution beyond the Pyrenees. Neither could the Moscow bureaucracy have permitted itself such a luxury. The most difficult questions would have been solved as they arose.

Instead of this, the anarcho-syndicalists, seeking to hide from "politics" in the trade unions, turned out to be, to the great surprise of the whole world and themselves, a fifth wheel in the cart of bourgeois democracy. But not for long; a fifth wheel is superfluous. After Garcia Oliver and his cohorts helped Stalin and his henchmen to take power away from the workers, the anarchists themselves were driven out of the government of the Popular Front. Even then they found nothing better to do than jump on the victor's bandwagon and assure him of their devotion. The fear of the petty bourgeois before the big bourgeois, of the petty bureaucrat before the big bureaucrat, they covered up with lachrymose speeches about the sanctity of the united front (between a victim and the executioners) and about the inadmissibility of every kind of dictatorship, including their own. "After all, we could have taken power in July 1936 ..." "After all, we could have taken power in May 1937..." The Anarchists begged Stalin-Negrin to recognize and reward their treachery to the revolution. A revolting picture!

In and of itself, this self-justification that "we did not seize power not because we were unable but because we did not wish to, because we were against every kind of dictatorship," and the like, contains an irrevocable condemnation of anarchism as an utterly anti-revolutionary doctrine. To renounce the conquest of power is voluntarily to leave the power with those who wield it, the exploiters. The essence of every revolution consisted and consists in putting a new class in power, thus enabling it to realize its own program in life. It is impossible to wage war and to reject victory. It is impossible to lead the masses towards insurrection without preparing for the conquest power.

No one could have prevented the Anarchists after the conquest of power from establishing the sort of regime they deem necessary, assuming, of course, that their program is realizable. But the Anarchist leaders themselves lost faith in it. They hid from power not because they are against "every kind of dictatorship" – in actuality, grumbling and whining, they supported and still support the dictatorship of Stalin-Negrin – but because they completely lost their principles and courage, if they ever had any. They were afraid of everything: "isolation," "involvement," "fascism." They were afraid of

France and England. More than anything these phrasemongers feared the revolutionary masses.

The renunciation of the conquest of power inevitably throws every workers' organization into the swamp of reformism and turns it into a toy of the bourgeoisie; it cannot be otherwise in view of the class structure of society. In opposing the goal, the conquest of power, the Anarchists could not in the end fail to oppose the means, the revolution. The leaders of the CNT and FAI not only helped the bourgeoisie hold on to the shadow of power in July 1936; they also helped it to reestablish bit by bit what it had lost at one stroke. In May 1937, they sabotaged the uprising of the workers and thereby saved the dictatorship of the bourgeoisie. Thus anarchism, which wished merely to be anti-political, proved in reality to be anti-revolutionary and in the more critical moments – counter-revolutionary.

The Anarchist theoreticians, who after the great test of 1931-37 continue to repeat the old reactionary nonsense about Kronstadt, and who affirm that "Stalinism is the inevitable result of Marxism and Bolshevism," simply demonstrate by this they are forever dead for the revolution.

You say that Marxism is in itself depraved and Stalinism is its legitimate progeny? But why are we revolutionary Marxists engaged in mortal combat with Stalinism throughout the world? Why does the Stalinist gang see in Trotskyism it chief enemy? Why does every approach to our views or our methods of action (Durruti, Andres, Nin, Landau, and others) compel the Stalinist gangsters to resort to bloody reprisals. Why, on the other hand, did the leaders of Spanish anarchism serve, during the time of the Moscow and Madrid crimes of the GPU, as ministers under Caballero-Negrin, that is as servants of the bourgeoisie and Stalin? Why even now, under the pretext of fighting fascism, do the Anarchists remain voluntary captives of Stalin-Negrin, the executioners of the revolution, who have demonstrated their incapacity to fight fascism?

By hiding behind Kronstadt and Makhno, the attorneys of anarchism will deceive nobody. In the Kronstadt episode and the struggle with Makhno, we defended the proletarian from the peasant counterrevolution. The Spanish Anarchists defended and continue to defend bourgeois counterrevolution from the proletariat revolution. No sophistry will delete from the annals of history the fact that anarchism and Stalinism in the Spanish revolution were on one side of the barricades while the working masses with the revolutionary Marxists were on the other. Such is the truth which will forever remain in the consciousness of the proletariat!

Role of the POUM

The record of the POUM is not much better. In the point of theory, it tried, to be sure, to base itself on the formula of permanent revolution (that is why the Stalinists called the POUMists Trotskyists). But the revolution is not satisfied with theoretical avowals. Instead of mobilizing the masses against the reformist leaders, including the Anarchists, the POUM tried to convince these gentlemen of the superiorities of socialism over capitalism. This tuning fork gave the pitch to all the articles and speeches of the POUM leaders. In order not to quarrel with the Anarchist leaders, they did not form their own nuclei inside the CNT, and in general did not conduct any kind of work there. To avoid sharp conflicts, they did not carry on revolutionary work in the republican army. They built instead "their own" trade unions and "their own" militia, which guarded "their own" institutions or occupied "their own" section of the front.

By isolating the revolutionary vanguard from the class, the POUM rendered the vanguard impotent and left the class without leadership. Politically the POUM remained throughout far closer to the Popular Front, for whose left wing it provided the cover, than to Bolshevism. That the POUM nevertheless fell victim to bloody and base repressions was due to the failure of the Popular Front to fulfill its mission, namely to stifle the socialist revolution – except by cutting off, piece by piece, its own left flank.

Contrary to its own intentions, the POUM proved to be, in the final analysis, the chief obstacle on the road to the creation of a revolutionary party. The platonic or diplomatic partisans of the Fourth International like Sneevliet, the leader of the Dutch Revolutionary Socialist Workers Party, who demonstratively supported the POUM in its halfway measures, its indecisiveness and evasiveness, in short, in its centrism, took upon themselves the greatest responsibility. Revolution abhors centrism. Revolution exposes and annihilates centrism. In passing, the revolution discredits the friends and attorneys of centrism. That is one of the most important lessons of the Spanish revolution.

The Problem of Arming

The Socialists and Anarchists who seek to justify their capitulation to Stalin by the necessity of paying for Moscow's weapons with principles and conscience simply lie unskillfully. Of course, many of them would have preferred to disentangle themselves without murders and frame-ups. But every goal demands corresponding means. Beginning with April 1931, that is, long before the military intervention of Moscow, the Socialists and Anarchists did everything in their power to check the proletariat revolution. Stalin taught them how to carry this work to its conclusion. They became Stalin's criminal accomplices only because they were his political cothinkers.

Had the Anarchist leaders in the least resembled revolutionists, they would have answered the first piece of blackmail from Moscow not only by continuing the socialist offensive but also by exposing Stalin's counterrevolutionary conditions before the world working class. They would have thus forced the Moscow bureaucracy to choose openly between the socialist revolution and the Franco dictatorship. The Thermidorean bureaucracy fears and hates revolution. But it also fears being strangled in a fascist ring. Besides, it depends on the workers. All indications are that Moscow would have been forced to supply arms, and possibly at more reasonable prices.

But the world does not revolve around Stalinist Moscow. During a year and a half of civil war, the Spanish war industry could and should have been strengthened and developed by converting a number of civilian plants to war production. This work was not carried out only because Stalin and his Spanish allies equally feared the initiative of the workers' organizations. A strong war industry would have become a powerful instrument in the hands of the workers. The leaders of the Popular Front preferred to depend on Moscow.

It is precisely on this question that the perfidious role of the Popular Front was very strikingly revealed. It thrust upon the workers' organizations the responsibility for the treacherous deals of the bourgeoisie of Stalin. Insofar as the Anarchists remained a minority, they could not, of course, immediately hinder the ruling bloc from assuming whatever obligations they pleased toward Moscow and the masters of Moscow: London and Paris. But without ceasing to be the best fighters on the front, they could have and should have openly dissociated themselves from the betrayals and betrayers; they could and should have explained the real situation to the masses, mobilized them against the bourgeois government, and augmented their own forces from day to day in order in the end to conquer power and with it the Moscow arms.

And what if Moscow, in the absence of a Popular Front, should have refused to give arms altogether? And what, we answer to this, if the Soviet Union did not exist altogether? Revolutions have been victorious up to this time not at all thanks to high and mighty foreign patrons who supplied them with arms. As a rule, counterrevolution enjoyed foreign patronage. Must we recall the experiences of the intervention of French, English, American, Japanese, and other armies against the Soviets? The proletariat of Russia conquered domestic reaction and foreign interventionists without military support form the outside. Revolutions succeed, in the first place, with the help of a bold social program, which gives the masses the possibility of seizing weapons that are on the territory and disorganizing the army of the enemy. The Red Army seized French, English, and American military supplies and drove the foreign expeditionary corps into the sea. Has this really been forgotten?

If at the head of the armed workers and peasants, that is, at the head of so-called republican Spain, were revolutionists and not cowardly agents of the bourgeoisie, the problem of arming would never have been paramount. The army of Franco, including the colonial Riffians and the soldiers of Mussolini, was not at all immune to revolutionary contagion. Surrounded by the conflagration of the socialist uprising, the soldiers of fascism would have proved to be an insignificant quantity. Arms and military "geniuses" were not lacking in Madrid and Barcelona; what was lacking was a revolutionary party!

Conditions for victory

The conditions for victory of the masses in the civil war against the army exploiters are very simple in their essence.

1. The fighters of a revolutionary army must be clearly aware of the fact that they are fighting for their full social liberation and not for the reestablishment of the old ("democratic") forms of exploitation.

2. The workers and peasants in the rear of the revolutionary army as well as in the rear of the enemy must know and understand the same thing.

3. The propaganda on their own front as well as on the enemy front and in both rears must be completely permeated with the spirit of social revolution. The slogan "First victory, then reforms," is the slogan of all oppressors and exploiters from the Biblical kings down to Stalin.

4. Politics are determined by those classes and strata that participate in the struggle. The revolutionary masses must have a state apparatus that directly and immediately expresses their will. Only the soviets of workers', soldiers', and peasants' deputies can act as such an apparatus.

5. The revolutionary army must not only proclaim but also immediately realize in life the more pressing measures of social revolution in the provinces won by them: the expropriation of

provisions, manufactured articles, and other stores on hand and the transfer of these to the needy; the redivision of shelter and housing in the interests of the toilers and especially of the families of the fighters; the expropriation of the land and agricultural inventory in the interests of the peasants; the establishment of workers' control and soviet power in the place of the former bureaucracy.

6. Enemies of the socialist revolution, that is, exploiting elements and their agents, even if masquerading as "democrats," "republicans," "Socialists," and "Anarchists," must be mercilessly driven out of the army.

7. At the head of each military unit must be placed commissars possessing irreproachable authority as revolutionists and soldiers.

8. In every military unit there must be a firmly welded nucleus of the most self-sacrificing fighters, recommended by the workers' organizations. The members of this nucleus have but one privilege: to be first under fire.

9. The commanding corps necessarily includes at first many alien and unreliable elements among the personnel. Their testing, retesting, and sifting must be carried through on the basis of combat experience, recommendations of commissars, and testimonials of rank-and-file fighters. Coincident with this must proceed an intense training of commanders drawn from the ranks of revolutionary workers.

10. The strategy of civil war must combine the rules of military art with the tasks of the social revolution. Not only in propaganda but also in military operations it is necessary to take into account the social composition of the various military units of the enemy (bourgeois volunteers, mobilized peasants, or as in Franco's case, colonial slaves); and in choosing lines of operation, it is necessary to rigorously take into consideration the social structure of the corresponding territories (industrial regions, peasant regions, revolutionary or reactionary, regions of oppressed nationalities, etc.). In brief, revolutionary policy dominates strategy.

11. Both the revolutionary government and the executive committee of the workers and peasants must know how to win the complete confidence of the army and of the toiling population.

12. Foreign policy must have as its main objective the awakening of the revolutionary consciousness of the workers, the exploited peasants, and oppressed nationalities of the whole world.

Stalin Guaranteed the Conditions of Defeat

The conditions for victory, as we see, are perfectly plain. In their aggregate they bear the name of the socialist revolution. Not a single one of these conditions existed in Spain. The basic reason is – the absence of a revolutionary party. Stalin tried, it is true, to transfer to the soil of Spain, the outward practices of Bolshevism: the Politburo, commissars, cells, the GPU, etc. But he emptied these forms of their social content. He renounced the Bolshevik program and with it the soviets as the necessary form for the revolutionary initiative of the masses. He placed the technique of Bolshevism at the service of bourgeois property. In his bureaucratic narrow-mindedness, he imagined that "commissars" by themselves could guarantee victory. But the commissars of private property proved capable only of guaranteeing defeat.

The Spanish proletariat displayed first-rate military qualities. In its specific gravity in the country's economic life, in its political and cultural level, the Spanish proletariat stood on the first day of the revolution not below but above the Russian proletariat at the beginning of 1917. On the road to victory, its own organizations stood as the chief obstacles. The commanding clique of Stalinists, in accordance with their counterrevolutionary function, consisted of hirelings, careerists, declassed elements, and in general, all types of social refuse. The representatives of other labor organizations – incurable reformists, Anarchists phrasemongers, helpless centrists of the POUM – grumbled, groaned, wavered, manuevered, but in the end adapted themselves to the Stalinists. As a result of their joint activity, the camp of social revolution – workers and peasants – proved to be subordinated to the bourgeoisie, or more correctly, to its shadow. It was bled white and its character destroyed.

There was no lack of heroism on the part of the masses or courage on the part of individual revolutionists. But the masses were left to their own resources while the revolutionists remained disunited, without a program, without a plan of action. The "republican" military commanders were more concerned with crushing the social revolution than with scoring military victories. The soldiers lost confidence in their commanders, the masses in the government; the peasants stepped aside; the workers became exhausted; defeat followed defeat; demoralization grew apace. All this was not difficult to foresee from the beginning of the civil war. By setting itself the task of rescuing the capitalist regime, the Popular Front doomed itself to military defeat. By turning Bolshevism on its head, Stalin succeeded completely in fulfilling the role of gravedigger of the revolution.

It ought to be added that the Spanish experience once again demonstrates that Stalin failed completely to understand either the October Revolution or the Russian civil war. His slow moving provincial mind lagged hopelessly behind the tempestuous march of events in 1917-21. In those of his speeches and articles in 1917 where he expressed his own ideas, his later Thermidorean "doctrine" is fully implanted. In this sense, Stalin in Spain in 1937 is the continuator of Stalin of the March 1917 conference of the Bolsheviks. But in 1917 he merely feared the revolutionary workers; in 1937 he strangled them. The opportunist had become the executioner.

"Civil War in the Rear"

But, after all, victory over the governments of Caballero and Negrin would have necessitated a civil war in the rear of the republican army! – the democratic philistine exclaims with horror. As if apart from this, in republican Spain no civil war has ever existed, and at that the basest and most perfidious one – the war of the proprietors and exploiters against the workers and peasants. This uninterrupted war finds expression in the arrests and murders of revolutionists, the crushing of the mass movement, the disarming of the workers, the arming of the bourgeois police, the abandoning of workers' detachments without arms and without help on the front, and finally, the artificial restriction of the development of war industry.

Each of these acts as a cruel blow to the front, direct military treason, dictated by the class interests of the bourgeoisie. But "democratic" philistines – including Stalinists, Socialists, and Anarchists – regard the civil war of the bourgeoisie against the proletariat, even in areas most closely adjoining the front, as a natural and inescapable war, having as its tasks the safeguarding of the "unity of the Popular Front." On the other hand, the civil war of the proletariat against the "republican" counterrevolution is, in the eyes of the same philistines, a criminal, "fascists," Trotskyist war, disrupting ... "the unity of the anti-fascist forces." Scores of Norman Thomases, Major Atlees, Otto Bauers, Zyromskys, Malrauxes, and such petty peddlers of lies as Duranty and Louis Fischer spread this slavish wisdom throughout our planet. Meanwhile the government of the Popular Front moves from Madrid to Valencia, from Valencia to Barcelona.

If, as the facts attest, only the socialist revolution is capable of crushing fascism, then on the other hand a successful uprising of the proletariat is conceivable only when the ruling classes are caught in the vise of the greatest difficulties. However, the democratic philistines invoke precisely these difficulties as proof of the impressibility of the proletarian uprising. Were the proletariat to wait for the democratic philistines to tell them the hour of their liberation, they would remain slaves forever. To teach workers to recognize reactionary philistines under all their masks and to despise them regardless of the mask is the first and paramount duty of a revolutionist!

The Outcome

The dictatorship of the Stalinists over the republican camp is not long-lived in its essence. Should the defeats stemming from the politics of the Popular Front once more impel the Spanish proletariat to a revolutionary assault, this time successfully, the Stalinist clique will be swept away with an iron broom. But should Stalin – as is unfortunately the likelihood – succeed in bringing the work of gravedigger of the revolution to its conclusion, he will not even in this case earn thanks. The Spanish bourgeoisie needed him as executioner, but it has no need for him at all as patron or tutor. London and Paris on the one hand, and Berlin and Rome on the other, are in its eyes considerably more solvent firms than Moscow. It is possible that Stalin himself wants to cover his traces in Spain before the final catastrophe; he thus hopes to unload the responsibility for the defeat on his closest allies. After this Litvinov will solicit Franco for the reestablishment of diplomatic relations. All this we have seen more than once.

Even a complete military victory of the so-called republican army over General Franco, however, would not signify the triumph of "democracy." The workers and peasants have twice placed bourgeois republicans and their left agents in power: in April 1931 and in February 1936. Both times the heroes of the Popular Front surrendered the victory of the people to the most reactionary and the most serious representatives of the bourgeoisie. A third victory, gained by the generals of the Popular Front, would signify their inevitable agreement with the fascist bourgeoisie on the backs of the workers and peasants. Such a regime will be nothing but a different form of military dictatorship, perhaps without a monarchy and without the open domination of the Catholic Church.

Finally, it is possible that the partial victories of the republicans will be utilized by the "disinterested" Anglo-French intermediaries in order to reconcile the fighting camps. It is not difficult to understand that in the event of such a variant the final remnants of the "democracy" will be stifled in the fraternal embrace of the generals Miaja (communist!) and Franco (fascists!). Let me repeat once again: victory will go either to the socialist revolution or to fascism.

It is not excluded, by the way, that the tragedy might at the last moment make way to farce. When the heroes of the Popular Front have to flee their last capital, they might, before embarking on steamers and airplanes, perhaps proclaim a series of "socialist" reforms in order to leave a "good memory" with the people. But nothing will avail. The workers of the world will remember with hatred and contempt the parties that ruined the heroic revolution.

The tragic experience of Spain is a terrible – perhaps final – warning before still greater events, a warning addressed to all the advanced workers of the world. "Revolutions," Marx said, "are the locomotives of history." They move faster than the thought of semi-revolutionary or quarter-revolutionary parties. Whoever lags behind falls under the wheels of the locomotive, and consequently – and this is the chief danger – the locomotive itself is also not infrequently wrecked.

It is necessary to think out the problem of the revolution to the end, to its ultimate concrete conclusions. It is necessary to adjust policy to the basic laws of the revolution, i.e., to the movement of the embattled classes and not the prejudices or fears of the superficial petty-bourgeois groups who call themselves "Popular" Fronts and every other kind of front. During revolution the line of least resistance is the line of greatest disaster. To fear "isolation" from the bourgeoisie is to incur isolation from the masses. Adaptation to the conservative prejudices of the labor aristocracy is betrayal of the workers and the revolution. An excess "caution" is the most baneful lack of caution. This is the chief lesson of the destruction of the most honest political organization in Spain, namely, the centrist POUM. The parties and groups of the London Bureau obviously either do not wish to draw the necessary conclusions from the last warning of history or are unable to do so. By this token they doom themselves.

By way of compensation, a new generation of revolutionists is now being educated by the lessons of the defeats. This generation has verified in action the ignominious reputation of the Second International. It has plumbed the depths of the Third International's downfall. It has learned how to judge the Anarchists not by their words but by their deeds. It is a great inestimable school, paid for with the blood of countless fighters! The revolutionary cadres are now gathering only under the banner of the Fourth International. Born amid the roar of defeats, the Fourth International will lead the toilers to victory.

Notes on Contributors

LEON TROTSKY
Trotsky was a revolutionary Marxist, a leader the Russian revolution of October 1917, and the founder of the Red Army. Trotsky initially supported the Mensheviks and then joined the Bolsheviks immediately prior to the 1917 October Revolution. After leading the struggle of the Left Opposition against the policies Stalin in the 1920s and against the increasing role of bureaucracy in the Soviet Union, Trotsky was expelled from the Communist Party in 1927, and deported from the Soviet Union in 1929. He helped launch the Fourth International in 1936 and was assassinated by an agent sent by Stalin in 1940 while living in exile in Mexico. He is the author of *The History of the Russian Revolution* (Haymarket), *Permanent Revolution* (Resistance Books), and *The Revolution Betrayed*.

JOHN RIDDELL
John Riddell has been active in the revolutionary socialist movement in Canada, the United States and Europe since the 1960s. He is the editor of a number of books publishing the key documents and resolutions of the congresses of Comintern, the international revolutionary socialist movement, from 1907 to 1923. Six volumes were published by Pathfinder Press under the title *The Communist International in Lenin's Time*. The others, *To the Masses* on the fourth Congress (1922) and *Towards the United Front* on the third Congress (1922) were published as part of Brill Academic Publisher's Historical Materialism Book Series.

DUNCAN HALLAS
Duncan Hallas was a leading member of the Socialist Workers Party (SWP) in Great Britain. Duncan Hallas joined the Trotskyist movement in 1940, and was a founder member with Tony Cliff of the Socialist Review Group, which was inside the Labour Party, in 1951. In 1968, Hallas joined the International Socialists (IS), the predecessor of the SWP. He is the author of *Trotsky's Marxism* (Pluto Press, London 1979) and *The Comintern* (Bookmarks).

TOM KERRY
Kerry was a lifelong member of the Socialist Workers Party in the USA. Kerry was inspired by the Russian Revolution of 1917 and became a Communist. He joined the Socialist Workers Party at its foundation in 1938. Kerry became one of its leading member for many decades and was a close collaborator James P. Cannon and Farrell Dobbs.

DANIEL BENSAID
Daniel Bensaïd was one of France's most prominent Marxist philosophers and wrote extensively on that and other subjects. He was for many years a leading member of the LCR (French section of the Fourth International) and subsequently of the New Anti-Capitalist Party (NPA). He was also a member

of the central leadership of the Fourth International, particularly following developments in Latin America - notably in Brazil - in the 1970s-90s. His books translated in English are *Marx for Our Time* (Verso), *An Impatient Life: A Memoir* (Verso), and *Strategies of Resistance* (Resistance Books).

MICHEL PABLO

Michel Pablo was the pseudonym of Michalis Raptis. He represented Greek Trotskyists at the founding conference of the Fourth International in 1938. After the war, Pablo became the central leader of the Fourth International and played a key role rebuilding the organization. Differences developed in the International over the nature of Stalinism and the revolution in colonial countries. This led to a split in the International in1953 in which Michel Pablo sided with Ernest Mandel, Pierre Frank, Livio Maitan. But Pablo's differences with the organisation deepened, and he left in 1964 after the re-unification of the International. He is the author as Michel Raptis of *Revolution and Counter Revolution in Chile* (1974) and *Socialism, Democracy & Self-Management* (1980).

STEVE BLOOM

Steve Bloom is a Brooklyn-based revolutionary activist and poet, member of Solidarity and of Scientific Soul Sessions. He has written widely on revolutionary theory and current events for journals such as Against the Current, International Viewpoint, and others. As a leader of the Socialist Workers Party in the 1980s, he fought the SWP's break with Trotskyism. He helped gather together US Trotskyists expelled from the SWP, to reconnect them with the Fourth International. In 1992, he joined Solidarity and has served in Solidarity's New York and national leaderships.

JAMES BURNHAM

In 1929 he became a professor of philosophy at New York University. He was a radical activist in the 1930s, and a founding member of the SWP when it was launched in 1938. Following the Stalin Hitler pact, James Burnham left Marxism to become an intellectual of the American right wing writing for America's leading conservative publication, *National Review*. He published in 1941 *The Managerial Revolution*, the book for which he is best known.

About the IIRE and Resistance Books
The International Institute for
Research and Education

The International Institute for Research and Education (IIRE) is an international foundation, recognised in Belgium as an international scientific association by Royal decree of 11th June 1981. The IIRE provides activists and scholars worldwide with opportunities for research and education in three locations: Amsterdam, Islamabad and Manila.

Since 1982, when the Institute opened in Amsterdam, its main activity has been the organisation of courses in the service of progressive forces around the world. Our seminars and study groups deal with all subjects related to the emancipation of the world's oppressed and exploited. It has welcomed hundreds of participants from every inhabited continent. Most participants have come from the Third World.

The IIRE has become a prominent centre for the development of critical thought and interaction, and the exchange of experiences, between people who are engaged in daily struggles on the ground. The Institute's sessions give participants a unique opportunity to step aside from the pressure of daily activism. The IIRE gives them time to study, reflect upon their involvement in a changing world and exchange ideas with people from other countries.

Our website is constantly being expanded and updated with freely downloadable publications, in several languages, and audio files. Recordings of several recent lectures given at the institute can be downloaded from www.iire.org - as can talks given by founding Fellows such as Ernest Mandel and Livio Maitan, dating back to the early 1980s.

The IIRE publishes Notebooks for Study and Research to focus on themes of contemporary debate or historical or theoretical importance. Lectures and study materials given in sessions in our Institute, located in Amsterdam, Manila and Islamabad, are made available to the public in large part through the Notebooks.

Different issues of the Notebooks have also appeared in languages besides English and French, including German, Dutch, Arabic, Spanish, Japanese, Korean, Portuguese, Turkish, Swedish, Danish and Russian.

For a full list of the Notebooks for Study and Research, visit http://iire.org/en/resources/notebooks-for-study-and-research.html

To order the Notebooks, email iire@iire.org or write to International Institute for Research and Education, Lombokstraat 40, Amsterdam, NL-1094.

Resistance Books

Resistance Books is the publishing arm of Socialist Resistance, a revolutionary Marxist organisation which is the British section of the Fourth International. Resistance Books publishes books jointly with the International Institute for Research and Education in Amsterdam and independently.

Further information about Resistance Books, including a full list of titles currently available and how to purchase them, can be obtained at http://www.resistancebooks.org, or by writing to Resistance Books, PO Box 62732, London, SW2 9GQ.

Socialist Resistance is an organisation active in the trade union movement and in many campaigns against the war, in solidarity with Palestine and with anti-capitalist movements across the globe. We are eco-socialist – we argue that much of what is produced under capitalism is socially useless and either redundant or directly harmful. Capitalism's drive for profit is creating environmental disaster – and it is the poor, the working class and the global south that are paying the highest price for this.

We have been long standing supporters of women's liberation and the struggles of lesbians, gay people bisexuals and transgender people. We believe those struggles must be led by those directly affected – none so fit to break the chains as those who wear them. We work in antiracist and anti-fascist networks, including campaigns for the rights of immigrants and asylum seekers.

Socialist Resistance believes that democracy is an essential component of any successful movement of resistance and struggle. With Britain and the western imperialist countries moving into a long period of capitalist austerity and crisis, deeper than any since the Second World War, Socialist Resistance stands together with all those who are organising to make another world is possible.

Socialist Resistance is the bi-monthly magazine of the organisation, which can be read on-line at www.socialistresistance.org. Socialist Resistance can be contacted by email at contact@socialistresistance.org or by post at PO Box 62732, London, SW2 9GQ.

International Viewpoint is the English language on-line magazine of the Fourth International which can be read on-line at www.internationalviewpoint.org.

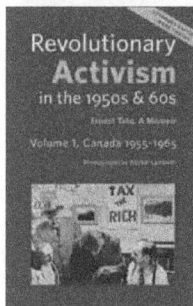

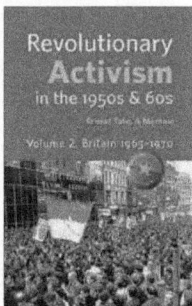

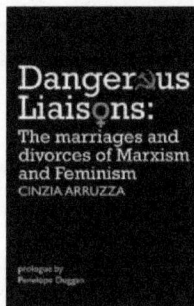

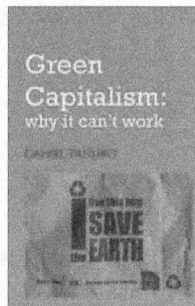

from
the International Institute for
Research and Education
& Haymarket Books

RETURNS OF MARXISM

Marxist Theory in a Time of Crisis

RETURNS

OF

Marxist Theory
in a Time of Crisis

MARXISM

IIRE

EDITED BY SARA R. FARRIS

In recent years we have witnessed a 'return of Marxism' as a younger generation of scholars and activists have rediscovered Marx as a crucial source for the critique of capitalism.

The title **Returns of Marxism** refers to this return but also to the rewards of the Marxist tradition when this wealth of ideas is re-appropriated and re-interpreted by a new generation of activists and scholars in contemporary struggles and research. Returns of Marxism brings together contributions from different traditions and generations working on the urgent renewal of radical critique.

Returns of Marxism includes essays discussing a wide range of topics ranging, examining Marxist thought and its uses for interrogating past and present. The volume is divided in six different sections, each containing contributions to broader discussions within the Marxist tradition:

- Reading Capital,
- Re-Reading Marx,
- Marxism and International Politics,
- Historicising Historical Materialism,
- Feminist and Queer Marxisms,
- Many Marxisms

Contributors include Guglielmo Carchedi, Riccardo Bellofiore, Michael Heinrich, Geert Reuten, Frieder Otto Wolf, Tom Rockmore, Wei Xiaoping, Joost Kircz, Jan Drahokoupil, Bastiaan Van Apeldoorn, Laura Horn, Gal Kirn, Jeffery Webber, Bertel Nygaard, Marcel Van Der Linden, Peter D. Thomas, Chiara Bonfiglioli, Peter Drucker, Katja Diefenbach, Steve Wright and Roland Boer. The volume is edited by Sara R. Farris.

The collection of essays presented in this volume demonstrate the richness, rigour and importance of Marx's thought for developing alternative worldviews and politics in the present.

to order:
visit iire.org